I, Candidate for Governor:
And How I Got Licked

UPTON SINCLAIR

Introduction by James N. Gregory

UNIVERSITY OF CALIFORNIA PRESS

Berkeley   Los Angeles   London

F
866
S59
1994

University of California Press
Berkeley and Los Angeles, California

University of California Press, Ltd.
London, England

Originally published by Upton Sinclair
© 1934, 1935 Upton Sinclair
Introduction © 1994 by The Regents of the University of California

Library of Congress Cataloging-in-Publication Data

Sinclair, Upton, 1878–1968.
I, candidate for governor, and how I got licked / Upton Sinclair ;
introduction by James N. Gregory.
p.   cm.
Originally published: New York : Farrar & Rinehart, © 1935.
Includes bibliographical references.
ISBN 0-520-08197-8 (alk. paper). — ISBN 0-520-08198-6
(pbk. : alk. paper)
1. Sinclair, Upton, 1878–1968.   2. Governors—California—
Election—History—20th century.   3. Mass media—Political aspects—
California—History—20th century.   4. California—Politics and
government—1865–1950.   I. Gregory, James Noble.   II. Title.
F866.S59   1994
324.9794'05—dc20   94-25599
CIP

Printed in the United States of America
9 8 7 6 5 4 3 2 1

The paper used in this publication meets the minimum requirements of
American National Standard for Information Sciences—Permanence of Paper
for Printed Library Materials, ANSI Z39.48-1984

INTRODUCTION

JAMES N. GREGORY

For a few weeks in the fall of 1934, events in California threatened to push Adolf Hitler off the front pages of American newspapers. An extraordinary political story was unfolding. The internationally known author and long-time socialist Upton Sinclair had captured the Democratic party nomination for governor on the strength of an audacious plan to "End Poverty in California." Riding on the hopes of hundreds of thousands of working-class and unemployed Californians who had endured four years of economic depression, Sinclair's EPIC movement had stirred an equally charged conservative opposition, who saw in it a threat to "sovietize California." The result was one of the angriest electoral contests in twentieth-century American politics and a collision that echoed far and wide. California's distinctive multifaction two-party political system was born in that encounter, as was the national media's fascination with California politics. In Washington, President Franklin Delano Roosevelt's New Deal administration came under new pressures as a result of EPIC, and the altered political priorities and social policies of 1935 show the impact. More significant, Sinclair's End Poverty movement and the Republican countercampaign that kept him out of the California governor's mansion may have changed the tools of American electoral politics. The first election in which Hollywood money and talent figured prominently, the 1934 contest has been credited with the birth of modern media politics.

The EPIC story belongs to a pivotal year in a pivotal decade. Like 1919 and 1968, 1934 was a year of exceptional turmoil and uncommon challenges to the political order—a year that convinced many Americans that society was poised on the brink of dramatic change or irreversible conflict. The early years of the Depression had been remarkably calm, particularly in comparison with Europe, where the crisis had turned the continent into a battleground between fascism, communism, and assorted other political passions. Americans reacted differently. All through the Hoover years, as the economy declined and jobs and homes were lost, the political life of

INTRODUCTION

the United States had remained largely undisturbed. Organized labor quietly absorbed its losses in the early 1930s. And while the tiny Communist party and still smaller Socialist party tried to stir the unemployed to action in the major cities, the radical left remained fragmented, weak, and easy to ignore. So quiescent was the American public that in most locales it was not until 1931 that incumbent officeholders began to pay a price at the polls, and not until 1932 that voter dissatisfaction finally cost the Republican party its majority following.

But 1932 was no climax. The election of Roosevelt and Democratic gains in Congress and in many state governments marked the beginning, not the high point, of political mobilization and conflict. Roosevelt's inauguration and the early New Deal plans he announced in the spring of 1933 opened the door to all sorts of nongovernmental initiatives, which soon threatened to overwhelm the New Deal administration. Labor unrest was part of it: 1934 saw a massive wave of union organizing and strikes roll across the industrial heartland, touching big cities and small, climaxing in full-blown general strikes in San Francisco and Minneapolis.

Paralleling conflicts at the factory gates were a variety of political movements that emerged suddenly to challenge the moderate economic policies of the New Deal. In the upper Midwest, a revived Farmer-Labor movement led by Minnesota's governor, Floyd Olson, demanded that Washington move toward social-democratic policies of public ownership and public spending to rebuild the economy. In the South, the flamboyant Louisiana senator Huey Long built a potentially potent network of "Share the Wealth" clubs with his slogan "Every man a king" and a vague plan to confiscate and redistribute the fortunes of the nation's millionaires. From Detroit, a Catholic priest, Father Charles Coughlin, kept an audience of millions tuned to his weekly radio broadcasts as he railed against the conspiracy of bankers that had driven the nation into bankruptcy. And that is only part of the list. The year also witnessed the beginnings of Francis Townsend's Old Age Revolving Pension movement, with its fanciful plan to end the Depression through generous pension spending. In Wisconsin, Senator Robert La Follette's sons built a new Progressive party, which soon controlled the state, and in Oregon and Washington, another left-wing political movement, the Cooperative Commonwealth Federation, began electing public officials. The far right was active too, as the Silver Shirts and other fascist groups claimed headlines and growing memberships. It was, in short, a year of explosive political initiative, much of it outside the old, established political parties, much of it ideologically unorthodox by standards of recent American politics, much of it as threatening to FDR's Democratic party as it was to the conservatives in the Republican party.

EPIC was part of this explosion. It started as a lark, one of a limitless number of schemes and projects tested over the years by America's best-known, if not always most respected, radical. Upton Sinclair was about to turn fifty-five in the summer of 1933 when the idea of EPIC began to take shape in his mind. His writings (among them *The Jungle* and more than forty other books) had fueled radical causes since 1904, and for most of that time he had carried a Socialist party card. Since 1915, he had made his home in Southern California, in faintly bohemian but decidedly upscale Pasadena, whose tranquility he managed now and then to disturb. Sinclair was an expert at gathering media attention. If his endless stream of books did not make headlines, his personal crusades on behalf of such disparate causes as civil liberties and mental telepathy always did. Californians had come to know him also as a perennial Socialist party candidate for statewide office, usually the governor's. He rarely campaigned in an active way, but his name, a speech or two, and a few I-dare-you-to-print-this letters to the state's major newspapers had usually earned him at least 50,000 votes, far more than other Socialist party candidates had received in recent years.

The idea for EPIC, Sinclair claimed, first came to him in the mail, in a letter from a Democratic party activist urging that he run for governor once again, but this time as a Democrat. But that was only part of it. He had been working on a plan—a bold, unorthodox blueprint for ending the Depression. California, along with the rest of the country, was suffering the greatest economic crisis in its history. The state's unemployment rate had stood at 29 percent when FDR assumed office six months before and had changed only slightly since. The administration's emergency relief spending was finally putting some money into the hands of the unemployed, but hundreds of thousands of Californians were still jobless, and tens of thousands were homeless. The New Deal was not going to solve the crisis, Sinclair was sure. The National Recovery Administration's policy of supporting corporate profits while restricting production made no sense, not when people were hungry and in need. Nor did the New Deal's massive relief programs, which Sinclair thought were wasteful and would ultimately bankrupt the government.

His Socialist party did not seem to be coming up with answers either. The party was in the midst of a comeback in 1933. It had almost disappeared in the 1920s, shattered by the split in 1919 that generated the Communist party and battered by the postwar Red Scare and the lingering climate of antiradicalism. The Depression had reenergized the SP, and Norman Thomas's 1932 presidential campaign had brought the party almost 900,000 votes. But in truth, the left was failing, Sinclair realized, despite the unprecedented opportunity at hand. With capitalism apparently crumbling all around, the American public still feared the term *socialism* and remained stubbornly wedded to its two old political parties. It was time to try something new, time to see what could be done working on the inside with an "Americanized" version of socialism.

So, in early September 1933, Upton Sinclair walked into the Beverly Hills city hall and changed his voter registration to Democrat. On his desk at home was a nearly complete draft of the platform he would bring to the California voters, his plan to end poverty in California. "I say, positively and without qualification, we can end poverty in California," it would announce. "I know exactly how to do it, and if you elect me Governor, with a Legislature to support me, I will put the job through—and I won't take more than one or two of my four years."

The plan had elements that later would appear sensible, like pensions of $50 a month for the elderly and disabled. Other provisions were within the realm of political possibility, such as one to replace sales taxes with sharply graduated income and property taxes. But the heart of the platform was an elaborate project that mainstream economists and orthodox Socialists alike would denounce as unworkable and conservatives would charge was more than dangerous. The new government would establish a network of cooperative colonies for the state's 700,000 unemployed, basing them in idle factories and vacant farmland, which the state would seize under its powers of eminent domain or through confiscatory taxes. The state would capitalize and manage these cooperatives, which would exchange their products within a giant, cash-free network. Modeled, although Sinclair did not say so, on Soviet collective farms, the EPIC colonies were not envisioned as temporary projects. They were to be the seedbeds of a new cooperative economy, an economy of "production for use" that would ultimately supplant the old economy of "production for profit" as workers, farmers, and even businessmen realized the efficiency and numerous personal and social advantages of cooperation.

Sinclair sketched his vision in a booklet that became the principal organizing tool of the campaign. Bearing the remarkable title, *I, Governor of California: And How I Ended Poverty: A True Story of the Future,* the 64-page pamphlet narrated its story backward from the future in the style of Edward Bellamy's utopian novel *Looking Backward* (1888). Writing from the fictional vantage point of 1938, "Governor" Sinclair details the steps that have brought California out of the Depression and made it the model for recovery for the rest of the nation and the capitalist world.

The booklet also depicted the campaign that had supposedly carried Sinclair into the statehouse. It proved to be a marvelous bit of forecasting. Apart from the final vote, events happened just about as he said they would. Publication of the booklet in October 1933 set off a flurry of interest. People from around the state ordered copies, distributed them to friends, and then set up EPIC clubs to discuss the plan and organize the campaign. By December, there were dozens of such clubs, and Sinclair had launched a weekly newspaper, the *EPIC News.* By May, when the number of clubs had grown to the hundreds, the old-line Democratic party began to understand the implications. Although desperate to fend off "the socialist carpetbagger," the party's bitterly antagonistic factions could not unite around an alternative candidate for the upcoming primary election. One of the contenders, Sheridan Downey, saw the handwriting on the wall and signed on as Sinclair's running mate for lieutenant governor. That left George Creel, who had been head of President Woodrow Wilson's Committee on Public Information during World War I, and more recently had served as West Coast chief for Roosevelt's National Recovery Administration, as the most credible opponent.

Sinclair had chosen his target well. California's primary election system permitted anyone to run for a party's nomination, and the Democrats, the junior party in the state since the 1890s, were particularly vulnerable to such a move. Democratic fortunes had reached an all-time low in the 1920s, when registration favored Republicans three to one. As late as 1931, not a single Democrat held statewide office, while Republicans claimed 12 out of the state's 13 congressional and Senate seats and an incredible 111 out of 120 seats in the state legislature. The Republican monopoly had started to disintegrate in 1932, when Roosevelt carried California, sweeping into office with him a sizable contingent of Democratic congressmen and legislators. But California's Democratic party still faced major problems. The leadership could not put aside the feuds between wet and dry and Catholic and Protestant factions that had complicated the 1920s. Equally important, they had done little to shape a liberal agenda. Always responsive to the ideological leadership of William Randolph Hearst, whose five in-state newspapers had been the voice of California Democrats for more than thirty years, the party leadership remained cautious and conservative at a time when Democrats in Washington and elsewhere were practicing active liberalism.

Now it was too late. By June, EPIC had nominated a slate of

candidates for the legislature and had built up a political organization the likes of which California had never seen. Operating out of a huge headquarters in downtown Los Angeles, scores of volunteers coordinated a network of over fifty district organizations and nearly eight hundred EPIC clubs. In addition to the weekly newspaper, which was distributed by the hundreds of thousands in local editions, the campaign operated speakers' bureaus, research units, women's clubs, youth clubs, and drama groups. It put on radio broadcasts, plays, and rodeos, was making a film, and drew big crowds to a lavishly staged EPIC pageant that depicted the lessons of production for use—all this in addition to a heavy schedule of campaign speeches and rallies.

Even so, the August 28 primary election results came as a surprise, not because Sinclair won but because of the scale of his support. He captured the Democratic nomination with more than 436,000 votes, more than any primary election candidate in California history, more than all of his Democratic opponents combined, and more than the Republican he would face in November, the incumbent governor, Frank Merriam. Standing with him in the general election would be Sheridan Downey and forty-nine EPIC endorsed candidates for the state legislature.

Who were these voters who had turned the Democratic party over to a former socialist? A scornful George Creel blamed Los Angeles, claiming in a widely quoted *Saturday Evening Post* article that EPIC appealed to the same sort of disoriented Southern Californians who had previously flocked to Aimee Semple McPherson's Angelus Temple and other dreamland "religious, political, and economic cults." Historians have generally concurred, echoing Carey McWilliams's assessment that EPIC belonged to the desperate unemployed and the disaffected lower middle class of depression-battered Los Angeles. But a close inspection of voting patterns shows something different. Southern California provided most of the votes, but EPIC belonged solidly, almost exclusively, to working-class voters.

The race had been close in many parts of California, and George Creel had actually won in the city of San Francisco, but in Los Angeles and the other counties of Southern California, Sinclair had buried the opposition, collecting two-thirds of all Democratic votes in Los Angeles County. Many of his voters were new Democrats (the party had added 350,000 registrants in the seven months prior to the election), and they were overwhelmingly working-class. It was in the blue-collar neighborhoods of central and east Los Angeles, and even more in the industrial suburbs stretching south to Long Beach that EPIC found its key support. In South Gate,

Lynwood, and Hawthorne, Sinclair won by margins of 80 percent and more, amid record-breaking turnouts. George Creel meanwhile owed what modest support he received in Southern California to hillside and westside middle-class neighborhoods, where Sinclair's message had been badly received, and where in the election to come Republicans would pile up a huge anti-EPIC vote.

Elsewhere in California, the patterns were somewhat more complicated, but Sinclair's support everywhere was limited by class. With the exception of some of the activists drawn into EPIC (many of them former socialists), he had little luck appealing to white-collar or well-educated voters. In the Bay Area, middle-class Democrats supported Creel in the primary, then defected to the Republicans in the general election. Working-class voters split between the two major Democrats: Sinclair enjoying a substantial lead among blue-collar voters in the East Bay; Creel getting a slight edge in San Francisco, thanks to the support of many of the city's labor leaders. But unlike Creel's middle-class supporters, those blue-collar votes—indeed blue-collar votes nearly everywhere—would go to Sinclair in the November election. Even more than the primary, the vote in that contest would break strictly on class lines.

What EPIC had done was reshuffle the electorate. For a generation, the Republican party had encompassed most of California's citizenry in a remarkably stable two-wing, cross-class coalition. Now Sinclair had stolen much of its progressive wing with a program that appealed very strongly to the less privileged segments of the population. In addition to finding a natural following among the unemployed, he had also struck responsive chords among employed blue-collar voters. California was returning to political alignments that it had not known for a generation. Like the Workingman's party of 1878, the Democratic party of the 1880s, and the Union Labor parties of the prewar period, EPIC had resurrected the politics of class.

Fear had also been resurrected. The road to the primary had been easy; the next two months had a different momentum. While national media turned up the spotlight, Sinclair's campaign met one obstacle after another. The first disappointment came from the White House. Fresh from his primary triumph, Sinclair had left for a cross-country speaking tour to capitalize on the headlines and seek an audience with the president. Roosevelt met with him, but would offer no endorsement, despite Sinclair's efforts to tone down some aspects of his plan. That rejection cleared the way for many of California's established Democratic party leaders to defect to the Republican camp.

Of equal import was the new role of the state's major newspapers, many of which were linked to the conservative wing of the Republican party. The press had been relatively quiet during the primary campaign, suspecting that Sinclair would be easier to defeat than the moderate Creel. But the huge primary vote for the former socialist raised the stakes; now it seemed that he might actually win. Joining in the panic that gripped conservatives throughout the state that summer and fall of 1934, the state's major newspapers pounced on the Democratic candidate in a display of partisan viciousness almost without parallel. Sinclair details the distortions and slanders in the account you are about to read.

Several missteps also hurt the EPIC cause. Sinclair's careless comment about the unemployed flooding into California if he won gave the opposition some of its best ammunition, while awkward attempts to soften the EPIC program to appeal to New Dealers and moderates pleased no one and cut into the campaign's credibility. To make matters worse, a third party candidate, Raymond Haight, running under the banner of the old Progressive party, was now making a claim to the ideological middle ground and picking up disaffected Democrats and moderate Republicans. By October, EPIC was in trouble. And the record-breaking voter turnout on November 6 confirmed it. Sinclair doubled his primary tally, but his 879,537 votes were well behind Frank Merriam's 1,138,620. The Republican had not, however, received an electoral majority. Raymond Haight collected 302,519 votes.

The election did not finish EPIC. Although his supporters were devastated, and Sinclair himself was exhausted, the year-long campaign had accomplished too much to be considered a loss. The idea that almost 900,000 Californians had voted for EPIC was electrifying: Sinclair had received almost exactly the number of votes in one state that Norman Thomas had gained in his nationwide Socialist party presidential campaign two years earlier. Those same California voters had also just elected thirty-eight Democrats to the eighty-seat Assembly, twenty-four of them EPIC nominees. Several EPIC-endorsed state senators and U.S. congressmen would also be taking office. In addition, EPIC candidates had captured Democratic central committee posts around the state, giving the movement effective control of the party machinery. Sinclair saw in this a beginning, not an end, to the EPIC story. Now, he decided, the time was ripe to take the message of "production for use" beyond California.

I, Candidate for Governor: And How I Got Licked was written as Sinclair contemplated that new campaign. Dashed off in five weeks of feverish writing, it was intended to spread the End Poverty plan far and wide. Offered as a daily series to newspapers that had been clamoring for Sinclair's story, the account was published in more than fifty papers across the country, representing millions of readers. But as a national movement, EPIC did not live up to its creator's dreams. Clubs sprang up in many states, but only in the Pacific Northwest did the movement catch on. End Poverty campaigns in Oregon and Washington surpassed the successes of California. In Washington, an EPIC spin-off called the Cooperative Commonwealth Federation elected congressmen and a U.S. senator, in addition to a variety of state officeholders, and went on to influence Democratic party affairs for the next decade.

Elsewhere, EPIC ran into too much competition. By 1935, the spectrum of radical reform proposals had become impossibly wide, as political movements of various descriptions jockeyed for members and headlines. Just as important, both the labor movement and the Democratic party were on the move, providing options for activists eager to push for comprehensive change. The 1934 elections had sent a message. Left-wing Democrats had won election to legislatures and Congress from a number of states, and now the machinery of formal politics was grinding out new New Deals in state capitols throughout the land. While EPIC ideas about cooperative production surfaced frequently in the year or two after the campaign, the movement itself got lost in the commotion, and outside the West, it never gained much of a foothold.

The organization faced difficulties in its home base as well. The campaign over, EPIC almost immediately began to fragment. Jealousies were part of it. The movement lost some of its ablest organizers in battles over Sinclair's excessive authority. Difficulties with the Communist party also took a toll. After viciously condemning EPIC during the 1934 campaign, the CP then tried to join and influence the organization, triggering a bitter expulsion struggle. Most damaging of all was the battle that erupted between EPIC's headquarters and some of its newly elected legislators over the proper role of each. State Senator Culbert Olson, leader of the EPIC legislative caucus and new chair of the state Democratic party, wanted EPIC to move to the background and fold most of its functions into the party. Sinclair and most of the activists resisted, arguing that EPIC had to remain an independent movement with its own agenda. The organization continued and had some success sponsoring candidates in the 1935 municipal elections in Los Angeles, but with Olson and the new Democrats taking a separate course, EPIC could not maintain its influence. A final miscalculation all but finished the movement in mid-1936. Still hoping to send a message to Washington, EPIC entered its own "production for use" slate in the California presidential primary in opposition to the official Roosevelt slate of delegates, although pledged to back the president on the second ballot. The gambit failed badly. California Democrats had had enough of Sinclair, and perhaps of EPIC. They voted seven to one for Roosevelt. Sinclair himself lost interest shortly afterward, and although the End Poverty League continued to exist for another decade, it very quickly became a small political sect.

EPIC's legacy was more impressive than its organizational half-life. The movement, the campaign, and the election each had a profound impact, certainly on California, very likely on the rest of the United States as well. Sinclair liked to believe that his movement strongly influenced the direction of federal policy after 1934, providing the ideas and impetus behind the creation of the Works Progress Administration, which in 1935 replaced the patchwork of emergency relief programs that Sinclair had loudly attacked. The WPA did not embrace production for use, but it was a massive program of public works, designed to put the unemployed to work at jobs that would contribute to societal needs. Federal policy might well have taken this turn without EPIC. The idea of work relief was far from new, and both Harry Hopkins and Roosevelt favored the principle, but events in California certainly helped push it forward. So, too, the New Deal's expanded support for producer and consumer cooperatives can be at least partly attributed to EPIC. Several federal agencies began to issue grants to cooperative projects for the unemployed in 1934. The Farm Security Administration experimented as well with rural cooperatives, setting up collective farms—including one in California—that in the planning stages resembled EPIC's proposed land colonies.

Much more significant were the ways in which EPIC transformed California, especially its politics and policy. A divided Democratic party was one of the legacies of the 1934 election. Political alignments were changing in many states in the early 1930s as Democrats built winning coalitions of working-class, ethnic, and urban middle-class voters. California followed the broad trend up to a point, joining other western states in developing a balanced two-party system for the first time in the twentieth century. But the Democrats never built the kind of stable coalition that became politically dominant in many other states.

EPIC had fixed a deep fault line within the Democratic party, one that would remain for the next twenty years. Sinclair's campaign marked the beginning of a powerful left-wing presence in the party. Although EPIC itself melted away, veterans of that campaign formed the nucleus of a Democratic party faction that was ideologically very liberal and soon closely tied to organized labor, especially the left-wing CIO. Powerful enough to win primaries and nominate candidates, that faction faced almost constant warfare from the antiradical wing of the party, a loose coalition that, like the left, had originated in the 1934 contest. Several hundred thousand Democrats, including many of the traditionalists who had been with the party during the lean 1920s, bolted in 1934 rather than vote for Sinclair, costing him the election. They would do so again repeatedly over the next two decades. Although able to turn out impressive majorities for Roosevelt in presidential elections, the new majority party in California could not function on the state level.

The election of 1938 almost proved otherwise. Culbert Olson, leader of what had been the EPIC legislative caucus and the favorite of left-wing and liberal Democrats, won the nomination and swept on to victory over a tired Frank Merriam. But the intraparty warfare resumed almost immediately in the legislature, as conservative Democrats joined Republicans to block Olson's legislative program and undermine his administration. Defeated when he ran for reelection four years later, Olson would remain California's only twentieth-century Democratic governor until Edmund G. "Pat" Brown won the office in 1958.

A revitalized Republican party was another legacy of 1934. Despite an electorate that became more and more Democratic in registration, in state politics the Republicans managed to hold on to power nearly continuously through the New Deal period. This made California unique among states with sizable metropolitan populations. Merriam's victory was one of the few GOP triumphs of 1934, a year that sent the Republicans reeling toward oblivion in most parts of the country.

Sinclair's incursion into the Democratic party had given the Republicans a rare chance to move to the middle, a strategy that paid off, not only in that election, but throughout the next two decades. Frank Merriam inaugurated the strategy with his belated and clumsy endorsement of the New Deal midway through the 1934 campaign. He more or less maintained that course during his next four years in office, supporting tax and relief programs much resented by conservative Republicans, while maintaining good relations with Washington. But even more than Merriam, it was the young Republican district attorney of Alameda County, Earl Warren, who best understood the lessons and opportunities of 1934. An adviser to Merriam and successful candidate for state attorney general in 1938, Warren crafted a liberal Republican politics that carried him into the governor's mansion in 1942 and kept him there for three terms.

In one sense, then, EPIC changed the course of California politics by returning things to their old channel: the Republican channel that so dominates the state's twentieth-century experience. In another sense, all the channels were new. California would never again be a one-party state, and rarely would its political life be contained within two cohesive parties: 1934 had given birth to the pattern of politics that still prevails, a politics of party factions and extreme variation, which ultimately became standard for Republicans as well as Democrats. The political system that later in the century would alternate liberal Democrats and conservative Republicans in the governor's mansion, while bringing still more extreme differences into congressional and legislative delegations, had its origins in the turbulent campaign of that year.

Although EPIC has been the subject of numerous articles, chapters, dissertations, and, most recently, of a fine book, *I, Candidate for Governor: And How I Got Licked* arguably remains the best source for understanding the campaign. Written immediately after Sinclair's November 6 defeat, it captures the intensity of the moment as no secondary account can. Its narrative of the events of the campaign is full, if a bit disjointed, and needs little annotation despite the passage of six decades. Most important, *I, Candidate* reveals the personality at the center of these events. Filled, as nearly all of his books are, with autobiographical detail, the book introduces the many sides of Upton Sinclair.

There is Sinclair the political wizard, concocting a program out of bits and pieces of earlier radical strategies. He borrowed much of the program's gradualist, consensus spirit and softened socialist terminology ("production for use") from Edward Bellamy, who over fifty years earlier had invented an "Americanized" socialism. The key electoral strategy of invading one of the old parties was also taken from the past, principally from the experience of the radical Non-Partisan Leagues that after World War I briefly captured Republican parties in several midwestern states. Inspiration also came from more recent projects. The Technocracy movement had generated great enthusiasm in Los Angeles in 1932 and 1933 with its plans for a nonmonetary economy of abundance based on scientific planning. Echoes of that efficiency ethos would appear in EPIC. The barter clubs that had sprung up by the score in Southern California in the early Depression were a still more important source of ideas, for it was there that Sinclair saw the basic model for the cooperative network that would be EPIC's answer to unemployment and California's gateway to socialism.

The wizard was also a brilliant publicist. The genius of EPIC was as much in the packaging as in the plan. Sinclair worked the media better than anyone on the left; he knew how to attract publicity. But what was ultimately more important was his ability to address the working-class audience that became EPIC's primary constituency. His writings had never aimed at highbrow readers. Sinclair had started out writing adventure serials for the pulps while still in high school, and one of his special gifts was storytelling; he could build drama into any scene. Another was pedagogy; he would turn the same scene into a lesson in radical politics. No one did it better. His books had educated two generations of radicals and were especially prized by the young and the modestly educated. In an age that had been inventing popular media, his books had been the reader's digests of American radicalism.

That special skill is evident in *I, Candidate,* as it was throughout the campaign. Master of the clever phrase and powerful slogan, Sinclair was unmatched in his ability to bring ideas down to the level of common sense, while persuading his audience that no other level was valid. The intellectuals of his day found his style annoyingly egocentric, but for hundreds of thousands of modestly educated Californians, his self-presentation as teacher-with-all-the-answers was powerful and self-affirming. He was the teacher, but he taught that they were the experts, insisting that the so-called economists were fools, and that the only kind of economics that made sense had to be based on common sense. Thus he set up his appealing equations: that cooperation was more efficient than competition; that capitalism begot overproduction, which in turn begot unemployment; that putting people to work made more sense than giving them handouts; that state management and planning would balance production and consumption; that "production for use" would end the Depression. It was all so straightforward. "I have spent my whole life studying the idea of production for use," he assured his audiences. "It is to me as obvious as arithmetic, as certain as sunrise. If you give hungry men tools and access to land, they will grow food; if you give them access to factories, they will turn out goods. Who but a lunatic—or a hireling—would question it?"

But was the teacher perhaps the real fool, or, worse, a charlatan? The plan made no sense to most economists, including many on the left. How would Sinclair finance enterprises employing half a million workers? Could the products really be distributed in such a way as to make them self-sufficient? Would the unemployed really join the cooperatives? What would keep private capital from fleeing the state, worsening the crisis? How would EPIC acquire the land and factories? How would it handle the unemployed from other states, who were sure to come west? To many analysts, of various political persuasions, Sinclair's plan seemed a prescription for state bankruptcy, for social chaos, and worse.

Did Sinclair really believe it would work? That is hard to say. Privately, he admitted after the election that he was relieved to have lost. He knew that he had none of the administrative talents necessary in government, and after a year of campaigning, he was dying to return to his writing. But it is also clear that he was thinking about and probably troubled by some of the criticisms of his plan. Indeed, during the campaign, he had modified quite a few provisions, making the twelve-point EPIC plan included in the appendix to this book substantially different from the original program. The difference is in the details, many of which had disappeared by the end of the campaign. In the version published here, there is no longer a calculation of what the plan will cost or how it will be funded. There is less detail, too, about Sinclair's tax-reform measures, which he had earlier promised would raise millions through steep taxes on wealthy estates and large incomes. More significant, he dropped the idea of confiscating idle factories and farmland; instead, the state would rent them. Also eliminated was the severely criticized proposal for a separate monetary system, the California Authority for Money, which under the original plan was to have issued scrip as a medium of exchange within the co-op system. By the end of the campaign, it had become the California Authority for Barter, charged with working out the procedures for distribution and exchange of goods. There were sound political reasons for these modifications, most of which were hammered out at the statewide Democratic party convention after Sinclair won the nomination. But they probably also represent some second thoughts on the part of the plan's original architect, who at precisely that moment was confronting the possibility that he might actually win and get a chance to try EPIC.

Sinclair did not yet realize it, and in fact would never realize it, but the campaign had changed him. By the time he wrote *I, Candidate,* he was on his way to becoming a New Dealer. Years more would pass before he felt completely comfortable with Roosevelt, and he would go to his grave three decades later still proclaiming his socialist faith, but those months of trying to end poverty in California in 1934 had begun to erode the clarity of his radicalism. The plan that he had devised in late 1933 as an alternative to the weak medicine of the New Deal was by the end of the campaign losing

its visionary force and becoming an extension or refinement of the general thrust of New Deal reform.

It had always had that potential. Part of the political genius of EPIC was its susceptibility to multiple readings. Putting the unemployed to work was an idea that mixed nicely with some very traditional values, and read narrowly the plan for cooperative work projects was not particularly radical, especially if they turned out to be self-sufficient, as Sinclair promised. Barter clubs and self-help groups had been functioning in California's major cities since 1932, sometimes modestly assisted with public funds. Was EPIC merely proposing a larger, better-funded version of that primitive cooperative network? Sinclair cleverly played both answers from the start, encouraging both radical and narrow interpretations of the plan. Just so he encouraged multiple readings of his relationship to the New Deal, early on claiming an affinity with and trading on the legitimacy of the Roosevelt administration, even while severely criticizing much of the New Deal program. But what began as a pair of strategic positions designed to lure moderate voters led ultimately toward more genuine ambiguity. By the time he wrote *I, Candidate,* Sinclair was seeing the New Deal in an increasingly positive light. He was still critical and still promoting his End Poverty plan as the solution, but now it was production for use within the framework of the New Deal rather than EPIC as replacement for the New Deal.

This subtle transformation in political values was not his alone; indeed, it was one of the big stories of the 1930s, shared by millions of Americans. Through the EPIC movement, and in other states through a variety of other political experiences, great numbers of Americans came to embrace the Democratic party and the welfare state liberalism that had become its creed. The converted came from various backgrounds, conservative as well as progressive, and among them was much of Sinclair's generation of radicals, former members of the Socialist and Progressive movements who discovered in the unfolding policies of an activist government major portions of what they had long fought for—rights for labor, sustenance for the poor, controls on the economy, a language of collective good and public authority. Some on the left remained very clear that welfarism was not socialism, but what Roosevelt offered was enough for many. As it opened wide over the course of its first four years, the New Deal became an ever-larger tent, drawing converts of many political faiths. EPIC had helped make that happen. Pushing the New Deal from the left, the various political movements of 1934 led large numbers of activists into the Democratic coalition, effectively bringing to a close the story of democratic socialism and electoral radicalism in the United States, leaving the Communist party as the only important voice of the left.

There is another side of Sinclair that fairly leaps from the pages of *I, Candidate:* the competitor, the pugilist, the warrior. He loved combat, or at least political combat, and the meaner the better. He had waged crusades all of his adult life, beginning with his stunningly successful exposé of the meat-packing business in 1906. For almost thirty years, he had practiced the art of muckraking journalism in dozens of books that exposed the insidious corruptions of capitalism. His targets were almost too many to list: journalism in *The Brass Check*; universities in *The Goose Step*; public schools in *The Goslings*; organized religion, *The Profits of Religion*; art and literature, *Money Writes* and *Mammonart*; banks, *The Moneylenders*; the courts, *Boston* and *Singing Jailbirds*; Hollywood, *Upton Sinclair Presents William Fox*; and we could go on. Each had been an exercise in literary combat.

So is *I, Candidate.* From the opening paragraph, Sinclair is on the attack, setting up to tell "the inside story" of the campaign, a story that reveals "what money can do in American politics." Actually, there are two inside stories. A narrative of his own campaign structures the book and dominates the first hundred pages. But intertwined with it, and gradually becoming the dominant story, is his account of the malicious countercampaign, the "Lie Factory," as he calls it, that pulled out all of the stops to save the "Plutocracy" and smash EPIC. This is where the book gains its power and its significance. And it is where Sinclair exacts his revenge. He may have lost the election, but through *I, Candidate* he won the battle for history, ensuring the EPIC would be remembered by future generations less for what it tried to do than for what was done to it, ensuring that his opponents would be remembered as the architects of modern American "dirty" politics.

The facts are clear enough. Almost the entire established media in California lined up against his candidacy, in what the *Nation* labeled "the worst press conspiracy we have ever witnessed." Balance and fairness disappeared entirely from many of the leading newspapers as they pummeled Sinclair mercilessly from front page to back. This was to be expected from the *Los Angeles Times,* whose ultraconservative owner, Harry Chandler, had passionately fought reds and liberals for decades. The surprise came when the powerful Hearst newspapers and the usually progressive McClatchy *Bee* newspapers joined the cause. Among the metropolitan dailies, only the *San Francisco News* and the *Los Angeles Illustrated Daily News* gave Sinclair anything like reasonable coverage, but there was some compensation from the small newspapers that served the blue-collar suburbs where EPIC thrived.

Historians have found greater historical significance in two other aspects of the anti-Sinclair campaign. One is the role of Hollywood, discussed briefly in the account that follows. When MGM's Louis B. Mayer dove into politics to save California from the threat of "Sinclairism" in 1934, he started a pattern of filmland involvement that would reshape American political life. Not that the heavy-handed perversions of media power of that year would become routine. As far as we know, neither the faked newsreels nor the extortionist fund-raising tactics have been repeated. But Hollywood and politics discovered each other in 1934 and have been married ever since. In the years to come, Democrats as well as Republicans would turn to the film community for money and celebrity power. Indeed, it was not long before Washington greeted its first actor-politician. Like the rest of Hollywood, Congresswoman Helen Gahagan Douglas, Democratic representative from Los Angeles for 1944–50, traced her political awakening back to the EPIC campaign. Her political demise at the hands of Richard Nixon in the 1950 senate campaign would be remembered as California's second encounter with the "Lie Factory."

The other innovation is extensively explored in Greg Mitchell's recent book *Campaign of the Century.* The anti-Sinclair campaign was orchestrated by media professionals. Hired by the prominent Los Angeles advertising agency Lord and Thomas, Clem Whitaker and Leona Baxter went into business as the first-ever professional campaign managers and quickly designed a strategy that became a model for modern "hit campaigns." Ignoring the colorless Merriam, whose record and personality offered little voter appeal, they built a campaign entirely out of negatives, exclusively around Sinclair and EPIC.

Sinclair makes reference to Lord and Thomas in the account that follows and in one important passage refers to "political chemists at work preparing poisons" to be delivered to the press and public, but he may not have been fully aware of the dimensions of their work. He certainly knew the end product. It was Whitaker and Baxter who devised the devastating tactic of using Sinclair against himself. Combing his massive bibliography for politically embarrassing quotations, they fed the press a stream of excerpts from his earlier writings that purported to show his extremist views. Featured in the famous front-page "boxes" of the *Los Angeles Times,* these quotations, bearing headlines such as "Sinclair on Marriage,"

"Sinclair on the Soviet Union," and "Sinclair on Christ," also appeared as pamphlets mailed to voters by Whitaker and Baxter under various phony organizational names.

And what was the effect of these and all the other opposition tactics? Sinclair asserts loudly that the election was stolen, that voters were tricked into rejecting EPIC by a cabal of powerful interests. Trickery and deceit there were, but it is by no means clear that Sinclair would have won a clean election. Even without malicious embellishment, his background and his program would have seemed very radical, and not just to a tiny business elite. Many Californians feared drastic change during the 1930s, especially those retaining middle-class jobs and social standing. Depressions, it must be remembered, distribute economic distress unevenly—and even in the Great Depression, it was only a minority of Americans who suffered significant unemployment. Political instincts were polarized accordingly, and with or without media manipulation, Sinclair would have had trouble assembling an electoral majority. Too many people felt they had too much to lose, too much to fear. In the end, Sinclair's 879,000 ballots represented no small accomplishment. They testify to the remarkable grass-roots political movement the writer-politician had built. Even more, that vote reminds us of the extraordinary fluidity of American politics in the pivotal year 1934.

ADDITIONAL READING

Blake, Fay M., and H. Morton Newman. "Upton Sinclair's EPIC Campaign." *California History,* Fall 1984.

Gregory, James, and Nancy Quam-Wickham. "Who Voted for Upton Sinclair? The EPIC Campaign of 1934." Paper delivered at the Southwest Labor Studies Association meeting in San Francisco, April 29, 1989.

Larsen, Charles E. "The Epic Campaign of 1934." *Pacific Historical Review,* May 1958.

Leader, Leonard. "Upton Sinclair's EPIC Switch: A Dilemma for American Socialists." *Southern California Quarterly,* Winter 1980.

McIntosh, Clarence Fredric. "Upton Sinclair and the EPIC Movement, 1933–1936." Ph.D. dissertation, Stanford University, 1955.

Mitchell, Greg. *The Campaign of the Century: Upton Sinclair's Race for Governor of California and the Birth of Media Politics.* New York: Random House, 1992.

Singer, Donald L. "Upton Sinclair and the California Gubernatorial Campaign of 1934." *Southern California Quarterly,* Winter 1974.

I, Candidate For Governor:
And How I Got Licked

by

UPTON SINCLAIR

PUBLISHED BY

THE AUTHOR

STATION A, PASADENA, CALIFORNIA

I, Candidate for Governor

AND HOW I GOT LICKED

By UPTON SINCLAIR

CHAPTER I

This is the story of the EPIC movement and the campaign to End Poverty in California; an "inside" story of events about which there has been much guessing. It is a revelation of what money can do in American politics; what it will do when its privileges are threatened. When I was a boy, the President of Harvard University wrote about "the scholar in politics." Here is set forth how a scholar went into politics, and what happened to him.

I am beginning this story three days after the election. Having known for a month what was coming, I had time to practice smiling. I write now in a mood of cheerful aloofness. To the gentlemen of great wealth who control the State of California I would not pay the compliment of grieving about anything they could do to me.

I grieve for the people. But the people have suffered for ages, and I have no way to help it. Whoever made this universe ordained it that people learn by suffering, and in no other way. The people of California have much to learn.

For the past fourteen months I have traveled up and down the State, addressing some two hundred meetings and facing half a million men and women. I spoke a score of times over the radio, so that practically every one in the State heard my voice. The substance of my message was this:

"All my life I have believed and preached democracy, in the broad sense of that word; the right and power of the people to govern their own affairs. I am proposing now that the people shall vote to End Poverty in California. I am willing to abide by the people's decision. If you have not suffered enough, it is your God-given right to suffer some more. All you have to do is to elect Governor Merriam, and he will see that you do it."

In three of my novels you may read what I have observed during nineteen years of residence in the State of California. The first, "100 Per Cent: the Story of a Patriot," deals with the broken promises of the World War. The second, "They Call Me Carpenter," pictures Jesus coming to "Western City," and not having a happy time. Finally, at the height of the Coolidge boom, I wrote "Oil!" a sort of panorama of Southern California life.

If you prefer facts to fiction, there are the opening chapters of "The Goslings," telling how I was arrested and kidnaped by the police of Los Angeles under a charge of "suspicion of criminal syndicalism"; the offense being an attempt to read the Constitution of the United States while standing on private property with the written consent of the owner in my pocket. Or read the chapter in "The Goose-Step," which deals with our State University, termed "The University of the Black Hand." Finally, in "The Brass Check," are chapters dealing with our newspapers, the same ones you will meet in this book, unchanged between 1919 and 1934.

For those who have no time to read books, let me say briefly that for nineteen years I observed my home State governed by a small group of rich men whose sole purpose in life was to become richer, and who subordinated all public affairs to that end. I saw them set aside the Constitution of State and Nation, and use the law enforcement officers as strikebreakers, kidnapers, torturers and killers. I saw the civil rights of workers and friends of workers abrogated. In seventeen counties of California it is against the law for more than three persons to congregate in any place, and it is against the law for poor men even to walk upon the highways. I saw the Governor of the State publicly justify the lynching of possibly innocent men; a Governor who was drinking himself into paresis, and petting his movie mistress in automobiles in the public streets. I saw our richest newspaper publisher keeping his movie mistress in a private city of palaces and cathedrals, furnished with shiploads of junk imported from Europe, and surrounded by vast acres reserved for the use of zebras and giraffes; telling it as a jest that he had spent six million dollars to make this lady's reputation, and using his newspapers to celebrate her changes of hats.

Side by side with such events I saw the extreme poverty which everywhere accompanies them. I saw old people dying of slow starvation, and children by the tens of thousands growing up stunted by the diseases of malnutrition—the very school teachers dipping into their slender purses to provide milk for pupils who came to school without breakfast. I saw hundreds of thousands of persons driven from their homes; the sweep of an economic process which has turned most of the land of California over to money-lenders and banks. I saw one colossal swindle after another perpetrated upon the public; and for every official who was sent to jail I knew that a thousand were hiding their loot.

In short, I have seen this fair State going the way of the slave empires of history; decaying with luxury at the top, and destroying the concept of democracy by ruthless suppression of the people's protest.

For nineteen years I put my State into books, telling myself that this was my way of service. But now and then my feelings would boil over, and I would go out and make a political speech, or attempt to make one, and get arrested. Three times I let myself be persuaded to run for public office, as a more immediate form of protest. Twice I ran for Governor, and once for United States Senator, always on the Socialist ticket, and the highest vote I ever polled was sixty thousand out of an electorate of a couple of million.

I was fifty-four years of age, and beginning to feel the effects of a lifetime of overwork. I said that I had done my share, and promised myself, and also my wife, that from then on I would be a writer and nothing else.

But then came Hitler; to me the most hideous phenomenon since the days of the Inquisition. I saw where our civilization was heading. I saw around me all the little incipient Hitlers—the Californazis. I put to myself the question: what is the use of taking a lifetime to build a Socialist movement, when our enemies can destroy it in twenty-four hours?

I sat down to rethink the problems of my lifetime. What was wrong with the Socialist party, that it had made no headway in America? First, it was a foreign movement, and had used long foreign words—proletariat, surplus value, dialectical materialism. I had always known that was a blunder, and had tried to prevent it, but with little success.

Second, the movement was based upon the working class. So far as concerned my home State, there was very little working-class mentality. Those who belonged to that class did not know it, and hated you for telling them. They were middle class in their thoughts and feelings, and even the most hopeless among them were certain that their children were going to get an education and "rise in the world."

I saw the middle classes suffering just as much as manual workers and farmers. The white collar people were losing their jobs and their homes; the small investors had been swindled out of everything; even the skilled technicians, the engineers, administrators, architects—were sitting idle in their offices, unable to pay their rent. Six hundred lawyers were being dropped from the Bar Association, because they could not pay their annual dues of seven dollars and a half. Thousands of doctors were no longer able to collect fees—so it went, wherever one turned.

If Fascism came to California it would be through these middle class people. If Democracy were preserved in California, it would be because these people had come to understand the depression and the remedy.

I wrote a little book, "The Way Out," intended to enlighten them. There came to me a young man, Richard S. Otto, a real estate subdivider, forcibly retired. He had a thousand acres of land which he would be glad to donate for a colony—there was nothing else that could be done with it. He read "The Way Out" and it met his mental needs. He spent a part of what money he had left to print an edition of ten thousand copies of this book. He was running two "Bellamy societies," and would sell the books or give them away at meetings.

That was August, 1933, and there came to me a letter from an elderly gentleman of Santa Monica, chairman of the County Central Committee of the Democratic Party in his assembly district. He suggested that I register as a Democrat and announce myself a candidate for the nomination for Governor on the Democratic ticket, putting forward a definite program to deal with the depression. I smiled, and marked the letter to receive the form answer prepared for those who invited me into politics.

But this old gentleman would not be put off. He wrote several times. He said that five of the seven members of his committee were for me; he said it would be the same all over the State. The Democratic Party was split into half a dozen factions, with half a dozen warring leaders, no one of them having any economic knowledge or any idea how to meet the crisis. He tempted me subtly; even if I did not run, would I not help prepare a program for those who wished to take action?

This started a process in my mind. Suppose the people of California wanted to do something, what could they do? I took all my thoughts on the subject and thought them over again, weighing them from a new point of view. I no longer had thirty years, perhaps not thirty months; something had to be done now—and what was it?

This ruled out all measures which were difficult to understand, or were foreign to the American mind. It ruled out all foreign movements, all foreign words. It ruled out all minor parties, all new parties.

I said to myself: "Fifty per cent of the people are going to vote a certain ticket because their grandfathers voted that ticket. In order to get anywhere, it is necessary to have a party which has grandfathers." That seemed to point to the Democratic Party, the oldest in the country, a party of grandfathers and of great-grandfathers. My own great-grandfather had been one of its founders—Commodore Arthur Sinclair, who commanded the first frigate built by our nation, the "Congress," in 1802.

I had left the Democratic Party, because as a youth in New York I had got close to Tammany Hall. Now it was proposed that I should come back, and endeavor to take the Democratic Party of California away from the graf ters and corporation agents. The idea began to interest me, and finally I yielded this far; I said to the old gentleman in Santa Monica: "I will prepare a program and see what you and your friends think of it."

That was how I fell into the trap, and ceased to be

an author and became a politician for fourteen
months—in spite of all the promises to myself, and the
still more solemn promises to my wife!

CHAPTER II

Somewhere in the writings of Robert Blatchford occurs the sentence: "When six men go out into a field to
catch a horse, it makes all the difference whether they
spend their time catching the horse or keeping one-
another from catching the horse." For thirty years that
sentence stayed in my mind as a final statement on the
subject of cooperation versus competition in industrial
affairs.

I know that we began in a competitive world, and I
have no quarrel with the past. I am looking toward
the future; and I say that when men compete with one
another for wealth they produce poverty for themselves. They duplicate plants, they over-produce, they
adulterate goods, they lie about their products, they
spy upon one another, they buy special favors from government officials, they subsidize lobbyists and politicians, and build up political machines, and ultimately
undermine the practice of Democracy. For all such
forms of waste the consumer pays.

For thirty years I have been pleading for production
planned by trained experts and distribution based upon
services rendered. Thirty years ago I asserted that by
such elimination of waste it would be possible to give
every worker $5000 per year for three or four hours
work a day. Thirty years have passed, and with our
new powers of production we could give every worker
twice that much for two hours' work a day.

I preached and taught this; I campaigned for office,
and great audiences came and applauded—and then
went away and voted for the old system. Why was it?
I sat down to think it out, and decided that the thing
sounded too good to be true. People did not really
believe it; they could see no way of getting from where
they were to the heaven I offered.

So I said: "Let us drop utopias from our program.

No more ideal commonwealths, no more perfect societies. Let us start from where we are."

In Los Angeles County there were, according to official figures, 509,000 persons dependent upon public relief. To keep these persons was costing a huge sum of money. Including food, rent, gas, carfare, and other necessities, it could not be less than fifty cents a day per person. One-quarter of a million dollars a day, or nearly a hundred million a year—that was the burden which my county, had to reckon upon.

Of course not all this money was paid by the county. Some of it came from the State, some from the Federal government, some from private charity. But in the long run it all came to the same thing; somebody was putting up a hundred million dollars a year, and it could only be those who still had jobs or incomes.

If you were no longer going to keep these persons as objects of charity, what else could you do? Manifestly there was only one alternative. You could put them at work and let them produce what they themselves were going to consume; make them self-sustaining, take them off the backs of the taxpayers, and stop the process of driving the State into bankruptcy.

A curious story came to me from the cotton country, the Mississippi Delta, where my wife's people live. For more than a hundred years these people had used the labor of the Negroes; the whites riding on the Negroes' backs. There was only one crop, cotton; it was cheaper to buy everything else outside. But now the depression came, and changed the situation in the oddest way. Cotton being no longer a cash crop, the planters had no money; but they had to feed their Negroes—it was the tradition, handed down from slavery days. So the Negroes were being kept in idleness—riding on the backs of the whites!

Of course it did not take the white people many years to realize this, and cotton ceased to be the only crop. The Negroes were made to grow corn and raise hogs for their own food. Production for use in the Mississippi Delta!

And now here were the people of Los Angeles county in the same position! They could not let their unemployed starve; they had to give them some food and clothing. How long would it be before they took the same step as the Mississippi planters, and set the idle workers at producing what they were going to consume?

Here seemed to be the emmediate issue, the program for this moment. Use the credit power of the State to give the unemployed access to land and let them grow their own food; give them access to machinery and let them produce their own goods. When they had produced, let them exchange among themselves, and so build up a system of production for use instead of for profit.

The State of California is well adapted to such an experiment. We have a vast area, with widely divergent crops, and whave many of basic natural resources. We can produce every kind of food except a few secondary things such as tea and coffee. We have lumber, cement, rock and gravel, clay and gold. We have no iron ore, but we have steel mills and copper smelters, and factories in which most of the common articles are produced. Needless to say, we have skilled workers in all these industries, and trained technicians and administrators, thousands of them idle.

The total number on relief in the State was about one million, which meant some four hundred thousand able-bodied workers. If we established a cooperative system for that many persons, there would be work of every kind, and each could do the kind for which he had been trained. The scale of the undertaking would be large enough to demonstrate the advantages of cooperation, and to the extent that we made a success of it the whole world would learn from California. It would be impossible to make an entire failure, for no one could deny that the unemployed would produce something, and whatever they produced would be that much saved to the taxpayers.

Such a procedure would help everybody and hurt nobody. It would restore the morale of the unemployed; it would make them self-sustaining and self-respecting citizens, paying their own way in the world; it would benefit the taxpayers because it would take the unemployed off their backs. It would help the workers who still had jobs, because it would take the unemployed off the labor market, and so stop the process of beating down wages. It would not hurt the business men, because the unemployed are no longer of any use to private business, having no money to spend. That which they spend with the merchants they first get from the taxpayers—which means the merchants and those who still have jobs.

If I was right in my belief that the crisis was a permanent one, the money paid by the State to feed the unemployed was an expenditure without end. But by making a capital investment for the unemployed, the State would solve the problem once for all. The unemployed would earn a surplus, and pay off the debt of the State, and then be in position to manage their own affairs in an independent cooperative society.

Here, then, was the way of making a start at the building of a new social order. It was a way adapted to our immediate needs; it was an American way, in accordance with our traditions of self-help and independence. It would be a Democratic way, depending upon mutual consent; it would be brought about by the votes of the whole people, in accordance with our laws and Constitution.

Nobody would be robbed and no property would be confiscated. There was any quantity of idle land, and our ten thousand factories were running on an average of only forty per cent of capacity. Many of the owners would be glad to sell or rent to the State. All that was necessary was to persuade the taxpayers and voters to make this capital investment.

It was a problem of mass psychology; and I cast about for a slogan. End Poverty In California came to me as a statement of our goal, and I noted that the initials spelled the word EPIC. We found that people liked that—it sounded impressive. The EPIC Plan it became, and the EPIC Plan it remains, and it is good not merely for California, but for Connecticut, Colorado, Canada, and even Kansas and Kentucky! Unfortunately not all of our States begin with C or K; but as our movement spreads, the rest of the world may interpret the name to mean End Poverty In Civilization. If any one can suggest a better version, I'll be glad to hear from him!

CHAPTER III

It is easy to imagine the unemployed of California in a system of production for use because of the efforts which they have made to establish such a system for themselves. All over the State self-help and barter groups have sprung up. There have been literally hundreds of them, and for a year or two I had been hearing stories of their achievements. In Compton, an industrial town south of Los Angeles, they served 19,745 meals at a total money cost of less than one-half cent a meal. My friend, Hjalmar Rutzebeck, author of "Alaska Man's Luck," was active in the UXA (Unemployed Exchange Association) of Oakland, and told me marvelous tales about the complicated procedure whereby a group of several thousand hungry men would manage to make something out of nothing. They would find a farmer with a crop of peaches rotting on the trees, and who needed to have his barn painted. They would find a paint merchant who would accept some canned peaches in return for paint. Some of these operations were extremely complicated, involving an elaborate circle of activities with a dozen different participants.

One would have expected such efforts at self-support to be welcomed by the entire community. The cooperatives of Los Angeles county maintained 150,000 members for five months on a cash expenditure by the Government of only seventeen cents per family per month. Since a family is found to average 3.6 persons, this was less than one-sixth of a cent per person per day. Here was Los Angeles county drifting into bankruptcy; here was the board of supervisors being besieged one day by hungry men demanding doles, and the next day by taxpayers clamoring against further taxes. For persons on the dole who did not belong to cooperatives the State of California was paying out in one way and another forty-five cents per person per day, or 270 times as much as the cooperatives were costing. One would have expected that everybody in the county would hail the cooperatives as the most progressive, the most American, the most helpful of all the developments of these depression years.

But it was not so. The cooperatives were handicapped and hamstrung in a hundred different ways. Their funds were cut off, their leaders were bribed, they were broken by dissentions deliberately fostered.

A story was told to me by one of the leading society ladies of Los Angeles. A self-help group had got hold of some old baking machinery and got it to working and were turning out several thousand loaves of bread per day. Another group had got some land and grown some vegetables. They had an old truck and were exchanging bread for vegetables; but the bakery concerns objected to the bartering of bread, and the produce concerns objected to the bartering of vegetables, and the politicians forced the relief workers to cut off the gasoline supply of the truck, and so the operation was brought to an end.

That is how it is in our blind, anarchic society. When the State gives money to the unemployed and they spend it for bread in a store, that amounts to a subsidy for the stores; and in their greed for that subsidy the store-owners are willing to see the taxpayers driven out of their homes and the State driven into bankruptcy.

Even relief itself has become a racket. As I write, Senator Borah tells the American people that of the money which the Government gives for relief of the unemployed not more than one-half actually reaches the unemployed. The rest goes to the politicians along the line. In Democratic States it goes to build up a Democratic machine and in Republican States it goes to build up a Republican machine. California has been a Republican State for forty years and remains so, and the relief money serves to build up a machine of President Roosevelt's enemies and to bring the New Deal to futility.

The society lady who told me the bakery episode had tears of vexation and despair in her eyes. Her story stayed in my mind, and was one of the factors which brought about my decision to try to break up this racket and set the cooperatives free to grow. It is interesting to note that after I announced my candidacy for Governor, this lady sent me messages of sympathy, together with apologies for her failure to help me. Her whole family was in arms against me, insisting that I was going to ruin them. Her daughter was actively campaigning, first for George Creel and then for Merriam. The mother kept silence.

It seemed such a simple thing to put the credit of the State behind these cooperatives and enable them to function, and take care of the people for half a cent a day instead of for forty-five cents a day. The plight of the people was so tragic, and their efforts to help themselves so infinitely touching! I visited a cooperative in Pomona, where I found a group of men and women working in an old garage. They had been permitted to gather peaches and tomatoes which were going to rot for lack of a market. They had set up three or four oil-burning stoves with wash-boilers to top; with this primitive equipment they had stacked up half the garage with crates of canned fruit. They were not permitted to sell any of it to me, but they were permitted to eat it, or to exchange with another place where old clothing was being repaired.

The possibilities of production were unlimited. All our cities are ringed around with idle land held out of use by speculators. In Germany every square foot of such land was planted with vegetables and small fruits. Why could not we in California have garden plots where now were burned-over patches of weeds?

"Americans don't want to work the land," said my objecting friends. "They leave that sort of work for Mexicans and Japs and Portuguese and Filipinos and Hindoos." The answer came in the shape of a photograph showing what a cooperative in Alhambra was doing. They had got a patch of land, and having no horse, four men had hitched themselves to the plow, and were pulling it while the fifth man guided.

I collected statistics as to factories. There were more than 10,000 of all kinds in California and they were working on an average of 40% of capacity. Some 16% were entirely idle. Many were dismantled; but how quickly the unemployed would have gone to work and put them into condition, and started them up to make their own shoes and clothes, and their own flour and sugar and butter and lumber and brick and cement!

I had no time to get statistics as to the financial condition of the factories, but it seemed obvious that no plant which was running at 40% of capacity was making money, and those which were closed down were falling into the hands of the moneylenders. It was so easy to imagine an enlightened Government saying: "Mr. Factory Owner, you cannot pay your taxes and the interest on your bonds. Let the State take over the running of your plant, guarantee you your fixed charges and a modest profit, and call in your own idle workers and set them to making goods for themselves. We will keep your own administrative staff and pay them the usual salaries. All we want is production. Instead of 40% capacity we will get 100%; indeed we will run it two or three shifts and make seven factories out of one."

I said to myself, "The time has come for the people to understand this proposition. They have got to understand it because the State is approaching bankruptcy and our taxpayers are losing their homes and their ranches. We cannot go on for more than a year or two longer; and it does no good to imagine that we are going to get help from the Federal Government, because California will owe its share of the national debt, and there is no use fooling ourselves with the idea that the people of Texas are going to pay our share. In Texas the people are fooling themselves with the idea that California is going to pay their share."

At that time, the autumn of 1933, we had a deficit of something like thirty-five million dollars in the State, due to our having elected as Governor a sunny gentleman whose qualifications for office were a smile, an excellent knowledge of good liquor, the ability to wear shiny boots and a gardenia, and to ride a horse backwards at county fairs. Fifteen months have passed since then, and now the State controller tells us that the deficit will be sixty-five million very soon, and this without counting any expenditure for relief. In the mean-time the national debt has been increased by ten billion dollars, and the number of the dependent in California has increased by another quarter million.

I said to myself, "Somebody has to make a start; and if I try in California, I will probably accomplish more than by adding another book to the forty-five I have written.

I said: "I will drop all the things I have taught and believed in the past thirty years. I will concentrate upon one simple and practical idea; to take the unemployed of California off the backs of the taxpayers, and put them at work under a system of producing for use. That, with a tax revision program and social insurance measures, will be the way to End Poverty In California, and I will offer my services to do the job, if the people want me."

CHAPTER IV

A proposal to put the half million unemployed workers of California at productive labor, would, of course, involve the expenditure of a considerable amount of money, either for rental or purchase of land and factories. This made it necessary that the EPIC Plan should include a tax program, and I set myself to the study of this.

I am not an expert on taxation; but it needs no expert to discover that our State system is not designed to remedy the inequalities of wealth distribution. Our present tax structure is a part of the system whereby the rich are made to grow richer and the poor to grow poorer.

Taxes upon bonds, public utilities and great corporations are very light, and those upon natural resources are still lighter. The great bulk of taxation is upon land and improvements, and the assessment methods are such that the small homeowner pays relatively several times as much as the great corporation. Many forms of manufacturing escape all taxing. For example, a firm in Hollywood manufactures a motion picture at a cost of a million dollars; the negative is shipped to New York and kept there, and it pays no taxes either in New York or in California.

The extravagances of "Sunny Jim" Rolph made necessary additional taxes in 1932. Two measures were proposed: a sales tax and a State income tax. The latter was designed to raise $45,000,000, but the senate cut it down to $15,000,000. The assembly then passed the sales tax and the income tax, the understanding being that the Governor would sign both; but he signed the sales tax and vetoed the income tax, and the people of the State "took it lying down," as usual.

The sales tax is supposed to be 2½%, but it begins with a tax of one cent on a 15 cent purchase, which is nearly 7%. Since the poor do more of their purchasing in small quantities, they pay the higher rates. In any case they pay most of the tax, and that is why it is favored by the rich. Its effect is to reduce purchasing power and make still worse the depression which it is supposed to remedy.

Manifestly any enlightened tax program would provide for the repeal of the sales tax and the substitution of the State income tax, also an increase in the State inheritance taxes. The maximum inheritance tax was reduced recently from 20% to 12%. It has been so easy to fool the people of California! I asked the question of many audiences and found that not more than two or three in a thousand knew that this reduction in inheritance taxes had taken place.

The next source of taxation would be, of course, the idle land. California has always been a paradise of real estate speculators. Everybody who had any money at all bought some lots, and was hoping to sell them for two or three times what they had cost. The result is that every city, town and village is surrounded with a belt of unoccupied land. In all the outlying portions there are more vacant lots than occupied lots, and this results in greatly increased costs for paving, water, gas, electricity and telephones. With homeless men by the thousands wandering our highways and with people starving by the thousands in every city and town, it required no tax expert to see that idle land should be taxed, and thus be taken out of the hands of the speculators and brought into productive use.

Finally there was the problem of the small ranch owners and home owners who were unable to pay their taxes. All over the State they were being turned out of their homes, or allowed to stay on as tenants of the banks. To deal with this problem I suggested that homes occupied by the owners and ranches occupied by the owners which were assessed at less than $3000 should be exempt from taxation.

Work for those who are able to work and State care for those who are unable to work—that seems to me the basic program for any enlightened country. I proposed the payment of a pension of $50 per month to every needy person over sixty years of age who had lived for three years in the State; the same for the blind and those physically incapacitated; also for the widowed mothers of dependent children.

Such was the EPIC Plan. It was designed to meet the immediate issues of this depression by methods which involved the least possible strain upon the propertied classes. Since it was designed to win majority consent, it necessarily had to appeal to the masses of voters. It was expected to win the unemployed, the small home owners, the small taxpayers, the old people, and the women. Since these various groups included 80% or 90% of all voters, the only question was whether these people could be persuaded to vote in their own interest, instead of in the interest of those who exploited their labor and disregarded their sufferings.

Having completed this program, I printed it and sent it to some fifty of the most qualified thinkers upon the subject. I asked for their comments, and several changes were made in the Plan to meet their objections. I mention this because one of the charges brought against me was that I had proceeded with rash impetuosity upon my own ideas. Among those who made these charges was a certain Catholic publication, so perhaps I should mention that one of those who gave me advice was Father John A. Ryan of the Catholic University of America.

I took the program to my Democratic friends in Santa Monica. I had not had much to do with Democrats since the days of my youth, and I did not know how they were thinking and feeling. I read the program to them, and was not a little surprised to find that they took what I had to say with enthusiasm. It was the unanimous opinion of the members of that county central committee that if my program were put before the Democratic party it would sweep the State and become California's share of the New Deal.

The old gentleman who lured me into this EPIC adventure is Mr. Gilbert F. Stevenson, who once owned the Miramar Hotel in Santa Monica, assessed at $2,136,000. The banks had got it during the depression, and we met in a cheap hotel across the street. Afterwards he gave me one of his books to read, a work on money reform, and I discovered to my distress that my political monitor had fallen under the sway of the anti-Semitic agitators, and believed in the so-called Protocols of Zion! It was the first of many complications which I found to be incidental to a career in the Democratic party.

"Go and register as a Democrat," whispered Mr. Stevenson, as we parted. "Do it at once, and do it quietly." So on the first of September, 1933, I slipped into the city hall at Beverly Hills, and signed a piece of paper to the effect that I had formerly been registered as a Socialist but was now registering as a Democrat. I didn't want anybody to know about it until I had written my book setting forth the program and the plan. But a couple of weeks later, while I was in the midst of writing, some newspaper reporter picked up the story and called on me for a statement.

It was embarrassing, because I needed a book to explain what was in my mind, and everybody wanted the explanation at once. My son and his wife, devoted Socialist party members in New York, sent me frantic telegrams, and from all over the country came peremptory letters demanding to know if this was one more "Brass Check" story, or had I really gone back upon the faith of my lifetime? All I could say was that I was writing a book, and would they please wait.

I had hit upon the lively idea of putting my program into the form of a story, imagining myself elected Governor and doing the job. I thought that people would be more apt to read it in that form. The title, "I, Governor of California, and How I Ended Poverty," sounded tempting, and I hoped it would lure them on. Above all I counted upon the fact that people were in need and it was a remedy for their troubles I was offering.

As I wrote the story it became more and more real to me. I began to see myself as Governor. If I had been the vain person which my enemies portray me, I might have been delighted with this rise to prominence. Being a person who hates more than any one thing to be bored, I found the vision terrifying, and it took all my courage to hold myself to the new task.

In the middle of September my wife and I had to travel to New York, to attend the opening of a motion picture, "Thunder Over Mexico," for which we had got ourselves responsible. I finished revising the manuscript of the book on the train, and left it with my printers in Chicago. In a few days the proofs of the book reached me in New York, and among my friends who read them was Norman Thomas. He felt it his duty to issue in the "New Leader" a repudiation of the Plan. I observe with sorrow the fallibility of the human brain as an instrument for arriving at truth. My old friend, Norman Thomas, has been writing now for fourteen months about the EPIC Plan, and I have yet to find in what he writes anything which I can recognize as the Plan I advocate.

Reading the proofs, and seeing the excitements of the New York newspapers on the subject, I realized once more the painful possibility that I might become the Governor of a State. I composed a brief paragraph to the effect that as I wrote this story it had become real to me, and I had been tempted into taking it seriously; now it was necessary for me to say that I purposed to remain a writer, and requested the readers of this book to take it as fiction. I pasted that onto the last page, and was about to mail the proofs to the printer, when my wife got hold of them and stopped me. "No!" she said. "You have publicly committed yourself! Terrible as it all seems, you must go on with it." So the paragraph was taken out and the EPIC movement started.

In the months that followed, how many occasions I had to be glad that my wife was a sharer in my guilt! Every husband will understand how fortunate we are when our wives are not in position to blame us for the troubles we have brought upon them. I was a candidate for Governor, and Mary Craig Sinclair, bless her heart, was candidate for Governess, in spite of being the least ambitious for fame of all persons in the State of California!

CHAPTER V

The book, "I, Governor of California: And How I Ended Poverty," was published in October, 1933. I returned from New York in the first days of November,

The Literary Circle in California

which gave me just a year for the political campaign. My home at that time was in Beverly Hills, and my secretary had a little five-room cottage near by; I arranged to use the front room as an office, paying half the rent. That became the headquarters of the "End Poverty League," a non-profit corporation, which we formed for our purpose. There my new friend, Richard S. Otto, and I answered letters, filled orders for the book, and received the visitors who came in a constantly widening stream.

The book "caught on" from the very outset; orders poured in, for single copies or for hundreds. People came every day to offer help. There was only one trouble about it; each person wanted to see me, and get his instructions from me, and his enthusiasm was conditioned upon that wish being granted. That remained the case up to the very end. I ought to have been able to grow by fission, like the amoeba; first there would have been two of me, and then four, then eight, sixteen, thirty-two—and so on until there were a thousand. Then I should have been able to receive all the visitors, make all the speeches, sign all the letters and autograph books—so, no doubt, I might have carried the election.

As I look back on that year, it was like living on board a ship in a hurricane. Another secretary had to be engaged, then a third and a fourth. The elderly lady who lived in the cottage vacated another room, and then, unable to stand the day and night turmoil, she moved to another house, and the End Poverty League had five rooms. A month or so later we moved into a house with seven rooms, each twice as big. In two or three months more we moved to downtown Los Angeles, a fourteen-room place which fifty years ago had been a mansion of the rich. From there we moved into a thirty-two-room office building, where we finished the campaign with something like a hundred and fifty volunteer workers, and a big warehouse near by serving as the wrapping and mailing rooms of our paper.

Telephones, telegrams, postage, stationery, literature—all these things take money; and money was our problem from the first hour. We solved it at first by using the cash which came day by day from the sale of the books—until I had run up a bill at my printers of something over $3,000. Then I generously presented the book to the End Poverty League—which meant that from then on Dick Otto had to do the worrying about money! He had told me at the outset that he had enough of his own to keep him and his wife for the year's campaign, and after that he didn't know what he would do. The year has passed now, and he is still on the job sixteen hours a day, and I have been too busy to ask him how he is managing, and he has been too busy to tell me.

I began making speeches; anywhere I was invited, to any sort of crowd which was willing to learn how to end poverty in California. I remember the annual banquet of the "Third District Association," a neighborhood improvement group. They had invited also our State treasurer, a popular political personage, "Gus" Johnson; he also was a candidate for the governorship, and he laid down the law that what the State of California needed was a "business man." "Well," said I, "I am running as a business man"—which excited great hilarity among the crowd. I told them my extensive experience; publisher of over a million books, not counting ten millions in foreign translations; producer of several plays and a motion picture; publisher of a monthly magazine; manager of a farm and also of a Socialist colony. I had handled several millions of dollars, and made close to a million in profits, and spent them on the causes I loved—I counted myself successful, whatever the world chose to think.

Presently we found that we could take collections at meetings, and so help out our suffering bank-account. Under the California law the people may use the schoolhouses for political and educational meetings, but no collections may be taken; however, they allow "voluntary dues," so we invited people to join the End Poverty League, and pay us whatever dues they could afford. A few would pay a dollar; others would pay a penny, or a collar-button.

I look back over that year, a blur of meetings, meetings, meetings. I shall never be able to pass a California high school building without remembering the time I spoke there, and the crowd which filled the last seat up in the balcony, and lined the walls all around, and stood outside, hoping to catch an echo. The way the people crowded in, the way they listened, and then went out and organized, and did the job in their neighborhood—later on it was called "a political miracle." But it wasn't that, it was just the pressure of the economic screw, and the fact that we had a program which met the people's needs and appealed to their sound judgment.

From the outset I made practice of answering questions from the audience. I would speak for an hour, and then answer questions for an hour. Some of our friends who had political experience were frightened by this; no candidate ever had done such a thing, the enemy would set traps for me, and so on. My answer was that I had been studying this subject all my thinking life, and I did not think anybody in the audience could ask me a question I could not answer. If they did, I might learn something myself. The question periods did educate me as well as the audience; they told me what the people were thinking, and helped me to prepare for the later attacks.

At the outset the Socialists would ask why I had deserted them, and did I think this was Socialism, and so on. But it was not long before the Socialists came to understand—the drop in their vote at the end showed that ninety-five per cent of them were with me. As to the Communists, their heckling was violent and bitter: did I think the capitalist class would surrender anything without a fight? did I imagine I would be allowed to take office if I were elected?—and so on. At some meetings they showered the audience from the gallery with leaflets attacking me; I would call for a copy of the leaflet, and read it to the audience, and answer it. The people showed such resentment at interruptions, and such an overwhelming resolve for Democratic procedure, that in the end the Communists gave up, and I do not recall any attempt at heckling during the last three months of the campaign.

I made it the rule to speak simply and quietly, without any attempt at oratory. I explained to the people the plight in which they found themselves, and what our program was, and what I believed it would do for them. I said, in substance: "I cannot end poverty in California, but you can, and what I offer is to show you how, and guide the procedure. But first and last it is your problem. I am not asking to be Governor of

California, I am not asking anybody to vote for me. I am offering my services, if you want them; but you have to go out and do the work. It means organization, education, and sacrifice for a year. It's up to you." I took to asking at the end: "How many are for this plan?" and the hands raised would be ninety per cent of those present.

I would tell them about an old fellow who spoke to me in the post office in Pasadena, a year or so after the depression started. "Sinclair," he said, "the people in this neighborhood don't know what is happening to them. Smith knows that he's in trouble, but he thinks that Jones is all right; Jones knows he is going under, but he thinks that Smith is still safe." So I would say: "Let's see how it is in Fresno"—or in San Diego, or Santa Rosa, or San Luis Obispo. "How many here are out of work?" Anywhere from one in three to one in five of the audience would raise their hands. In the farming communities it would be less, and I would say: "They have contrived it so that the farmer does not get out of work. What the farmer gets out of is money. How many in this audience are out of money?" Of course, there would be a roar of laughter, and everybody in the hall would raise his hand; many would raise two hands.

They would accept my challenge, and go out and organize. Often they would stay in the hall and organize that night. It spread so fast we could not keep up with it. Letters would come in, telling of new clubs formed, new headquarters opened; there would be more letters to answer, more orders to fill, literature, books, posters, stickers, buttons and what not—and our pitiful little office crowded with visitors all day, and Dick Otto having to take home armfuls of letters to answer at night.

To the audiences I said, over and over again: "There is only one thing you can do for me, which is to vindicate the faith in the people which I have held to all my life." And they did that; from that point of view it was a magnificent triumph, through the whole year. The people awakened; they studied and thought about their problems, they took charge of their own job. They formed nearly two thousand clubs; they opened and financed several hundred headquarters; they paid for and circulated nearly half a million booklets and ten or fifteen million newspapers; they organized thousands of meetings; they swept the Democratic primaries by the biggest vote ever polled, and ten weeks later they doubled that vote. And if anyone thinks they are through yet, he has something to learn about politics in the State of California!

CHAPTER VI

The only way you could understand what we went through in the early days of the EPIC movement is if you have built a house and lived in it at the same time. We had to do the work of running an office, and at the same time sort out the stream of visitors to find new people to do the double work that would be piled upon our shoulders the next day.

I have met men who claimed to be infallible judges of character, able to pick out the competent person at a glance. I looked in vain for such a miraculous one all through the campaign. We were obliged to follow the more painful process of trial and error. Men and women offered themselves, and some went to work and did what they said they would do; while others sat around and talked, and told stories and got in other people's way. Since they were all volunteers and fellow-idealists, we couldn't bear to hurt their feelings.

There came promoters with wonderful schemes for making money, and inventors with things we could put on the market and solve our financial problems at once. There came poets, and composers of campaign songs and marches, and authors of EPIC plays and painters of EPIC pictures, and astrologers to cast our horoscopes, and sculptors to make busts of us. There came efficiency experts, highly trained, ready to make us all over after the pattern of big business. One of these gentlemen worked day and night for a week, and brought a whole portfolio full of plans and charts, adapted to the requirements of a ten-million-dollar corporation with twenty-two department heads at a salary of twenty-five thousand per year each. We had fifteen dollars in the bank at that time and maybe a thousand in debts. What we wanted was somebody to sit at a desk and straighten out the tangles in my speaking dates, or go out and persuade the owner of some radio station that a talk on the ending of poverty in California would be economics and not politics.

Our one perpetual need was funds. We would pick out likely looking persons and tactfully suggest that they go out and try to find money for the ending of poverty in California. Almost invariably they would request that I give them a list of my friends who happened to have money. No. 1 was always Charlie Chaplin; Number 2 was Aline Barnsdall, whose father owned an oil company; Number 3 was Kate Crane-Gartz, whose father founded the Crane Company. We would patiently explain that if our friends had anything to give, they would be as likely to give it to us as to strangers.

There was money to be had for our campaign, but unfortunately always money that we could not take. As soon as it became evident that we had a real movement, we began to have visits from well-dressed, smooth-spoken persons familiar with politics, who offered us the solution to all our problems. The first was a representative of a group of men who conducted a gambling game, and at that time were taking sixty-five thousand dollars a day from the people of Los Angeles. All these people wanted to know was that if I was elected Governor I would let them alone. On that basis I could have "anything within reason." I never found out how much that was, because I told the gentleman that we were not making political promises, except those in our program.

Next came the "rock, sand and gravel people." The gentleman they sent to us was shrewd and took a lot of trouble. He studied our program, he was deeply interested, he came into our office and went to work; he helped to organize several clubs, and went out and tried to raise money for us honestly. After a while he came with an offer. The rock, sand, and gravel people understood that I was an honest man and would have nothing to do with any kind of corruption. They wanted to be on our side without any kind of pledge whatever; there were three different companies which wanted to pay fifty thousand dollars each to our campaign fund. Of course, I understood that these companies had been practicing collusive bidding for years, and I told our friend that we were not taking that kind of money. Soon afterward I learned that this man had run up a bill in our name at a hotel where we then had headquarters.

There came another who had been a hanger-on of our movement, doing a little work and feeling us out. He got me into a room alone and had a proposition that was "absolutely honest" and I need not be afraid of. I had become wise by that time, and when anybody told me he had something honest, I knew **he** wasn't honest. However, I listened to the proposition, and learned that the State of California insures certain of its buildings against fire with private insurance companies. If I became Governor I would be obliged to place this insurance, and there could be no question of rates because these were fixed; so there would be no loss to the State by my indicating which companies I would favor. If I would so indicate, this gentleman would get me fifteen thousand dollars from each of the companies concerned.

I said: "If I were Governor, the honest way for me to meet such a situation would be to find out how many qualified companies there were and then divide the business among them." The reply was, "Yes, but you wouldn't get any campaign funds that way." I said: "Is it not possible that there might be some insurance men who would like to have the business of the State honestly conducted?" The gentleman said that he doubted it, but would inquire. As he did not come back, I gather that he was right and I was wrong. No doubt he is sure of it by now, since I have failed of election.

All through the campaign we struggled with a load of debt, and had these fortunes dangling before our eyes. One of our San Francisco workers, a manufacturer ruined by the depression and living by the kindness of his son, received a visit from a representative of the gamblers of San Francisco, who offered us sixteen thousand dollars per month, not merely during the period of the campaign but during the four years of my incumbency. That worked out at close to nine hundred thousand dollars. Later on when I saw our opponents

"FOR WHATSOEVER A MAN SOWETH, THAT SHALL HE ALSO REAP"

By Jerry Doyle

From the New York "Evening Post"

pouring out unlimited treasure I was able to guess where it had come from.

These offers were no temptation to me, because I did not care that much about winning. But I was interested to observe the effect of them upon some of our workers. I have in mind a young man just recently out of college, a fresh, eager youngster, full of fine ideals. He worked for us for several months, living on the bounty of his father. He would think up wonderful plans which we could carry out if only we had the money; and he would be heartbroken because his plans were not carried out. He would blame our campaign manager and others for failing to do the things which they had not the money to do.

Finally, one Sunday morning he came out to see me at my home. "Upton, we gotta have the dough!" he cried. It was not the language they had taught him at the university, but the language of politics which he had taken up. "We gotta have the dough, I tell you. You can't win any election without dough." "But where can we get it?" I asked. My young friend blurted out: "I know an old gentleman who wants to be made fish and game commissioner, and he'll put fifteen thousand dollars into the campaign if you will promise him." I asked why an old gentleman wanted to be fish and game commissioner, and the answer was: "He likes to fish, and his friends like to fish, and it would be an honor. He's got a lot of money and he'd like to wear a ribbon or something." I said: "If he wants to wear a ribbon, that's all right, but suppose he wants to steal the fish?"

I turned down the young man's proposition, and he went away disgusted, and I have not seen him since.

An odd thing about the fish and game commissioner. I had made my remark about stealing the fish as a joke; but a few days later a friend took me sailing outside the harbor, and I put out a trolling line, and I did not get a strike, and remarked, "There do not seem to be many fish here." My friend replied that it was the commercial fishing that had ruined these fishing grounds. I asked if there were not laws on the subject, and my friend said: "Yes, but you see the commercial fisheries invite Jimmy Rolph down and give him a banquet once a year, and then they name the fish and game commissioners, and can do what they please."

AND HOW I GOT LICKED

I promised you the story of "a scholar in politics." As you know, I am now a scholar out of politics, because I refused to play this game according to the rules. All through the campaign I said to my audiences: "I have not made the promise of a single office, nor any other sort of pledge, except those which are in our platform. I have not taken one dollar with a string tied to it. On the night before election I intend to make that same statement over the radio to the voters of the whole State." I made it, and it was true; and because of that attitude and that conduct, we did not have the money to answer the millions of lies of our enemies, and so we did not get the votes. And so the scholar is out of politics.

CHAPTER VII

California is 650 miles from North to South, much too big for one state. I found it so in this campaign; I am sure that during the fourteen months I travelled enough miles to have taken me around the earth. I would set out on a trip to the North, and spend a week going from town to town, speaking every evening in a high school auditorium, and often in the afternoon also.

The first trip, just before Christmas, very nearly brought the EPIC movement to a sudden finish. We set out in an old car which I have driven for the past six years; two recent college graduates with me, and a load of literature to be disposed of on the way. We were in the mountains near Lompoc, on the coast route, and it was raining hard. On a curve we struck a muddy place, and the car skidded. It was a matter of a small part of a second: there were white painted posts set up on the edge of a precipice, and we hit one and knocked it out of the soft mud, and hit a second and knocked it pretty nearly out, and there we stopped, poised carefully on the edge. We scrambled out into the rain and mud; and presently came another traveller, whose tires were not worn quite so smooth as mine, and drove me to the next town, from which I sent back a tow-car. The next day I received a letter from my anxious wife, who did not approve of long campaign tours, saying that while asleep in the afternoon she had dreamed of our car going over a precipice on a mountain road.

We held our meeting in San Luis Obispo with several hundred people in a theatre on a rainy night, and we sold our quota of books to pay the costs of the journey, and went our way, knowing we had got a start in that valley. It was interesting to note the difference when we came back a couple of months later; we had an organization now, and twice as large an audience, and the questions showed they had read the book.

It would be that way everywhere. In Sacramento we started with 300 in the Methodist Church, and finished with 4000 in the Auditorium. In Fresno we started with 600 in the high school, and finished with the Auditorium packed to the doors. In San Francisco we started in the Veterans Memorial Hall, about half full, perhaps 700 people; we finished, a week before election, with a crowd in the Auditorium which the hostile newspapers estimated at from 16,000 to 20,000, and across the street in the plaza some 10,000 more listening to Kate O'Hare and Sheridan Downey.

San Francisco would be a hard nut to crack, they told us. It is a cosmopolitan city, proud of itself, and not friendly to cranks from Los Angeles. Justice Wardell and George Creel, my two leading rivals for the Democratic nomination, both lived in San Francisco; the former being the city's perpetual candidate for Democratic offices. It is a strong Catholic city, and the rumor spread quickly that I had written dreadful things about the church.

We made a start with half a dozen on our committee, and had a hard time finding anybody that anybody else approved of; our little group would have a bust-up every now and then. But in spite of this the movement spread; the railroad brotherhoods came over to us, and the labor politicians began to worry, realizing that we were taking their people from under them. A certain postmaster said to me: "The Federal brigade is all working against you"—meaning the office-holders. I replied: "The generals and the colonels are against us, but the privates are for us—and this is no Mexican army." He laughed, and admitted that I was right; every clerk and carrier in his place was an EPIC man.

AND HOW I GOT LICKED

By one means or another we were managing to get the book circulated. We were not permitted to sell literature in school-house meetings—it is one of the devices by which the reactionaries keep the people from getting new ideas. But there was no way to keep people from buying books on the sidewalk outside, nor to keep me from telling them that the books were on sale outside. The books cost about three cents a copy to manufacture, and the End Poverty League sold them for fifteen cents a copy, or six dollars a hundred. Many of the unemployed earned their keep by selling these books at meetings; they learned to follow me around, and one even made a trip to San Francisco in my wake.

The League printed edition after edition of "I, Governor of California." The total up to election day amounted to 255,000 copies. After several months of travelling and answering questions, I knew what the people wanted to know about the Plan, so I prepared a second booklet, "EPIC Answers." This told how the Plan would affect various groups: workingmen, farmers, businessmen, clerks, doctors, lawyers, women, the unemployed, and so on. It answered the questions which were asked over and over again at meetings. The sales have been 65,000.

As the campaign waxed hotter, I began writing letters answering the charges of this person or that newspaper. Presently there was quite a stack of such letters, and I collected them into a book, "The Lie Factory Starts." Our EPIC workers were waiting for it and took 50,000 copies in less than four months.

Finally, just after the primary election came "Immediate EPIC," setting forth the first steps we would make, and explaining various changes in the Plan. Of that there were printed 65,000. This makes a total of 435,000 books, and the End Poverty League must have made $10,000 or $20,000 from these four volumes. The money went for radio time, travelling expenses of speakers, the printing of leaflets, all the costs of a great educational job. From first to last none of our workers received any salary for what they did for the movement; we just didn't have it. When we found that some of our faithful workers were going without food in the middle of the day, we began giving them fifty cents for lunch.

I, CANDIDATE FOR GOVERNOR

The first big "lie factory" was set up in Pasadena. A man came to work in our headquarters there; I don't know if he was a "plant", or a genuine psychopathic case. Anyhow, he began quarreling with the people there, and threatened physical violence. I heard Dick Otto, our campaign manager, ordering this man to resign over the telephone; the man refused, and before we got rid of him the police had to be called in. While I was away on a trip, he called to see my wife, and with two other men spent several hours arguing with her. His demand was that Otto should be "fired", and himself placed in charge of the campaign; otherwise, he said, "I will see that your husband does not become Governor of California." My wife replied: "My husband does not wish to become Governor on those terms."

So the man went out, and a few days later there appeared in a wretched advertising sheet which is left on the doorsteps of everybody in Pasadena, an interview with this man, in which he quoted my wife as saying that her husband did not care to become Governor of California, but was using the campaign just to advertise his books.

Then, a little later, an elaborate article in the Los Angeles "Times," in which this man told the "inside" details about the fortunes Upton Sinclair was making out of the EPIC movement. My profits from the "Governor" book were "expected to net around $40,000." The fact was that the League owed me about $1,700, which I in turn owed to my printers, and still owe. I was said to be expecting to make $25,000 out of the "EPIC News." The fact was that I had never had one cent from the paper, and have not had since. I was said to have "augmented" the sales of my former books by the campaign; the fact being that in 1933 the sales of my books averaged $1720 per month, while in 1934 they averaged less than half that.

The story went on: "And so on down the line, motion pictures, plays, shows, rodeos, food and other merchandising, auction sales, banquets and what nots! And for the personal profit of Sinclair to the potential tune of a quarter of a million dollars." The answer to all this is that I had never had anything to do with any of these attempts of the End Poverty League to earn money for

THE EARLY BIRD EXCITES THE BARNYARD
San Francisco "News"

its work, and had never derived a cent of profit from any of them; at that time I had personally contributed more than $3,000 to the work of the League in one form or another, and when I have finished the writing of this present book, and turned it over to the League to help earn money to pay its debts, I shall go on a lecture tour to earn money to pay the debts which I myself have incurred.

This mess of falsehoods was taken up and reprinted all over the State of California. Three supposed to be respectable newspapers of the central part of the State, the Sacramento "Bee", the Fresno "Bee", and the Modesto "Bee", published and edited by C. K. McClatchy, who doubtless thinks he is a gentleman—all three of the "Bees" printed this libel. Mr. McClatchy resents the statement that he got it from the "Times", and claims the dubious honor of having published it first. All right, Mr. McClatchy! You think you have done your full duty because you allowed me to deny the slanders in your columns—but with no retraction or apology from you. What I ask is, why, before publishing grave charges against a man's honor, not give the man a chance to say whether there is any basis of fact in them? The answer is, because you wanted to discredit the man, and you didn't care what means you used.

CHAPTER VIII

One of the first needs of the End Poverty campaign was, of course, a newspaper. I was modest, and hoped for a weekly bulletin. But in the first weeks of the campaign there came a man who introduced himself as an old Hearst editor; he had some money and thought that publishing a weekly paper for our movement could become a commercial proposition. He was willing for me to control the editorial policy of the paper, and I signed a contract providing that a share of any profits of the enterprise was to come to me.

That was the only basis for the charge that I was "expecting" to make money out of the campaign. Of course, I was hoping to get some money for our growing movement; but I never got any. During the five months that he published "End Poverty" this gentleman never rendered a statement, and we found at the end that his procedure was to take the income and leave the bills unpaid. The clash between the profit motive and the idealistic one in our organization was incessant, and finally we asked the publisher to cancel the contract and quit. When he failed to do so, we just dropped that paper, and started a new one with a new name, "EPIC News." This was from the beginning the property of the End Poverty League, and no one has ever made a cent out of it.

The price was five cents per copy, and we got a thrill out of hearing the newsboys crying EPIC on the streets. One bold crusader took his stand in front of the "Times" building, and it was not long before a plain-clothes man came from police headquarters across the street and ordered him away. But the crusader refused to obey, and the detective thought it over, and the sacred right of selling the "EPIC News" in front of the "Times" building has stood unchallenged ever since.

I contributed an editorial to the paper every week, explaining our program, and dealing with the various issues of the campaign as they arose. The first number contained most of the "I, Governor" book, and in subsequent issues "EPIC Answers" ran as a serial, and then "Immediate EPIC." The paper was sold at meetings, and bundle orders came from our clubs all over the State; we published the news of the progress of our movement in California and in the rest of the country.

Our direct sales from the beginning amounted to about 20,000 weekly. After a few months we hit upon the idea of getting out special editions for different localities. The paper was eight pages, tabloid size, and we would print an outside sheet of four additional pages, dealing with the news of San Fernando Valley or Oakland or whatever the place might be. Our clubs would get local advertising for these special four pages, sufficient to pay for an edition of ten thousand or more. They would then distribute the papers free from door to door. This proved a fruitful idea, and it was not long before we were printing special editions for big affairs, such as a meeting in the Pasadena Rose Bowl or the Civic Auditorium at Long Beach, and distributing thirty or forty thousand papers over the city and the neighboring towns. By such means the paper continued to grow, until two weeks before the primary we printed what was probably the largest edition of a newspaper ever printed in California, 1,450,000 copies, more than eighty separate editions. Before the general election we beat that with two issue of nearly two million each.

The clubs distributed the paper and the paper made new clubs. There were so many that I could not keep track of the growth. Every time I would boast of the number in a speech, I would be told that I was behind the times. At the date of the primary there were close to a thousand, and before the general election there were nearly two thousand.

It was a mass movement, springing directly out of the needs of the people. They did the work, and they did the thinking, and brought in so many new ideas that I did not know what was going on. I would come back from a speaking tour and be told that we had a play in rehearsal, or that I was to appear at a rodeo. The nearest I came to feeling like a real Governor was at this last affair, when I had to drive my car around the ring and wave to a roaring mass of people. We had a barbecue, and feats of horsemanship and steer-roping, and then a string of candidates poured their eloquence into a loud speaker in the middle of the dusty field.

I must not forget "Depression Island." In my book, "The Way Out," written before the EPIC movement started, I had used the illustration of three men cast ashore upon a tropical island; I imagined what would happen to them while they were free, and then the situation if one of them came to own the island. I made a story out of it—three or four pages—and when the EPIC movement got going people began begging me to take up this idea and make it into a play or motion picture. I wrote it as a scenario for a picture, a two-reel comedy.

Since the picture producers refuse any story which suggests any thing wrong with the profit system, we decided to raise the money and make "Depression Island" for ourselves. I spent five days visiting in the palaces of the rich, begging for a loan of thirty-five hundred dollars. I was able to get pledges amounting

But the Dog Can't Vote

CARTOON FROM THE "EPIC" NEWS

to seventeen hundred—of which five hundred was withdrawn two or three days after it was pledged! So the motion picture version of "Depression Island" still waits.

Some of our people demanded it as a stage show, which could be made to pay for itself. So in due course the Shrine auditorium was rented and our clubs were put at work selling tickets. We borrowed the "set" of a tropical island from a motion picture concern, and one evening an audience of three or four thousand assembled.

The curtain went up on three castaways searching for water and something to eat. There was an entirely practical cocoanut tree and highly realistic fish, both fresh and dried. There magically arose a hut. The three men were happy, because if Abie charged too many cocoanuts for a fish, Bing and Crunk could go out and get their own fish; and the same with cocoanuts and huts.

The only trouble was they became bored and took to gambling, and Crunk, a realtor from Los Angeles, won the ownership of the island and also the fishing rights. At once everything was changed, for Crunk put Abie and Bing to work for him, and paid them only one cocoanut and one dried fish per day for their labors. He made them pile up dried fish and cocoanuts for him, and when they had piled up more than he could use, he told them he was very sorry but there was no more work for them. When they asked the reason, he said there was a depression on the island, and when they wanted to know what they should do about it, he told them that was their problem, not his. Crunk was a believer in "rugged individualism."

So of course there arose the problem of social unrest. Abie, a little Jewish song writer from New York, insisted upon helping himself to cocoanuts, whereupon Crunk, owner of the island, hired Bing as policeman and ordered him to put Abie into jail. When Abie tried to persuade Bing that this was all nonsense, and that he and Bing should take the island away from Crunk, the latter called that criminal syndicalism, and urged Bing not to listen to any of that red talk. Bing was a taxicab driver from Chicago, and told Abie that he was a Democrat and a patriot, and believed in law and order; he obeyed the owner of the island, and Abie had to surrender, and be put on a dole of half a dried fish and half a cocoanut a day.

You can imagine how an audience of EPIC enthusiasts roared over these sallies. The story went on to satirize all the developments of the depression. When Crunk started to publish a newspaper and hired Abie to write editorials to tell Bing that the social system was ordained by God, the actors had to stop and wait for the audience to get over laughing.

Finally Abie hit upon the idea of persuading Bing to political action. Bing, a loyal one hundred per cent American, would not listen to red talk, but he was quite ready to hear that they needed an election on that island. So they founded the Democratic party, and Abie wrote a platform, and elected himself Governor and Bing Lieutenant-Governor, and proceeded to impose an income tax on the rich, to cover the deficit and pay the salaries of the public officials.

The master of ceremonies at this show was my friend, Lewis Browne, and he helped in the ending of the play. I had really been too busy to think up an ending, and had quit at the point where Crunk refused to recognize the government, and he and Bing got into a civil war. At that point the master of ceremonies came running onto the scene protesting that brawling would not solve the social problem. The actors said that that was as far as the script went, and it was up to the author to tell them what to do next. So then there was a shout, "Author! Author!" and the author of "Depression Island" was dragged onto the stage, and persuaded to tell the audience how this problem of want in the midst of plenty could be solved by majority consent.

It was just one more EPIC speech; but everybody agreed that we had provided a new sort of introduction, and there was a clamor for "Depression Island" to be shown all over the State. But by then the primaries were only a month off, and our club members had to do precinct work, and we had to rule out the drama and all other cultural arts.

That ruined another fine enterprise, the "EPIC Pageant", which my young friend Youldon Howell had got up among his art pupils in the Pasadena schools. It was a deeply stirring picture of poverty and the people's struggle against it, and some forty amateurs acted it with great effect before crowded audiences in our city and others nearby. What talent there is among the people; and what possibilities of happiness for them, when once the great nightmare has been banished from their lives!

CHAPTER IX

I must not omit the story of the EPIC movement on the air. Early in our crusade I tried my beguilements upon the owners and managers of radio stations, and succeeded in persuading Mr. Guy Earl of KNX that fifteen minutes about EPIC would be educational and not political. Mr. G. Allison Phelps, who conducts an hour on a small station from his home, also gave my ideas a hearing, and reported that his audience called for more. But the big stations and "hook-ups" towered above us like snowy mountain-tops; humble peasants in the valley, we gazed at their summits, never hoping to attain them.

Among my friends was Will Kindig, business man and tireless propagandist of social justice. Mr. Kindig owned a lot, worth sixty-five hundred dollars in the dear, dead days beyond recall. If anybody could find a purchaser for that lot for two thousand dollars, Kindig would lend the money for radio time. We sought, but could find no purchaser of lots in our one-time paradise of realtors.

But Kindig was not to be thwarted. He found a small radio station willing to take his lot in exchange for $750 of time at, one dollar per minute. This gave us fifty broadcasts of 15 minutes each; we could beg for money over the air and perhaps get enough to pay Kindig the $750.

Such was our humble beginning. I spoke half a dozen times over that small station, and Kindig and Otto would do most eloquent begging. Other talent appeared, and we kept going.

Then came Aline Barnsdall from a winter in Japan.

AND HOW I GOT LICKED

Miss Barnsdall's grandfather drilled the second oil-well in the State of Pennsylvania, and her father, "Thee" Barnsdall, drilled more oil-wells than any other man in the United States. His daughter still has some of his money, and attributes the fact to me. She read my books, and realized that I was right—the Coolidge boom was not going to last. So she put her money into Government bonds!

Aline Barnsdall inherited from a rugged "independent" a habit of thinking for herself, and also a sense of fair play. When Tom Mooney was jailed, she made up her mind that it was a "frame-up", and has been his tireless defender ever since. Her property, Olive Hill, in the heart of Hollywood, has been kept covered with Mooney billboards, of Miss Barnsdall's composition; and of course she did not fail to make note of the fact that in my book, "I, Governor of California", I had promised that my first action upon taking office would be the pardoning of Mooney.

There is a wide difference of opinion on this case in California. Either you are for Mooney or against him, and you are apt to be violent in either case. My own position was set forth throughout the campaign as follows:

I take no position regarding Mooney's guilt or innocence. I was not present when the crime was committed, and I do not have access to Mooney's mind and conscience. But I do know that he was convicted upon perjured testimony. I have been told that by the judge who tried him. Judge Griffin's integrity has never been impugned by anybody, and I have listened to his story, how certain he was that Mooney was guilty, and later on was forced to realize that every particle of the evidence had been manufactured. All the jurors who still survive have come to the same conclusion, and any one who reads the Densmore report, by disinterested Federal investigators, will be forced to the same conclusion.

So I said throughout the campaign; and my conclusions have not been weakened by having the same men who employed perjurers against Mooney employ perjurers against me.

Miss Barnsdall offered to pay for some radio time, and the EPIC candidates spoke several times with "hook-ups", and half a dozen times over KNX. One trying feature was that I was forced to submit copy in advance; and having to read a speech takes all the life out of it for me. But the big stations asserted that Federal regulations required this. I noticed, when I went East after the primaries, that Federal regulations did not apply. In Chicago, Washington, and New York I was invited six or eight times to speak over nation-wide hook-ups, and they left me free to say whatever I pleased. I noticed that on election night the barriers went down even in California, and both Columbia and NBC chains gave me time and told me to "shoot the works."

Early in our radio campaign there came forward a quiet-mannered little man by the name of Gus Ingles, who had been a motion picture publicity man and was familiar with the radio field. It was magical the way somebody turned up who knew about everything! Whenever I went down to headquarters I would find new men and women installed at desks or tables, working at some new job. Gus and his wife call themselves "mind students," and have studied to good effect, hating learned serenity and kindness. They took me on one of my Northern trips in a Packard limousine, purchased in those happy days when, as Gus explained, you went into an automobile place and said: "Give me that one." Gus became our "radio man", and made all our bargains, and kept all our schedules, and saw to it that I was there and my script too. When the newspapers refused to give mention to our EPIC programs, and some even refused to take advertisements of our programs, Gus attended to printing hundreds of thousands of slips which went out to all EPIC workers. These took to organizing parties in headquarters and in their homes, so when I went on the air I had a multiplied audience. I used to meet those people at our meetings and hear what they thought about talks which I had already forgotten.

In North Hollywood lived a young man, formerly a labor organizer by the name of Oliver Thornton. We heard of great results in the organizing of North Hollywood. They had a meeting in the high school, and the janitor said there had never been such a crowd since the building was erected. I learned that Oliver and his wife had polled one entire precinct of North Hollywood for a test, and that we had 73% of the votes.

AND HOW I GOT LICKED

We brought this able organizer down to headquarters, and he had charge of our meetings and dates. Every time I arrived at a hall there was Oliver waiting on the curbstone with a bodyguard. There were literature sellers, a program figured to the minute, and a squad of boys and girls to take up the collection.

I could tell about scores of devoted men and women who came to work in our main headquarters, or whom I met in towns and cities of California. To know such people was to have one's faith in humanity restored. To see the cheering crowds packing the great auditoriums, to note the quickness with which they got every point, the determination they registered when called upon for action—it was a new birth of Democracy. All over the place men and women would rise and ask keen, penetrating questions, going to the heart of the problems. How pleased they were when I gave a satisfactory answer; and how quickly they showed annoyance at a stupid or unfair question. I used to think of my friend Mencken, with whom for twenty years I have been carrying on a debate on the subject of the people, their right and ability to manage their own affairs. Mencken's name for them is the "booboisie", and I wished I could have him with me, to see what the people of California were thinking and doing.

In the last stages of the campaign I used to ask three questions of all the audiences: first, how many are out of work?—and about one-third would raise their hands; second, how many have read the book, "I, Governor"?—and about two-thirds would raise their hands; finally, at the end of the evening, how many are for the EPIC Plan?—and 90% would declare for it.

They would crowd up to the platform to shake my hand; they would catch at me and try to touch me as I went out. I shall never forget those hands—the big hard-crusted hands of farmers, the hands of mechanics with fingers missing, the thin, skinny hands of toil-worn women. I see before me a blur of faces, tens of thousands of California's people. I see them rise to their feet as I come upon the platform. They took to doing that early in the campaign, and people told me I ought to be proud, but it made me humble; I was no longer a person, I was a symbol of the hopes and longings of millions.

One of our meetings in the Shrine Auditorium in Los

I, CANDIDATE FOR GOVERNOR

Angeles: the curtain was down and behind it on the stage some two or three hundred people, our leaders and organizers. We sat chatting, until there came a signal, and everybody fell silent. The curtain started, and when it had risen about six inches, a roar broke, like the sea in a storm. The curtain went higher, and gradually there came to view that ocean of faces, arms, hands, hats and handkerchiefs. The crowd was on its feet, and we rose, and our eyes went up to the gallery, the topmost seats—it was like seeing people on a mountain. The roar continued until I raised my hands and explained that we were going on the air; they must wait for the signal and then give a fresh cheer—but not too long, because it cost thirty dollars a minute!

CHAPTER X

The Republican party has named the Governors of the State of California for more than forty years, and during that period the Democratic party has been a small and feeble minority. It has been strongest in San Francisco, on account of the labor unions; there the party has played the part of office boy to Republican reaction. I was familiar with that bi-partisan combination of graft from the days of my youth in New York City, where I saw Tammany working hand in glove with the upstate Republican crooks, the two groups always ready to unite against any progressive candidate.

The California Democracy consisted of elder statesmen who had managed its affairs for thirty years or more, and naturally they did not relish the intrusion of a Socialist. They were split among themselves, living in the memory of old-time factional fights. There was a Catholic group who had fought for Al Smith; these were led by Justus Wardell, a stock-and-bond dealer of San Francisco, and were in a deadly feud with the partisans of Senator McAdoo, who had blocked Al Smith's hopes, and was accused by his enemies of being a "Kluxer." This fight was irreconcilable, and anybody whom the Wardell crowd favored would be fought by the McAdoo crowd.

In the South Wardell was represented by an elderly attorney for the Southern Pacific railroad, Isidore Dockweiler, who early took occasion to denounce my intrusion and say that if I got the nomination he would vote for a Republican. Papa Isidore's position was complicated by the fact that his son was a congressman running for re-election, who announced that he would support any Democratic nominee.

The McAdoo faction was supposed to be allied with the friends of John B. Elliott, an oil operator of Los Angeles, vice-chairman of the party; but it developed that there was a minor feud between McAdoo and Elliott. The latter indicated a wish to confer with me, and I listened while he told me that the State was in a terrible plight, and he did not know what to do about it, and didn't believe anybody could do anything. Apparently that remained Mr. Elliott's position to the end.

Various Democrats were urged to sacrifice themselves and unite the party against the "Socialist interloper." One feeble boom after another was launched, but apparently there was nobody whom everybody would accept. Dr. Malaby threw his hat into the ring, a physician of Pasadena who had been a Democrat when he was the only one; then Milton K. Young, a lawyer of Los Angeles, who had been the party's successful candidate in 1930. President Roosevelt had brought new hopes to Democracy, and naturally these elder statesmen felt entitled to the reward of their years of service.

There began to be talk about George Creel. I had known Creel since early youth, when we had both been writing jokes and sketches for the editor of the New York "Evening Journal." I had met him again at the time of the Colorado coal strike, when he was, or I thought he was, a radical like myself. He was now acting as administrator of the NRA on the Pacific coast, and I called to see him, and listened to harrowing tales of the inefficiency of that organization, and how the politicians in Washington were betraying Creel. He told me he was sick of politics and through forever.

A couple of months later he announced himself as candidate for the Democratic nomination for Governor. Immediately there started a bitter row with the Wardell faction; these two had been doing some negotiating, and each claimed that the other had promised to keep out. Wardell now dug up the testimony which had been extracted from Creel by a Senate investigating committee, to the effect that he had taken five thousand dollars from Doheny. Creel answered in kind, and our EPIC people behaved like the pioneer who came back home and found his wife in hand-to-hand conflict with a bear, and took a seat on the fence and said, "Go it, woman; go it, bear."

When the primaries closed in July there were eight Democratic candidates in the field. Besides myself were George Creel, Justus Wardell, Dr. Malaby, Milton Young, a lawyer of Hollywood named McNichols, a physician of Los Angeles named Dowie, and a business man of Culver City named Evans.

Dr. Dowie had come into our organization, and had publicly pledged funds at one of our banquets, and promised to finance the motion picture, "Depression Island". But then it developed that what was on the doctor's mind was to run for Lieutenant-Governor on our ticket. He had a program of his own devising; he wanted to put all the police of the State under control of the Governor, and then have the Governor declare martial law and wipe out all the crooks. When Dr. Dowie discovered that we did not favor him as a candidate, he lost interest in our movement.

The story of William H. Evans, "Fighting Bill" as he calls himself, is a still odder one. "Fighting Bill" came early into the field, with a little pamphlet in which he announced himself as a true progressive and intimate friend of the President and other eminent Democrats. He published the evidence, consisting of such formal notes of thanks as one gets by writing to men in public positions. His program had, if I remember correctly, eleven points, whereas our EPIC program had twelve; and apparently he had arrived at his ideas by taking ours and toning them down. Thus, we proposed to exempt homes assessed at less than three thousand dollars; "Fighting Bill" said two thousand. We proposed to give pensions at sixty years; "Fighting Bill" said sixty-five. All this did not worry me, because I had predicted in the "Governor" book that the politicians would take our ideas.

It did worry me somewhat when "Fighting Bill" took to writing long letters to my friends, urging that I withdraw in his favor, as he was the only progressive who could be elected. Later on he came to see me—a little round, bald-headed man of the high pressure salesman type—to say that he intended to support me if I carried the primaries. He went away, and a day or two later I received a long telegram signed "A Friend," or "A Well-wisher", or something like that, urging me to withdraw in favor of William H. Evans, the only progressive who could be elected. I cannot prove that "Fighting Bill" sent this telegram, but I have a strongly rooted suspicion.

A few days later he announced his retirement in favor of Creel; and I heard that he was attacking me over the radio. Then he sent me a telegram urging me to listen-in, because he was going to defend me against the unjust charges of my enemies. I listened, and learned that his way of defending me was to say that to be sure I had been a free-lover once upon a time, but I had repented of my sins, as was proved by the fact that I had changed my novel, "Love's Pilgrimage", in later editions. I wrote "Fighting Bill" informing him that no changes had ever been made in "Love's Pilgrimage", and begging him never to defend me again, but to go on attacking me.

After the primaries, when I got the nomination, he publicly stated that I would be a candidate for the Presidency in 1936. When I rebuked him for this impertinence, he wrote me humbly, asking if I meant to read him out of the party. A few days thereafter he came out for Merriam; and that is the last I have heard from "Fighting Bill".

My relations with George Creel through the campaign were equally amusing. One of our people sent out a circular asking for samples of the atrocity stories which Creel had invented during the War. I wrote this man a letter saying that we were not dealing in personalities or in history, and asked him to stick to the EPIC Plan. I sent a copy of this letter to George, because I wished him to know my attitude; he replied that he had never invented any atrocity stories, and that he also meant to exclude personalities from his campaign. But soon afterwards there was widely distributed in the churches a circular containing extracts from "The Profits of Religion", and signed by "The Catholic Friends of George Creel."

On my first speaking trip to Oakland, I learned that

I, CANDIDATE FOR GOVERNOR

Creel had been there the previous day. Somebody got up in my audience and stated that he had said: "Sinclair has the brains of a pigeon. I answered: "I don't know much about the anatomy of pigeons, and I doubt if George Creel does either; but this I know, that nobody ever saw ten million pigeons starving to death while the ground was covered with corn and the trees were full of cherries." This report crossed the ocean; the "New English Review" commented that it "had wings."

I wrote George another note reminding him of his promise, and telling him to go easy, because "as a good and loyal Democrat you are going to be supporting me after the primaries." He replied that he had only made the remark about the pigeon's brains once, and again he renewed his promise to be good.

But it is hard to be good when you want something very much and somebody else is taking it away from you. On the Sunday before the primary elections, two young members of the Communist party came rushing into our headquarters in a great state of excitement. How dared we claim that Communists were endorsing us? We asked what they were talking about, and they exhibited leaflets which were being distributed in front of churches all over the city. The leaflet contained my photograph, side by side with the red flag and the hammer-and-sickle of Soviet Russia, and a ringing call to the voters to support Upton Sinclair in the name of the "Young People's Communist League of Los Angeles." Of course we hastened to assure the Communists that we had nothing to do with this document. They had made a note of the license number of the truck which was doing the distributing, and we set to work on the mystery.

The circulars had appeared simultaneously all over Southern California and in the Bay cities. Boys had received armfuls to distribute, and were promised fifty cents each for the service—though many of them never got the money. There was no such organization as the "Young People's Communist League of Los Angeles." There is a "Young People's Socialist League" and a "Young Communist League", but neither had anything to do with this matter. The address printed on the circulars (as required by law) was a lodging house; the person named in the circular—Vladimir Kosloff—was unknown, but a person who worked in the Creel headquarters lived there.

We followed this and other clues and found the shop where the circular had been printed. It had been ordered from the Creel headquarters. The whole affair had been prepared in the office of one of the largest law firms in Los Angeles. I shall name them later.

I have no idea how many votes this fraudulent circular frightened away from us. It must have been judged successful, for it was reprinted again and again before the November elections. Of course we exposed the fraud over the radio, and also in our "EPIC News". Our people wanted to put the blame on the Creel headquarters, but I vetoed this, telling them what I had told Creel—that he would be supporting us before long!

CHAPTER XI

Soon after the announcement of my candidacy for the Democratic nomination I learned that a lawyer of Sacramento, Sheridan Downey, had also announced himself, and that his program was in some ways like my own. He had published a book entitled "Onward, America", and I read it. Mr. Downey had dealt more with national problems, especially the private control of credit. All my life I had declared that to be the main problem, but in our EPIC campaign I was dealing with what the people of one State could do by themselves.

Mr. Downey and I started a correspondence, and later he came to see me and we threshed out our differences. We never did get entirely together. Downey was able to see production for use as the final goal, but he believed that it would have to be on a national scale, by the taking over of our great productive enterprises; the idea of starting at the bottom, by cooperative action of the weaker and less competent of our population, using the idle plants and putting them into condition by their own labors—this program appalled Sheridan Downey, and he spent much time pointing out to me the difficulties which would result. Of course I was prepared for difficulties; but then it is difficult for people to starve, and they have to choose between the two kinds of trouble. I would point out to Downey how spontaneously all over the State hundreds of such cooperatives had actually set to work at self-help; but he would come back to the idea of getting the Federal Government to use its control over credit to make the great trusts into national productive institutions.

Needless to say, I shall be more than glad to have it come that way; I believe that the need of our people will force President Roosevelt to act in the end. But I saw no chance of a national start in the immediate future, and as candidate for the governorship of California, I was planning to do what I could with the resources of one State.

Downey questioned gravely whether we could win the farmers of California to any program which might appear to involve State competition with them. To meet his doubts, I put into the "I, Governor" book a six-point statement of exactly what our Plan could do for the farmer; I emphasized the point that the farmer was in the same position as the businessman—the unemployed were of no use to him, because they had no money to buy the food he raised. The only way they could get purchasing power was from the State, and the State had to get it from the farmer in the form of taxes; so it would be better for the farmer to make up his mind that the unemployed are out of it, and let them grow the food which they themselves are going to eat.

It was my hope that Downey would consent to join us and run for Lieutenant Governor. I was shy about suggesting it, because he had been in the field ahead of me and had considerable support from the State Granges and the railroad brotherhoods. He was a lawyer of wide experience; he had represented a committee of the State senate, investigating graft under the Rolph regime, and he knew the State affairs far better than I.

He proposed that we wait two or three months and see how our campaigns developed. Finally we had another conference, and to my great joy Downey came into our movement as my running-mate. From that time on we cooperated loyally, and wherever there were

We Appeal to the Exploited Masses!

"Help Us Save the State"

UPTON SINCLAIR

Emblem of Freedom

UPTON SINCLAIR | X

for GOVERNOR

SPONSORED BY THE

Young People's Communist League

VLADIMIR KOSLOFF, Secy., 234 N. Chicago St., Los Angeles

big meetings we appeared on the platform together. Downey is a practised orator; he told my wife that it was his life's ambition to deliver the great American oration, and the crowds in many halls thought that he succeeded during the campaign.

We had the task of picking a whole "slate", and this fell upon us in the last three or four weeks before the nominations closed. Our organizations had not been strong enough before that and we had not known the people. We tried to find candidates for treasurer and controller and attorney general, and for members of the board of equalization, and director of public instruction, and so on down the list, including eighty candidates for the assembly and twenty for the senate.

We wanted most of these candidates to be Democrats; for of course we knew the enemy was going to say that ours was a Socialist ticket in disguise. We could not keep the Socialists from coming into our camp and going to work for us, neither could we change the fact that they were the best organizers, and most clearly understood production for use. Likewise we were powerless before the fact that they were honest and disinterested.

Members of our campaign committee used to tell me comical stories about the old-time Democratic workers in Los Angeles and San Francisco, who came to sell us their services, and were dumfounded to discover that we expected them not merely to work without pay but to raise the money for their headquarters—and without even the promise of a job if we won! "Whose campaign is this, Sinclair's or mine?" demanded one ward heeler from San Francisco—and was quite taken aback when he was assured that the campaign was not Sinclair's. It is pleasant to record that some of these fellows saw the point after a while, and pitched in and worked as enthusiastically as anybody.

We had a complicated time with one of our State candidates, a Democrat of long standing, with the highest connections. Only after we had accepted him and he had started his campaign, did we make the painful discovery that he sometimes imbibed too freely before appearing on public platforms. So it was necessary for me to take up my old role of temperance reformer. I wrote this gentleman a most eloquent letter, pouring

Uppie and Downey

out my heart to him, giving him his choice between retiring as candidate or taking the pledge. He met the proposition in a fine spirit and apparently kept his word, so I can feel that I accomplished something, even if I did not become Governor.

Among those whose support I wooed was my old friend, J. Stitt Wilson, formerly mayor of Berkeley on the Socialist ticket. Stitt is a magnificent campaigner of the Christian Socialist type. He is seventy years young or thereabouts, but he can still take off his black frock coat on the platform and lift the crowd to ecstasies. He hesitated for a long time, but finally joined our camp. Then it was proposed that he should run for state controller, but the Democrats rose up in arms—"No more Socialists on our ticket!" Stitt took it in good part and campaigned for us as devotedly as ever. I came into a committee meeting one day and commanded our friend, Will Kindig, to become candidate for controller. He looked a little startled, but obeyed like a good soldier and came within an ace of nosing out Riley, whose sole title to fame is that he is the author of our sales tax.

I could take many pages to tell the troubles we had finding our assembly candidates. We wanted to proceed democratically, and invited our local clubs to make their selections. The difficulties began when half a dozen candidates would get themselves selected in one assembly district, and then make haste to file. All these candidates would appear the same afternoon to be interviewed by our campaign committee. Democratic incumbents would come, offering their pledges to help end poverty in California, and we had the problem, could we believe them or not? If we tried to believe them, we were certain to receive agonized protests from our local groups, who declared that they were nothing but old-style political self-seekers. The most painful problem, to choose between a Democratic politician who could get elected and an EPIC worker who couldn't! In the last few days I suppose I received a hundred telegrams begging me to intercede in this or that local fight; and here was I, scheduled for a big meeting every night, and writing magazine articles, and giving newspaper interviews, and helping with the "EPIC News", and trying to answer ten pounds of letters every day.

AND HOW I GOT LICKED

Somehow or other the selections were made; and now before long we shall find out if we were right or wrong. For the new legislature is to meet in January, and of the EPIC candidates whom we nominated and the Democrats whom we endorsed, some thirty-eight have been elected, and we shall see how they stand by their pledges. We shall not be able to pass any laws in the face of a hostile senate, but we can draft our measures and force them to a vote, and put the partisans of special privilege on record. And back in the districts our clubs will tell the people how their legislators are voting—and if they vote wrong, believe me, they will hear about it!

CHAPTER XII

All through the primary campaign efforts were being made to get the old-line Democats together. There were conferences in private, and others with reporters present; the lesser candidates met day after day in a hotel in Hollywood, but all that resulted was the discovery that each was certain that he would win if the others would withdraw. George Creel and Justus Wardell kept aloof; each hated the other more bitterly than he hated the possibility of seeing me win.

There appears to be some peculiar disease which affects the judgment of political candidates. Justus Wardell has run four or five times for Democratic nominations, and has never come anywhere near winning, but he felt certain of success this time. George Creel was even more so, as I learned from his intimates. He appeared to have plenty of money, and had the support of the entire "Federal brigade." I was told that his main source of unhappiness was that he had promised so many jobs that he had lost track and promised them several times.

All these candidates were ardent in support of the New Deal, and all spent most of their time denouncing the "Socialist interloper." George Creel called me a "rainbow-chaser", and added that "the Democratic party will never permit a Socialist hitch-hiker to thumb his way to Sacramento." Soon after that on a trip

North my old car broke down, and I had to do the very thing which George had said I couldn't do!

Mr. Wardell was not satisfied to call me a Socialist—he called me a Communist and undertook to prove it. There had recently been published a sort of "Who's Who" of the radical movement, entitled "The Red Network"; it was edited and published by a woman, and you can judge her intelligence by the fact that among the dangerous radicals of America she listed Mrs. Louis D. Brandeis and Mrs. Franklin D. Roosevelt. She did not dare to list the husbands, but the wives were fair game!

I do not know how she got her data, but apparently she collected the names of all humanitarian organizations in the world and shook them out of a pepper-pot. She has listed me as an official of organizations I had never heard of, and Mr. Wardell took this list and printed it in a leaflet and distributed it all over the State of California. Later on the Republicans took it up, and the "United for California League", and the "Save Our State" League, and all the other reactionary organizations.

Having been a Socialist for thirty-two years, and having set forth my ideas in a score of books and hundreds of magazine articles, I really thought I was safe from being called a Communist. I have been tireless in my insistence upon majority consent, and in my rejection of every suggestion of violence and dictatorship in bringing about social change. Early in the campaign the "Western Worker", organ of the Communist party on the Pacific Coast, described the EPIC Plan as "one more addled egg from the blue buzzard's nest." Robert Minor, editor of the "Daily Worker", described it as the most reactionary plan ever put forward; and surely that ought to have saved me from being identified with the Communists.

Soon after the Soviet revolution the Communists formed a number of camouflage organizations, leagues for defense of political prisoners, and so on, and all well-known liberals were invited to join these organizations. So I became a member of the "International Labor Defense", and of the "International Workers' Aid". Later, when these groups came to be controlled entirely by Communists and were used to attack Socialists, I

Boo!

severed all connection with them; but of course that did not help me with the lady editor of "The Red Network", and it did not help me with Mr. Justus Wardell, who even changed the titles of these organizations to make them sound more terrible. He listed them as the "National **Communist** Committee for International Labor Defense" and the "National **Communist** Committee for International Workers' Aid".

Another terrible sounding one was "The Emergency Committee for Soviet Political Prisoners." After some prodding of the memory, I recalled this as an organization founded by Roger Baldwin for the defense of those unfortunate Socialists who were imprisoned by the Communists of Russia. All Communists consider this an anti-Soviet organization—but here was Mr. Wardell citing it as proof that I was "an agent of Moscow"!

Also they had me as a contributor to the "New Masses." First there was the "Masses", a Socialist publication, and of course I wrote for it. When the "New Masses" fell into the hands of the Communists and became that party's organ, it began to attack me, like all other Communist organs; and of course I have no connection with it.

They had me as secretary of "The Revolutionary Writers' Federation." Whether this Federation ever existed I don't know. As to my being its secretary, my answer is that I have never been the secretary of any writers' federation; I have been a whole writers' federation by myself, and have needed several secretaries.

Of course no red-baiters ever failed to list the American Civil Liberties Union. This is an organization of the finest idealists in the United States, who devote their energies to defending the basic principles of our Constitution. Its supporters include such men as John Dewey and Felix Frankfurter, John Haynes Holmes, Harry F. Ward, and Father John A. Ryan. It is true that we frequently defend the civil liberties of Communists; we have also defended the civil liberties of the Salvation Army and the Reverend Bob Shuler, but that does not identify us with the doctrines and beliefs of these people.

I thought I knew something about the dishonesty of political campaigning, but my fellow-Democrat, Mr. Justus Wardell, taught me a lot of new tricks. He took

TAKEN FOR A RIDE

From the Chicago "Tribune"

one sentence from "Letters to Judd", reading: "We are going to take over the industrial plant of the United States and run it as one planned enterprise for the benefit of the whole people." He went on to assert that this meant confiscation; when the fact is that the next five pages of the book are an argument against confiscation and in favor of constitutional procedure. One of the arguments ends with the sentence, "So you see why I am in favor of compensation". But Mr. Wardell did not quote that sentence!

He went on to quote what he called "the incredibly shocking statement", as follows: "I say if there is violence, let the capitalists start it, and then you, Judd, and the rest of the workers can finish it". Mr. Wardell got a shock from reading that sentence, and I got a shock when I looked into my book, "Letters to Judd", and saw that the sentence was taken from an elaborate argument in favor of constitutional procedure. The sentence immediately preceding it reads: "I have pointed out the way to make a change under the Constitution." How could Mr. Wardell have brought himself to omit such a sentence?

I was pointing out to my readers what had happened in American history. Abraham Lincoln had fought the slave power, using constitutional means; he had carried an election, and left it to the slave power to attempt to revolt against the people's verdict; so he had kept the moral forces of America on his side. In "Letters to Judd" I was pleading with American workingmen to display the same wisdom in obtaining their rights. I was appealing to the people of California to display that same wisdom—and my fellow-Democrat was lying about what I had written!

One of the Wardell onslaughts was really funny. Speaking at a banquet of old-line Democrats he called me an atheist, and said that I had "defied the power of Almighty God." I answered next morning that I did not know what he meant; like every human being, I lived by the power of Almighty God, and in my campaign to End Poverty In California I expected to succeed by the power of Almighty God. It was not until later that I learned what was in the poor stockbroker's mind. He said that I had stood in the pulpit of a church and taken out my watch and said, "If there is a God, let him prove it by striking me dead within the next three minutes." So I realized that Justus had got me mixed up with Sinclair Lewis! I wasted a three-cent stamp telling him that I was not Sinclair Lewis, and that God would not hold me responsible for the actions of Sinclair Lewis.

I explained all that in a letter, and I published it in a pamphlet, "The Lie Factory Starts". I reached many voters in that way—but not enough of them; for the lies were taken up and reprinted in millions of leaflets, and put into the hands of every voter many times over. All those wretched fabrications of "The Red Network", all those garbled quotations from my books—millions of dollars were spent to spread them; and how could I, having only a few dollars, attempt to answer? Our opponents had hundreds of daily newspapers; we had one tabloid weekly. They had hours on the radio to our minutes; and if I used up my time answering false-hoods, what chance would I have to explain how to End Poverty In California? What our enemies wanted was to put me on the defensive, and have me making explanations and apologies, instead of dealing with the thing the people really cared about—their own troubles and the remedy.

CHAPTER XIII

The greatest single handicap I had to face in the campaign was "The Profits of Religion." This book was written and published in 1917, in the midst of the World War, and has the bitterness universal at that time. I saw millions of peasant boys being led out to slaughter in the interest of the governing classes of Europe; I saw priests of Jesus blessing the flags, and inciting the mass destruction of the human race. I sat down to study religion from a new point of view—the use, or rather the abuse which had been made of it, "as a source of income and a shield to privilege". The book is a de-fense of true religion, its purpose being to take the churches out of the hands of ruling classes and exploit-ers of all kinds.

I, CANDIDATE FOR GOVERNOR

I have before me the campaign literature of the so-called "United for California League." Here is a four-page leaflet entitled "Upton Sinclair on the Catholic Church"; another entitled "Upton Sinclair's Opinion of Christian Science"; another entitled "Upton Sinclair, Defiler of all Churches and All Christian Institutions." Originally this label was "Dynamiter;" on page two they still keep that word. Of these three leaflets nearly ten million were distributed in our State. A set was mailed to every voter.

The "Defiler" pamphlet starts off with this quotation from the "Profits of Religion": "There are a score of great religions in the world, each with scores or hundreds of sects, each with its priestly orders, its complicated creed and ritual, its heavens and hells; each damns all the others and each is a mighty fortress of graft."

Yes, that is the thesis of the book; and that it is true is my sorrow, not my fault. The proofs were all taken from history, and from the utterances of all the churches.

John Haynes Holmes wrote me: "I must confess that it has fairly made me writhe to read these pages, not because they are untrue or unfair, but on the contrary, because I know them to be the real facts. I love the church as I love my home, and therefore it is no pleasant experience to be made to face such a story as this which you have told. It had to be done, however, and I am glad you have done it, for my interest in the church, after all, is more or less incidental, whereas my interest in religion is a fundamental thing." In the course of seventeen years I have received hundreds of letters from clergymen telling me this same thing. A few were brave enough to come forward and say it in California.

I quote again from the leaflet: "It is the thesis of this book that 'Religion' in this sense is a source of income to parasites, and the natural ally of every form of oppression and exploitation. (P. 17)." If you read that sentence carefully you will note that the crucial words are "in this sense". What do these words refer to? You have to read the book to find out. The average voter of California hasn't time to read books, and hasn't a dollar to spare for "The Profits of Religion".

If he goes to the public library, he finds that all my books are out and there is a long waiting list—sometimes a hundred names. Those who print garbled quotations know this situation.

Here is the whole of page 17 from my book; read it, and understand how the people of California were lied to.

"It is the fate of many abstract words to be used in two senses, one good and the other bad. Morality means the will to righteousness, or it means Anthony Comstock; democracy means the rule of the people, or it means Tammany Hall. And so it is with the word 'Religion'. In its true sense Religion is the most fundamental of the soul's impulses, the impassioned love of life, the feeling of its preciousness, the desire to foster and further it. In that sense every thinking man must be religious; in that sense Religion is a perpetually self-renewing force, the very nature of our being. In that sense I have no thought of assailing it, I would make clear that I hold it beyond assailment.

"But we are denied the pleasure of using the word in that honest sense, because of another which has been given to it. To the ordinary man 'Religion' means, not the soul's longing for growth, the 'hunger and thirst after righteousness', but certain forms in which this hunger has manifested itself in history, and prevails to-day throughout the world; that is to say, institutions having fixed dogmas and 'revelations', creeds and rituals, with an administering caste claiming supernatural sanction. By such institutions the moral strivings of the race, the affections of childhood and the aspirations of youth are made the prerogatives and stock in trade of ecclesiastical hierarchies. It is the thesis of this book that 'Religion' in this sense is a source of income to parasites, and the natural ally of every form of oppression and exploitation."

I quote again from the leaflet: "He says the church is a 'sepulchre of corruption' (P. 94)". Again I ask you to read the entire paragraph from which this quotation is taken. Bear in mind that I am describing my own childhood as a pious little Episcopalian boy in New York, attending the great Fifth Avenue churches, and hearing the words of Jesus read, and looking at the worldly congregation; watching politics and business, learning about Tammany Hall, and how it is being used as a tool by the same fashionably dressed gentleman in the pews of these churches. Now read the paragraph:

"So little by little I saw my beautiful church for what it was and is: a great capitalist interest, an integral and essential part of a gigantic predatory system. I saw that its ethical and cultural and artistic features, however sincerely they might be meant by individual clergymen, were nothing but a bait, a device to lure the poor into the trap of submission to their exploiters. And as I went on probing into the secret life of the great Metropolis of Mammon and laying bare its infamies to the world, I saw the attitude of the church to such work; I met, not sympathy and understanding, but sneers and denunciation—until the venerable institution which had once seemed dignified and noble became to me as a sepulchre of corruption."

Again the pamphlet quotes from page 282: "From that time on **Christianity has been what I have shown in this book, the chief of the enemies of social progress.**" In the pamphlet all this sentence except the first four words is printed in black letter. Manifestly, the four words may be important. Why were they left obscure?

The chapter in which the sentence occurs is entitled "Christ and Caesar", and tells how the early Christians were primitive communists, having "all things in common, except women." They tell how the devil tried to tempt Jesus, and failed to get him, but came again to get his church. The Roman Emperor became a Christian, "and Satan went off laughing to himself. He had got everything he had asked from Jesus three hundred years before; he had got the world's greatest religion." How came it that the compilers of the pamphlet failed to note that designation of Christianity as "the world's greatest religion?" And why did they stop with one sentence? Why not finish the paragraph? Listen:

"From that time on Christianity has been what I have shown in this book, the chief of the enemies of social progress. From the days of Constantine to the days of Bismarck and Mark Hanna, Christ and Caesar have been one, and the Church has been the shield and armor of predatory economic might. With only one qualification to be noted: that the Church has never been able to suppress entirely the memory of her prole-

tarian Founder. She has done her best, of course; we have seen how her scholars twist his words out of their sense, and the Catholic Church even goes so far as to keep to the use of a dead language, so that her victims may not hear the words of Jesus in a form they can understand.

"'Tis well that such seditious songs are sung

Only by priests, and in the Latin tongue!"

The leaflet quotes from page 290: "This book will be denounced from one end of Christendom to the other as the work of a blasphemous infidel. (P. 290)." At the risk of boring the reader I will complete that paragraph also:

"Yet it stands in the direct line of the Christian tradition: written by a man who was brought up in the Church, and loved it with all his heart and soul, and was driven out by the formalists and hypocrites in high places; a man who thinks of Jesus more frequently and with more devotion than he thinks of any other man that lives or has ever lived on earth; and who has but one purpose in all that he says and does, to bring into reality the dream that Jesus dreamed of peace on earth and good will toward men.

"I will go farther yet and say that not merely is this book written for the cause of Jesus, but it is written in the manner of Jesus. We read his bitter railings at the Pharisees, and miss the point entirely, because the word Pharisee has become to us a word of reproach. But this is due solely to Jesus; in his time the word was a holy word, it meant the most orthodox and respectable, the ultra high-church devotees of Jerusalem."

The book then goes on to quote the twenty-third chapter of Matthew, but substituting American names for those whom Jesus denounced, and using American language instead of King James English. In the last days of the campaign I had the curious experience of hearing a well-known lawyer of Los Angeles read this entire passage over the radio; he thought the sentiments were mine! And how dreadful they sounded:— "Woe unto you, doctors of divinity and Methodists, hypocrites! for you send missionaries to Africa to make one convert, and when you have made him, he is twice as much a child of hell as yourselves."

AND HOW I GOT LICKED

The crowning infamy of this leaflet is still to be mentioned. Here are a couple of sentences, taken from page 313 in "Profits of Religion":

"Who does not know the genius of revolt who demonstrates his repudiation of private property by permitting his lady loves to support him? **Who does not know the man who finds in the phrases of revolution the most effective devices for the seducing of young girls?**"

What do you make of these two sentences, thus taken out of their context? What is anybody to make of them? The last sentence is printed in black letters; and why? Manifestly, the ignorant reader is supposed to draw the conclusion that I am in favor of the seducing of young girls, and am recommending the "phrases of revolution" as useful for that purpose. What other reason could there be for the quotation?

And now for the facts. Having been brought up in the Church, and holding to the ideals of Jesus, I have been considered an old-fashioned Puritan by several generations of young rebels whom I have seen pass through Greenwich Village. At the end of "The Profits of Religion" I preached a sermon to these young people; I pointed out to them that the need of changing the social system does not obviate the need for a personal morality. Read my words to the young radicals of America, and judge whether I am advocating vice:

"It is our fundamental demand that society shall cease to repeat over and over the blunders of the past, the blunders of tyranny and slavery, of luxury and poverty, which wrecked the ancient societies; and surely it is a poor way to begin by repeating in our own persons the most ancient blunders of the moral life. To light the fires of lust in our hearts, and let them smoulder there, and imagine we are trying new experiments in psychology! Who does not know the radical woman who demonstrates her emancipation from convention by destroying her nerves with nicotine? Who does not know the genius of revolt who demonstrates his repudiation of private property by permitting his lady loves to support him? Who does not know the man who finds in the phrases of revolution the most effective devices for the seducing of young girls?

"You will read this book to ill purpose if you draw the conclusion that there is anything in it to spare you

[69]

the duty of getting yourself moral standards and holding yourself to them. On the contrary, because your task is the highest and hardest that man has yet undertaken—for this reason you will need standards the most exacting ever formulated".

What was the effect of all these falsehoods? Franklin K. Hichborn, well-known California publicist, tells me of talking with two Portuguese fishermen on the beach. They had registered Democratic, and voted for me in the primary, but were going to vote for Merriam in the finals. "They say that if we vote for Sinclair, the Virgin will be angry." Another friend writes: "You were beaten by the Catholic and Christian Science vote."

CHAPTER XIV

Soon after the EPIC movement started I was invited to address the Los Angeles Democratic Club, and a stern-looking elder statesman, General Somebody, arose and demanded to know whether I had voted for Al Smith for President. I told him that I had never voted any but the Socialist ticket in my life. He then asked sarcastically if I did not think it presumptous of so young a Democrat to aspire to party leadership in the great State of California. I answered in the words of Pitt to Walpole: "The heinous crime of being young, with which the honorable gentleman has charged me, I shall attempt neither to palliate nor to deny." However, the problem of who was to lead the Democratic party was one which the voters would decide, and all good Democrats would abide by their decision.

The California law permits the voter to register as a member of any party, and he can file as a candidate on any ticket, regardless of how he is registered. In order to vote for EPIC candidates at the primaries, the voter had to be registered as a Democrat; and we took to having deputy registrars in the lobby at every meeting to take the changes. After our big meeting so many people would change that the registrars in that town would run out of blanks. In Pomona the deputy registrar was a strong Republican, and became indignant at having to take the depositions of so many deserters from his party. He refused to take more, and when this was reported to the county registrar he said that the solution of the problem would be to make one of our people a deputy.

President Roosevelt had been the cause of many new voters joining the Democratic party in 1932, but this had stopped after his election. Now had come a new wave of changes. Between January 1 and July 19, 1934, nearly 350,000 new Democrats came into the party; and we EPICS thought we knew what they meant. We were getting precinct reports from all over the State, and learned of two or three precincts in which every registered Democrat was for us. In a conservative town like Santa Barbara, our precinct workers reported 52% of Democrats for us on the first visit, and after we had left some literature and come back again, 90% were for us.

Our rivals for the nomination made earnest efforts to persuade me to withdraw; they made efforts to get the help of the Administration, and claimed success whether they had it or not. Postmaster General Farley came to open a new postoffice; and since he was also Chairman of the Democratic National Committee, all candidates owed him their respects and clamored for his blessing. Seven of them clamored for him to repudiate the "Socialist interloper."

I was invited to attend a luncheon given in his honor by Warner Brothers, the only Democrats among the motion picture magnates; an elaborate affair, served on a set prepared for a picture of Hawaii, with music and entertainment and little speeches by the local political celebrities. Truly funny were the precautions taken to deal with all the eight would-be governors upon an equal basis. They were placed at exactly the same distance from Mr. Farley's throne, and a safe distance apart from one another. Each was called upon in turn to take a bow, but none was permitted to speak. The Socialist interloper shook hands with Mr. Farley and chatted for a minute or two—whereupon the reporters came running up to ask what we had talked about. Mr. Farley said that we had talked about the weather, and I agreed with him.

I, CANDIDATE FOR GOVERNOR

Farley went away without giving any sign as to his attitude; a procedure which broke the hearts of all the other seven candidates.

General Johnson of the NRA came a few days later, fresh from having helped to smash the San Francisco strike. He was George Creel's boss, and gave the Creel crowd his blessing; whereupon all the other candidates gnashed their teeth and despised General Johnson.

I had stated my attitude towards the Administration at the very outset. We were trying to get California's share of the New Deal by our own efforts. I personally made no secret of my disapproval of parts of the New Deal—the destruction of food, the limitation of production,—the turning of the NRA into a price-fixing machine for big business. Another feature, the Tennessee Valley experiment, I hailed with delight, and called on the people of California to do something like that for themselves.

I had a formula about the President which I had been repeating all over the State. I repeated it to him when we met. "I might have joined the Republican party, but I saw that it was the party of Herbert Hoover, and I thought Mr. Hoover might be unhappy if I joined his party. I looked at the Democratic party and saw that it had given us in the White House a man who has not merely a kind heart but also an open mind." There would be applause at this; and I would add: "That is a rare combination in a statesman, and it's a lot better luck than you deserve. If you had known in 1932 what Franklin Roosevelt was going to do to you, you would all have voted for Hoover.

Many of my friends urged me to learn from Roosevelt's example, and not tell everything I knew. But I have spent my whole life learning to say what I think. The purpose of the EPIC campaign was to teach the people of California the idea of production for use. I told them exactly what was in my mind, and I told them it was far more important for them to understand the causes of the depression than for me to be elected governor. Because of that, I am able to take comfort in our enormous vote. Those people really knew what they were doing.

Even our bitterest opponents know in their hearts that we conducted an honest campaign. We did not reply to personalities—unless with laughter. We thanked them for advertising our cause instead of their own plans. We answered every question of our audiences—I figure somewhere between five and ten thousand questions.

We advised people to question the other candidates—and this worried the candidates greatly. George Creel, speaking in a theatre, would step back when he finished, and have the curtain drop quickly. On occasions he and Wardell tried to argue with our people, and lost their tempers and left the platform; one of our speakers then took over the meeting. If you turned on the radio in the closing days you heard nothing, but EPIC for or against. An unprecedented thing in a primary—the rival Republican candidates stopped denouncing one another, and took to telling their audiences how absurd and un-American and anarchistic and atheistic was the promise to End Poverty In California.

The primary election came on the 28th of August, and our people closed the campaign in a whirlwind of enthusiasm. We had literally hundreds of meetings every night of the last week. I could not doubt our precinct reports, and had made up my mind two months ahead that we were going to win. The margin proved to be so great we knew the result half an hour after the polls closed.

The vote for the Democratic nomination was: Sinclair, 436,000; Creel, 288,000; Wardell, 48,000; Milton K. Young, 41,000; and a few thousand for each of the others. The Republican votes were divided among four candidates. Merriam, who had been Lieutenant-Governor, and had become acting Governor when Rolph died, received 346,000. Former Governor C. C. Young received 231,000; Quinn, a supervisor of Los Angeles county, 153,000 and Raymond L. Haight, 84,000. The total Democratic vote was slightly greater than the Republican, and the vote for the "Socialist interloper" exceeded that of all his seven rivals. The extent of the "Red" peril in California may be judged from the fact that the Communist vote was 1072, and the Socialist 2521.

CHAPTER XV

The news that a former Socialist had captured the Democratic nomination by the biggest vote ever polled in a California primary, of course created a tremendous sensation throughout the country. Everybody agreed that it was a portent. To the conservatives it meant that the New Deal was marching straight into Communism; to forward-looking persons it meant that we had found how to win the American people. My vote was seven times what I had been able to get in the best of my three previous ventures into California politics.

To me personally it meant that my home was turned overnight into a mad house. While we were answering the telephone the front doorbell was ringing, and before we could get away from the door the telephone was ringing again. Our living room became a motion picture studio, a photograph gallery, a newspaper office, a conference place for politicians. All the Democrats of California wanted to see me; they would come, and find me standing on the lawn making speeches before newsreel cameras, or being photographed at my desk or my typewriter, or hoeing weeds in my garden, or gathering figs from my fig tree, or shaking one finger or two fists at imaginary audiences.

I seldom make such gestures, but I had to look as if I were making them at the horde of photographers. My wife insisted that the newspapers picked out the very worst of those photographs and sent them over the country—the ones in which I was frowning because of the sun, or in which I looked haggard and wild because of the flashlight, and because I was tired and harrassed. Considering everything else the newspapers did to us, this suspicion did not seem unreasonable.

From the moment I read the election results my thoughts turned to Washington and New York. I was seeking to influence not merely California but the whole country. Our slogan, End Poverty In California, really meant to me End Poverty In Civilization. New York was the centre of the country's thinking; the big magazines went out from there, and I wanted them to tell about our movement.

Also I wanted to see President Roosevelt, and explain my purposes to him. As a nominee of his party,

A Great Help He Turned Out to Be!

I, CANDIDATE FOR GOVERNOR

I felt that I owed him the courtesy of a call. Equally important was the fact that if I became Governor, I would have to deal with his administrators in Washington; the men who held the purse-strings, and would decide the fate of our EPIC program. I wanted to meet these men face to face, and get their reaction to my ideas.

The President was spending his vacation at his mother's countryplace in Hyde Park, up the Hudson river. I had written to say that if I carried the primary, I would seek the privilege of meeting him. On the day after election I sent a telegram asking for an appointment. In reply came a long message from Secretary McIntyre, explaining the President's attitude. He had publicly declared his position, that he would take no part in State elections. If I called to see him, he would be glad to meet me, but politics would not be discussed.

Of course I understood what that meant, and telegraphed immediately that I accepted the conditions, and would leave on Thursday, arriving in New York on Monday, and seeing the President the next day.

I appreciated Roosevelt's position fully. He had to carry the November elections, not merely in California but throughout the nation. The nomination of an ex-Socialist put him very much "on the spot". The Democrats of California had endorsed me, and I would come running eagerly to him, wearing this large and shiny medal, and expecting him to receive me with open arms. If he did so, what would be the reaction of the other forty-seven States, which had not nominated any Socialists? What would the Republican National Committee make of the incident? What would be said by the newly organized American Liberty League—which I had described as a league of liberty for millionaires? The President had a host of congressmen and senators to think about, and if he gained the California delegation and lost those of New York, Massachusetts, and Pennsylvania, it would be a poor swap.

I traveled with Robert Brownell, a Stanford graduate who had joined our campaign committee, and Crane Gartz, son of Mrs. Kate Crane-Gartz. We were started off by a cheering crowd, and of course the usual group of reporters, and photographers with flashlights which fail to go off and make it necessary for you to shake

ON THE WEST COAST

From the Los Angeles "Examiner"

your finger or your two fists all over again. It seemed as if there was hardly a station between Pasadena and New York at which we did not receive a telegram; requests for interviews, requests for magazine articles, bulletins from our committee, a message from my wife informing me that the Los Angeles "Herald" had quoted me as saying that our EPIC Plan was the same as the Russians were doing, and to please deny it immediately.

In between stations I gave a final revision to the manuscript of "Immediate EPIC", and mailed it back in installments for our paper. Bob Brownell sat in another compartment and pounded away at his portable typewriter. After a year of practice, Bob had learned to write EPIC interviews and articles so successfully that nobody could tell them from mine, and if I ever sort out those boxes of clippings I won't have an idea which is which.

There came a telegram from Edward Nockels of the Chicago Federation of Labor, asking if I would stop at the Fair and address a Labor Day meeting on Sunday afternoon; the radio station owned by the Chicago workers would be at my disposal with a nation-wide hook-up. I accepted, and asked if I would have to prepare copy, and so made the discovery that the "Federal regulations" which had been applied to me in California were not known in Chicago.

Mayor LaGuardia of New York was in Chicago, intending to speak to the same audience on Monday. I spent an hour in his hotel room, and he asked all about EPIC, and I pointed out how he could start the idle shoe and clothing factories of his city at making goods for the unemployed, and exchanging them for the surplus food produced upstate by the farmers. I conjured before his mind a trucking system which would take the factory products to the country and bring back the food to the hungry people of the New York tenements. Mayor LaGuardia was deeply interested but feared it would take a long time to get such a project started. I was not able to see why it should take a long time, and I never have seen but one reason—that public officials are more afraid of the money of big business than they are of the votes of ignorant and misguided and helpless poor people.

AND HOW I GOT LICKED

LaGuardia has in New York City exactly the same situation as we in California; the same population—six or seven millions, and the same number of unemployed workers; the same deficit, and the same clamor by the taxpayers against piling up of debts. I told him I would start a New York EPIC Committee, and I herewith commend it to the attention of all who read this book. The address is 112 East 19th Street, and the persons in charge are my friends, Horace A. Davis and Philip Hurn.

It was a rainy day in Chicago. An outdoor meeting had been planned, and the thousands who came could not get into the hall. However, the radio was there, and I talked for half an hour to the audience of WCFL, the Chicago Federation of Labor, and then for another half hour to the same audience plus a chain of other stations. In the first half hour I told how we had built up the EPIC movement; the second speech dealt with our plan to End Poverty In California, and how this could be applied by the people of other States and of the whole nation. From the audience in the hall I had the same reaction as in California; intense interest, and an instant response to every point. Let no politician have any doubt in his mind—the American people are awake, and are going to find a solution to the problem of want in the midst of abundance.

We arrived at the Pennsylvania Station in New York, and a deputation of reporters met us; we repaired to the Algonquin Hotel, and for an hour or so answered questions about the EPIC movement. After you get through there is always a belated reporter, and then another; they present apologies and beg your indulgence, and you tell your story and answer the questions all over again. Meanwhile there are six or eight cameramen telling you to uncross your legs, or to hold the telephone receiver, or to stand against this dark curtain; and the flashlight bulbs that don't flash, but make more delays and apologies. Then the newsreel men, who take an hour or so to set up their apparatus, and blind your eyes with their kleig lights; you made your two minute speech about the meaning of EPIC, and they ask you to make it again for a close-up, and they ask the second half again, because one camera ran out of film, or something. Meanwhile the telephone is ringing every two minutes in three different rooms and three secretaries bring messages, and magazine editors come to contract for articles, and an artist to sketch your portrait, and your old friends stand around and wait for a chance to say hello.

This is the price of taking part in public life in America. You have to learn to think on your feet, and to think about several things at once. You speak knowing that if you make a single mistake, you have lost your cause, and the hopes of a million people. You have to have a cast iron stomach, or else be wise enough not to eat until the excitement is over. You must go on without knowing that you are exhausted. Fortunately for me, I had a whole year in which to learn my EPIC lesson; fortunately, also, I have studied psychology and practiced what I learned, so that when I go to bed at one or two o'clock in the morning with a dozen dynamos whirring in my brain, I am able to stop them and go to sleep without drugs.

CHAPTER XVI

I had telephoned the President's secretary, Mr. McIntyre, at Hyde Park, and confirmed the appointment for the following afternoon. I said to him: "I want to make it plain that I appreciate the President's position and don't intend to embarrass him. I am not coming to make his home into a sounding-board for my ideas. I want him to feel free to say what he pleases to me, and you may assure him that he may count upon my discretion." I was not asked to say this, but volunteered it, and I have no doubt that it accounted in part for the President's frankness at our meeting.

A friend drove our party the eighty miles or so up the Hudson, and I saw the autumn woods for the first time in years. The fifth of September is early, but already the sumach was turning red. In woods like these I used to hunt rabbits, partridges and deer, and once in my youth I rode a bicycle over that road up the Hudson and into the Adirondacks. The Albany post-road it used to be called; they have paved it since then, but it still wanders here and there through old towns like Yonkers, following paths that were laid out by cows three hundred years ago.

A State trooper met us at the gate and checked us in. Franklin Roosevelt is a country squire with many acres and a beautiful home where he has lived all his life. His ways have been made smooth, and it is only natural that when men of his own class come to see him he should find it easy to understand their point of view and yield to their persuasions. It is always a task to make real to such a person the sufferings of the millions of forgotten men who own no estates and no homes, and do not know where they are to get the food for their wives and children next day.

I must explain my attitude toward Franklin D. Roosevelt. I do not think I have ever been more curious about any man in my life. I had watched him as Governor of New York and as candidate for the Presidency. I had seen him confront the breakdown of our banking system, the most difficult situation faced by any incoming President since Lincoln's day. I had watched for eighteen months his efforts to bring back prosperity. My knowledge of economics taught me that a few of these efforts were sound, while most were completely futile. There were two possibilities: he might be blindly groping; or he might be a wise man, letting the people have their own way and learn by their own blunders. Which was it?

Of one thing I was and still am certain: the whole future of America depends upon what is in that man's mind. The profit system is crumbling before our eyes, and there are only two alternatives—social ownership and operation of the industrial plant, or else Fascism, which I have defined as "capitalism plus murder." And Roosevelt is going to decide which it shall be. Nothing except his death can keep him from being re-elected in 1936, and by 1940 the issue will have been fought to a finish.

So I went into that fine old home possessed with an intense curiosity; also of a resolution, which was modest, I hope, but firm. All my thinking life I have been studying depressions, and for more than thirty years I have been claiming to know the cause and the remedy. To a hundred audiences up and down my home State I had said, without any hesitation or apology: "I know how to end poverty." There were several things that I wanted to tell the President, and meant to tell him if he could be got to listen.

The particular situation which put him "on the spot" is now past. He has got his election, an overwhelming majority in both the Senate and the House—in spite of his having shown courtesy to a "Socialist interloper." Also, I am out of his way, so there is no longer any harm to be done by my telling about that interview— especially since I have nothing but kind and grateful things to say. Of course I shall not tell any of the personal things that he said, either about himself, or about his aides in Washington, or about the Democratic politicians of California (how some of their ears would burn!) or about the great bankers of San Francisco (even though they put up the money to frustrate my cause!)

I was escorted into a library with logs burning in the fireplace. The President was sitting in a large leather chair which has a brass plate with some kind of inscription—a gift, I suppose, to one of his forefathers. He had a table before him with a stack of documents a foot or two high. His first remark was: "You see how far behind I am in my work." I told him we all marveled that he was so far ahead with it.

He is a powerfully built man with a large head, and his physical infirmity is not apparent unless you look for it. He is a warm-hearted and genial person; you feel that he likes you and is interested in talking to you. He could hardly keep that up all the time unless it was genuine on his part.

He likes to talk. He tells stories with gusto, elaborating the details. The ones he told me were all to the point, and I did not have to feign interest in them. He told me what happened when all the banks closed; how in San Francisco a group of insiders attempted to use the Federal Reserve Bank to put two of their rivals out of business. I found afterwards that this story is generally known in financial circles, so it cannot do any harm for me to mention it—except for what the President told me about his own part in the affair. When he got through I said: "I have met two Presidents in my life. The other was Theodore, and I don't know which of you is the more indiscreet." He threw his head back and laughed heartily.

From the San Francisco "News"

I, CANDIDATE FOR GOVERNOR

Of course there was nothing to the pretense that we were not going to talk politics. I found that he knew all about the California situation, and I asked him if he had all the other forty-seven States as well in mind. He told me about politics in Washington, and told me whom to see there; I afterwards learned that he had arranged for them to see me. In short, he was as kind to me as a man could have been.

But do not think that I was taken in by personal charm, or the honor of being cordially received by a President. I had all my thoughts concentrated upon one question—how much does this man know? How well is he equipped mentally for the tasks he has to perform? No good stories and no personal favors were going to keep me from getting that information.

I found that he had read my book and knew the EPIC Plan. I told him our situation regarding unemployment. I told him my firm conviction that he had ten million permanently unemployed men and their families to care for. To keep them on the dole would pile up the public debt and drive the nation into bankruptcy. There was only one possible solution, to put them at productive labor and let them produce what they were going to consume. He understood all that clearly, and after we had discussed it at length he said about as follows:

"My advisers tell me that I have to talk to the people again over the radio and explain to them what I am doing. I am going to give that talk in two sections. The first will deal with general problems, and the second will deal with unemployment. I am coming out in favor of production for use."

To that I said: "If you will do that, Mr. President, it will elect me."

He said, "That is what I am going to do. It will be somewhere about the 25th of October."

You can imagine that from that time on the 25th of October was a prominent day in my thoughts! Later on I shall tell what happened.

We discussed the crisis and its meaning, and I had a chance to cover all the points I had in mind. We are piling up the public debt, and when it comes to the point that we cannot borrow any more, we shall have to start inflation—real inflation, not merely pretended, as we have had so far. When that money is printed, it can be spent for doles, and we have got no further with our problem; but if we spend it as a capital investment for the benefit of the unemployed, we make them self-supporting, and we solve the problem for the present. In the process of inflation we should be doing to the stock-and-bond-owning classes no more than they have been doing to us throughout American history. They got possession of the productive machinery by watering stocks and bonds and manipulating markets. We would get possession back to us by watering the currency.

We discussed the Central Valley project, and the method by which the EPIC movement would undertake it upon a production for use basis. Also our EPIC tax—a tax payable at the option of the State in goods and services. With the great productive plant of California running at forty percent of capacity, it is hard for the corporations to pay taxes in cash, but they could pay in production, and in so doing would put tens of thousands of laborers at work, and at the same time the State would have for the Central Valley project great quantities of lumber, cement, rock and gravel, steel, oil, etc. We would have all the utility services, light, heat, power, telephones and telegraphs, and transportation by truck and railroad.

This EPIC tax was new to him, and it gave me a test of his mind. He went straight through it; it was like seeing a bunch of firecrackers go off. "Yes, it would be this way; but what would it do to that, and how would it affect such and such?" He answered the questions himself, or took the answers out of my mouth. I saw it was his own mind working, not just things which other men had brought to him.

With all the other matters I found that he was familiar. I started on one, and he said, "Yes, that's important. I was talking with So-and-so about it yesterday." I began on another and he said: "Yes, I am having So-and-so prepare me a paper on that." Finally I laughed and said: "I see you don't need me."

His attitude towards social changes was summed up in one sentence, "I cannot go any faster than the people will let me." That, of course, fitted in with what I had been saying to the people of California: "It's up to you."

I, CANDIDATE FOR GOVERNOR

I said to the President: "The people of my State will let you know what they are thinking!"

I have never read Miss Emily Post, and did not know how long one was supposed to visit a President. I had entered at five o'clock and expected to leave at about six; but the President was talking, and seemed to be interested in what he was saying, and it didn't seem courteous to stop him. I do not know how long he might have gone on to entertain me, but when the clock showed seven I thought it was really time to act, so I got up and thanked him for his kindness, and assured him that if any part of the burden fell upon me I would cooperate.

One thing more I wanted to say to him; some foolish persons in California and New York had been talking about me as a candidate for the Presidency, and I wanted to assure him that I myself was not numbered among those foolish ones. He did not want to let me say it; he said he wouldn't mind putting the burden off on somebody else, and coming back to Hyde Park and writing books. But I insisted on saying my say, which was that he had his job and was doing it, and if I should become Governor of California, he would have no more loyal supporter in 1936.

That was my attitude on September 5th, and it is my attitude on November 17th, as I write these words. I believe that the Squire of Hyde Park will give the people of America production for use as fast as they understand it. I think the eight hundred and seventy-five thousand who have just voted for our EPIC program are a part of that demand, and I feel certain that Roosevelt has heard it.

CHAPTER XVII

On the way driving up to see the President a wise friend had said to me: "The whole country is waiting to know how Roosevelt receives you. No matter what he says, and no matter how you really feel, you must look cheerful when you come out. The reporters will be watching every sign." But I did not have to act for the reporters. The interview had lifted a great load off my mind; and not because I wanted the job of being Governor, but because my whole being is concentrated upon the idea that there shall be no Fascism in the United States in my lifetime.

The President's secretary had told me to stop by at the Nelson House in Poughkeepsie, so we drove there and found a score of reporters and half as many cameramen. They took us up to the executive offices, and we had a half hour session. Of course, there were two things they wanted to know—first, what I had said to the President, and second, what the President had said to me. I told them that I could not tell those things, and the rest of the time was spent in sparring. They tried every sort of question that would get them a hint; and I would smile and ask them to be easy on me.

A few crumbs I was able to give them—harmless things such as what the President had said about "The Jungle"—how his mother had insisted on reading it to him at the breakfast table, and naturally it had spoiled his appetite. I would tell them anything they wanted to know about the EPIC Plan—except what I had told the President about it! Of course, there was one point on which I did not have to leave them in doubt, and that was that I was satisfied. Another was that I liked the President. They had noted the length of the visit, and drew their own conclusions from that.

One amusing episode: they kept insisting that it was all right for me to tell what I had said to the President; it was the established convention, that visitors were permitted to say what *they* had said. But I argued that I was a special kind of visitor. Finally I said: "This is what you can do: call up Secretary McIntyre and ask him, and if he says it's all right for me to tell what I said to the President, I will do it." They began to laugh, and one said: "There he is over there,"—pointing to a young man in a corner of the room. He had been watching the proceedings all the time, unknown to me!

I apologized and asked him what I should do. He said: "I think things are very well just as they are"— and so the interview ended.

I had a radio date in New York at 10:15 that evening. We were not familiar with the road and it took us longer than we expected; I would be ashamed to tell how fast we drove through the Bronx and down Riverside Drive. If we had met a traffic officer, we had an unusual excuse—that the President of the United States had kept us two hours. But nobody stopped us and we reached the radio station seven minutes late. It is one of the major crimes to be late for a nationwide hook-up! It seemed to me there were a dozen men between the sidewalk and the microphone, all waiting to hurry me along.

I talked the rest of my period and thought I was through. But the radio man said, "Go on." Every five minutes I would stop and ask him again, and he would say: "Go on some more." That is the way when you have just come from the Great White Father's throne!

I had an engagement to meet Mr. Farley immediately after the broadcast. It was after eleven o'clock, but there is no such thing as night in New York, and he was waiting for me at Democratic headquarters in the Biltmore Hotel. "Call me Jim," was the first thing he said, and when the reporters asked about the interview I told them that, and it caused a good deal of amusement; they have changed Mr. Farley's name from James to "Call-me-Jim." I hope he doesn't mind.

He did not seem to mind anything that night. He is a large, rosy, and genial gentleman, and gave me good political advice. At the outset he told me that he had just listened to my radio talk and found it interesting; also that Secretary McIntyre had told him that I had handled the press interview very satisfactorily.

Mr. Farley is the political manager of the Democratic party, and got his training in Tammany Hall. I got my training just outside, where I could peek through the windows, as it were, and see what was going on. We are about the same age, so we observed the same phenomena. Richard Croker was the boss of Tammany in my youth, and I wrote with true puritanic fervor that I would be willing to spear him on a pitchfork and thrust him into the fires of hell. This was in my early days, when I thought that graft was caused by grafters, and before I understood it was caused by big business. Not long after that my rich uncle revealed to me how he was paying Richard Croker to get the business of New York City for his company. My uncle was a prominent pew-holder in a fashionable

Episcopal church—so you see where "The Profits of Religion" began, and why I could not take all the political advice which my new friend Jim presented to me.

One thing the able political manager and I have in common, and that is loyalty to Franklin D. Roosevelt. Jim wants to get him re-elected in spite of the intrigues of every kind of enemy. I for my part am looking farther ahead; I want to keep him from wrecking his administration by yielding to the blandishments of those greedy interests which have either owned or wrecked every president of the United States since the Civil War.

We took the night train to Washington, and at noon a luncheon at the National Press Club, a most interesting occasion. There must have been five hundred men present—I was told afterward that as many more had to be turned away. A difficult audience, friends had warned me; all the Washington correspondents were there, and a great many public men and honored guests. Ten or fifteen feet in front of me sat Mr. Fletcher, Chairman of the Republican National Committee; looking, of course, for everything he could get on the Administration. Newspaper men are supposed to be hard-boiled and cynical, and those in Washington know all there is to know about the wiles of politicians and publicity seekers.

The first fifteen minutes of my talk was a Columbia broadcast. I had wired our California headquarters about these various "hookups," in order that our workers might be notified. It is interesting to note that this National Press Club was the only one that was broadcast in California, and it happened only because my wife, who had missed the other talks and was indignant about it, got busy on the telephone and brought so much pressure to bear upon the radio people in California that they did not dare to turn her down. The Los Angeles newspapers published the wrong hour, so that nearly everyone missed my talk.

I told about the EPIC movement, how we had built it up and what it meant. I spoke for fifteen minutes over the radio, and then for another half hour or so to the audience alone, after which I answered questions for an hour. I don't know how long they would have kept me if I had not had a series of other engagements.

AND HOW I GOT LICKED

I was told afterwards that Paul Mallon had sent a confidential bulletin to the United Press papers, saying that all newspapermen had been deeply impressed by my talk and astonished by my readiness in answering the most difficult questions. He said there was only one experience they could compare it with, their conferences with Franklin Roosevelt.

I do not mind repeating this, for the reason that the explanation is amusing. I was taking an unfair advantage of those supposed-to-be-hard-boiled correspondents. None of them realized the course of training through which I had been put by the people of California. I had been rehearsing that speech almost every night for a full year. I had made it in two-minute newsreel form; I had made it in two-hour oration form. I could cut it and fit it while in action. I had practiced over the radio so as to end it literally on a certain second. If the announcer told me that I had twelve minutes and a half, that was all right; or if he changed his mind and said I had thirteen minutes and fifteen seconds, that was equally all right.

I had tried all my jokes and polished their points with audiences of every kind of person you could think of: the Hollywood Chamber of Commerce, the Lawyers' Club, the Ministerial Association, the Graduate Students of U. S. C., the youngsters of Los Angeles Junior College, the Society of Cost Accountants, the County Medical Society, the League of Women Voters, the Junior Ebell Club, the Compton Cooperative, the employees of the Los Angeles Street Railways—I am naming them as they come to memory. I had talked to audiences of farmers in every one of the great valleys of California; I had talked in theatres, school-houses, churches, picnic grounds; in sun and in rain; in competition with automobiles and motorcycles and airplanes and crying babies and playing children and drunken men and Communists—again I am remembering all the adventures. I used to say that I could make my EPIC speech in my sleep or standing on my head.

As for the questions, I had answered every variety that ever came into all those different kinds of heads. It is literally true that this picked Washington audience, the cream of the country's journalistic and political life, failed to think of a single question which had not been asked many times in California. So, of course, I was ready, and of course I was at ease, and of course I had plenty of witty retorts—and of course those naive and simple-minded newspaper correspondents thought I was was the world's wonder!

CHAPTER XVIII

I spent the rest of that day and all the next interviewing Cabinet members and officials whom the President had told me to see. He had listed two kinds, to be seen privately or to be seen publicly. The first included a young member of the "brain trust," and I spent that evening in his home. He is a good-looking and genial fellow—I hope that won't identify him too completely—and there were present a Cabinet member, an executive official, and a legal adviser. Nobody had forbidden us to talk politics, and we talked nothing else. They thought I should have Administration support, that the pretense otherwise was all "the bunk," and they advised on the tactics of procedure. Incidentally they gave me amusing sidelights on the queer situation of a President who has advisers on the right and advisers on the left, and is pulled vigorously in both directions, and would like to travel in both, out of the sheer kindness of his heart.

In giving me a list of others I should see, the President said with a twinkle in his eye to "turn the spotlight on them"—or some such phrase. None of them seemed to object to the procedure, for wherever the cameramen came, the officials consented to be photographed with me. Several newspapers used these photographs—mostly Republican, if I remember. Mr. Jesse Jones of the RFC moved closer at request, and placidly ate his sandwich and drank his glass of milk while the cameramen flashed their magnesium bulbs in his office. Afterwards some correspondent remarked that I was probably the first Socialist Mr. Jesse Jones had ever met in his whole life. Very certainly Mr. Jesse Jones was not the first of his kind whom I had met; large, amiable, elderly gentlemen from the far South having been familiar to me from childhood.

AND HOW I GOT LICKED

Mr. Harry Hopkins, FERA administrator, is a different type. I don't know where he comes from, but I know his point of view. He and I face the fact that there are millions of unemployed men in the United States, that they are likely to be unemployed for a long time to come, and that it is necessary to give them jobs without any ifs, ands or buts. I did not have to tell Mr. Hopkins much about our California situation, because it is his job to know about all the States. I pointed out to him that a lot of the unemployed were coming our way this winter, because it is less easy to freeze to death here, and he readily agreed with me that the Federal Government would have to feed them wherever they were. He assured me that if I became Governor of California, and wanted to put the unemployed at productive labor for their own benefit, I might expect cooperation from his Department.

I went away happy at having met a clear-minded, frank-spoken, honest young man in the public service. In his organization I met several old friends. Jacob Baker, formerly editor of the Vanguard Press, is in charge of subsistence homesteads, and he told me about the Ohio plan, under which the cooperatives were doing much the same kind of thing as we advocate for California. He showed me a couple of pairs of shoes and a very good coat made in the factories of these cooperatives, and also a sort of Sears-Roebuck catalogue of the useful articles they had to exchange with one another. Our newspapers had seen to it that the people of California had never heard of the Ohio plan. I promised myself the pleasure of telling about it.

Another old friend is William E. Zeuch, formerly president of Commonwealth College, now entrusted with some $25,000,000 of Federal funds to be expended in behalf of self-help colonies. Zeuch called in all the people on his floor, some twenty or thirty young men and women, to hear about the EPIC Plan, and they plied me with questions for all the time I had to spare. I asked if they had any faults to find, and was happy not to hear of any.

And then Mr. Morgenthau, Secretary of the Treasury: It was raining, and the taxicab driver took me to the wrong door, which turned out to be the right one— the Secretary's private entrance, guarded like a jail. Mr. Morgenthau is an amiable and kindly young man, and told me I could have anything I wanted. To hear that in the United States Treasury appealed to my sense of humor; but Mr. Morgenthau would not join in my unseemly laughter. He told me earnestly how he had gained his training in social ideals at the Henry Street settlement. The President is quoted as saying that under the Morgenthau regime the United States Treasury is in Washington instead of Wall Street for the first time in two generations. From Morgan to Morgenthau seems progress to me.

Also Mr. Thomas of the Federal Reserve Bank, and Mr. Fahey of the Home Owners Loan Corporation. The propositions I put up to these gentlemen were new, and they had to call in their legal staff to ask if it could be done, and their legal staffs didn't know either. For example, the Federal Reserve Bank can lend money only to—I think the phrase is "established industrial enterprises." Well, is the State of California an established industrial enterprise? I was able to point out a number of industrial undertakings which our State was managing, and assuredly we have been established for quite some time. Could or could not a State government borrow money to build, let us say, a cement mill, to break the monopoly which bleeds our people? Turning to the Home Owners Loan Corporation, could the State of California borrow money to build a village for a cooperative of fishermen and fish-canners, to break another most cruel form of exploitation?

Secretary Ickes of the Department of the Interior is a lawyer who spent many years fighting the Insull gang in Chicago. Now miraculously he is in charge of the development of Federal public works, and the President asked me to tell him about our plan to put through the Central Valley project on a basis of production for use. The San Joaquin valley, which includes most of the central part of California, depends for its whole future upon this project. The water for irrigating crops is pumped up from an underground lake, and the level of this lake is constantly sinking and the lands are going dry and being abandoned. It is necessary to dam the Sacramento River and bring the water a great distance and build an elaborate irrigation system. The estimated cost of this project is $175,000,000. The people have voted the bonds, but cannot get the funds. Mr.

Ickes turned down California's application for a loan, on the ground that the Government could not spare that much on one State.

Under our EPIC Plan we would send fifty thousand unemployed men to work on this project. The farmers would bring their surplus crops to feed them, taking State credits which would be good for water and power when the project was completed. By our EPIC tax, payable in goods and services, we could get the materials, and so all the money we would have to ask from the Federal Government would be for such things as California could not produce. Mr. Ickes said: "That is a novel and important idea, and if it succeeds it can be applied all over the country."

After our talk I said to him: "There are newspaper men waiting in the outer office and I wish you would tell me exactly what I am to say." He thought for a minute or two, and then told me to say that he had been interested in the program I had put before him, and that if an application were made to him on that basis the Department would be glad to reconsider its decision. I went out and stated this word for word; I said that and nothing else whenever I told about this interview. But when I got back to California, the newspapers would not have it that way. They developed a regular technique of misquoting what I said about Washington officials, and then sending their Washington correspondents to ask if the officials had said the misquoted words; of course, the officials would deny it, and once more Sinclair had been "repudiated."

When I reached New York next day, the "Evening Sun" quoted what I had said about Secretary Ickes, but put over it a headline which did not conform to the text. I telegraphed Mr. Ickes, calling his attention to this familiar procedure, and when I got back to California I found a letter from him saying that he had no fault to find with anything I had given out about our interview. Soon after that I read in Chester Rowell's column in the San Francisco "Chronicle", among a list of my insanities, this: "He remembered things regarding his conversation with Father Coughlin and Secretary Ickes which these gentlemen emphatically say they do not remember."

Immediately after the election, the Los Angeles

I, CANDIDATE FOR GOVERNOR

"Times" published an editorial, quoting Mr. Ickes as saying that there had been "a great deal of mendacity" regarding his attitude to the Central Valley project. The "Times" gave its readers to understand that Mr. Ickes was repudiating me, so I at once wrote to him, and received in reply a letter which seems to cover the case completely.

THE SECRETARY OF THE INTERIOR
WASHINGTON

November 20, 1934.

My dear Mr. Sinclair:

I have your letter of November 13, to which was attached an editorial from the Los Angeles Times. I did not accuse you of being "mendacious" with respect to the Central Valley Project in California. As a matter of fact, what I intended to say, and what it seems to me is clear that I did say, was that, after you had visited me and discussed this project, it was charged by others that I had made promises which I had not made to you and which you never said that I had made. I am glad to attest that your record in this matter is entirely clear and straight. You never misquoted me on this matter but certain newspapers tried to make it appear that you and I had made some sort of a deal. It was that that I was striking at.

With personal regards

Sincerely yours,

(Signed) Harold C. Ickes,

One more story about Washington. Several months back we had heard reports of a movement by the commissioners who govern the District of Columbia, to set up a system of production and barter for the eighty thousand unemployed of the District. Naturally we had been gleeful over that report; taking it as proof that the EPIC plan had been noted by the Administration. We had published the story in our "EPIC News," and I had been asking my audiences the unanswerable question: "If it is statesmanship in our national capital, why should it be Communism in California?"

Of course, this gave offense to the reactionaries of our State, and our three "Bees," of Sacramento, Modesto, and Fresno, had published a dispatch from their Washington correspondent, to the effect that none of those in charge of the District of Columbia's affairs

Doing the Light and Very Fantastic ✦ By Korburg

knew anything about the plan which Upton Sinclair was telling about. So of course one of my tasks in Washington was to make sure.

I called upon two of the three commissioners who manage the affairs of the District of Columbia, and was received very cordially and told all about their plan. They had not got very far with it; Commissioner Allen, who had it in charge, said that he had been away for two months. But our "EPIC News" had not said that the plan was in effect, merely that it was intended. Commissioner Allen gave me a certified copy of the articles of incorporation of the governing body which was to have charge of the project, and he told me of the application to the FERA for a grant of funds. They had made a start with the repairing of shoes and clothing by the unemployed, and I visited their workshop, and a photograph of it was published in our "EPIC News."

An amusing detail: It turned out that the "Bees", which had printed a denial of my story about Washington, had previously published a Washington story affirming the whole thing. One of our supporters, who apparently read the Fresno "Bee" more carefully than the editors themselves, sent me a clipping from the issue of July 20, in which their Washington correspondent, Ira Bennett, had written as follows:

"Scrip—The District of Columbia is the seed-bed for a new experiment in unemployment relief. A co-operative concern to be called the District Rehabilitation Corporation will draw funds from the Federal Relief Administration.

"Farm colonies will be established in nearby Maryland and Virginia, managed by district unemployed. They are to raise food for the 80,000 unemployed of the district. Non-profit factories are to be set up in which others now unemployed will make bedding, clothing, furniture, etc. Chain stores will be installed. Workers on these farms and factories will be paid in scrip which they can exchange at the relief stores for grub or what have you. The unemployed will get scrip until they can be absorbed in self-sustaining rehabilitation work."

I wrote the "Bees", calling their attention to this little joke on themselves. I further called their attention to the fact that Governor Merriam had just discovered that the peach crop of California was rotting on the ground, and he was trying to arrange for the cooperatives to can part of it for themselves. Maybe Governor Merriam didn't know that was the EPIC Plan; and maybe the "Bees" didn't know it!

In this, and a hundred other cases, I patiently supplied the facts to the California newspapers; but it did no good. It was something—I was to learn about the rest of the campaign—facts no longer mattered. I might gather as many as I pleased, but no notice would be taken of them, and the wholesale publication of falsehoods would go right on. This was a war, and we were in the stage of "atrocity stories"—soldiers crucified to barn-doors, and Begian babies with their hands cut off.

CHAPTER XIX

In telling of my experiences with the California newspapers during the campaign, I have to repeat the explanation which I made in "The Brass Check." I am not just venting a grievance; I am not assuming that my personal misfortunes are a matter of importance to the public. The significance of this story derives from the fact that I was trying to show the people of California a way of escape from poverty. The newspapers were not lying about me because they objected to the color of my eyes, nor because some particular editors were angry with me; on the contrary, some of them were my friends, and apologized to me for what they were doing, even while they went on doing it.

The importance of this story derives from the fact that the campaign of lying about Upton Sinclair was ordered by the biggest business men in California and paid for with millions of their dollars. It was carried out by the best newspaper brains, the best advertising brains, the best motion picture brains, the best political brains—so on all the way down the line. In putting the facts before the public I am not whining, or seeking sympathy; I am telling the people of California what was done to *them* by their big business masters; I am telling the people of the other forty-seven States what they have to expect when their turn comes. For this old dying system has a great deal of vicious life in it yet. It will fight to its last gasp, and this is the way it will fight; all this bitter sneering, these slanders and forgeries, these cruel falsehoods taken up and repeated millions of times over, pounded into the feeble minds of poor people who are overworked and over-driven, and have very little education, and often no power to absorb education.

If you take this book rightly you will consider it a textbook of military strategy; a book of maps and other data needed for the planning of forty-nine campaigns of the future: forty-eight of these to take our States out of the hands of organized greed and knavery, and the forty-ninth, the biggest of all, to take our nation out of the same hands.

Now a little story for Catholics, and how they were persuaded to desert their Democratic party, and vote a reactionary Republican into office.

On the way back to California we stopped off to call on Father Coughlin, the "radio priest." We drove some eighteen miles to the town of Royal Oak, and called by appointment at the modest cottage where Father Coughlin lives with his mother. The hour of our coming had been misunderstood, and the Father was saying mass; so we sat and chatted with another priest, presumably his secretary. This gentleman remarked that Father Coughlin had been studying production for use and was keen about it.

When Father Coughlin himself came in he took me into his study alone and we talked for half an hour. He is a fine, upstanding man, and our conference was in every way satisfactory. He agreed fully that the unemployed must be put at productive labor for their own benefit. He was heart and soul for that program, and said he was going to broadcast in favor of it. I told him that it was the backbone of our EPIC Plan. He asked me for the rest of the program, and I outlined it point by point: income tax, increase in inheritance taxes, repeal of the sales tax, exemption of small homes from taxation, tax upon idle land to bring it into productive use, pensions for the aged, the blind and disabled, and the widowed mothers of dependent children. To each one of these plans Father Coughlin said, "I am for that," or "That is right," and at the end he said, "I approve that program, and you are authorized to state that I endorse it."

Furthermore, in the course of our conversation he said: "You may say that I am willing to forgive you for anything you may have written against our church seventeen years ago. Tell them about Paul who persecuted the Christians and later joined them." I said that the situation was a little different in this case, because the Christians were joining me; the various churches were adopting programs of social justice, coming nearer and nearer to what I had been advocating for thirty years. I spoke of the last encyclical of the Pope on this subject, and said I wished that all the Catholics knew what was in that utterance. Father Coughlin agreed with me, saying that not even priests realized how radical the doctrines of the Church were—all Catholics needed to be educated on the subject.

That ended our interview, and we went out and sat down to a good-looking Sunday dinner. I cannot say how it tasted, because as soon as I was seated at the table I looked at my watch and discovered that we had barely time to get back to our train. One of the young priests undertook to drive us, and it was fortunate that we had not delayed, for half way down the boulevard he discovered he was out of gas, and we had to hail a passing car and be butted along a mile or so to a filling station.

On board the train I wrote an account of that interview. My memory was fresh, and I have an unusually good memory for that sort of thing; it is my habit as a writer to go over in my mind what I want to write, and I have learned to retain several thousand words correctly. I am sure that I quoted verbatim what Father Coughlin said.

The story was put into the "EPIC News," and, of course, our enemies took it up. They were trying to represent me as an atheist and a bitter foe of Catholics, and naturally it was intolerable to them that our program should have the endorsement of the most prominent Catholic priest in America.

What the newspapers did was the same thing as in

the case of Secretary Ickes; they distorted my words and made me say what I had not said. First, I was quoted as saying that Father Coughlin had endorsed me for Governor of California; second, I was quoted as saying that he was going to broadcast in favor of my candidacy. Then some Catholics in San Francisco wrote to him saying that I had said these things, and asking if they were true. Of course, Father Coughlin replied that they were not true, and so I was branded as having misquoted this Catholic priest.

I had never dreamed of asking Father Coughlin to endorse me for Governor of California. As a priest he was not supposed to take any part in politics, and certainly not in the politics of another State. As to his broadcasting, he had said that he was going to urge that the unemployed be permitted to work and produce necessities for themselves. In a letter quoted in the San Francisco newspapers, Father Coughlin said he was "so ignorant" that he had not read any of my books. I was not surprised by that; for they are probably not included in the reading courses of Catholic seminaries.

When the priest's letter was published, I telegraphed him, explaining the device of my opponents. I subsequently made an affidavit as to what had transpired in his home, and I sent a copy to him, saying that I hoped my recollection was in accord with his. He did not reply. No doubt there was heavy pressure upon him, and I do not blame him for keeping out of the controversy. I do not believe he will ever deny having said to me the things which I quoted him as saying.

Six years ago Al Smith sought to become the President of the United States, and the Ku Klux Klan and others raised the religious issue, and the Catholics were outraged. In 1934 Upton Sinclair sought to become Governor of California, and some Catholics raised the religious issue and helped to defeat him. By so doing they sacrificed their moral position.

I have before me one of the leaflets of the "United for California League" of Los Angeles, entitled "Upton Sinclair on the Catholic Church." Across the top is the motto: "Out of His Own Mouth Shall He Be Judged," and at the top of the second page is the heading: "The Church of the Servant Girls." Of course, that designation, applied to the Catholic Church, sounds insulting,

SHALL THE STAMP OF SINCLAIRISM CRUSH CALIFORNIA?

and is calculated to infuriate Catholics. But as usual, if you read the book you discover that it has a different meaning.

I am telling how, as a child, I opened my eyes to religion. I was scrubbed and shined and dressed in my best Sunday clothes, a tight little derby hat and painfully tight kid gloves, and escorted by my father and mother up Fifth Avenue to one of the fashionable churches. On one side was St. Thomas' where the fashionable ladies went, and across the street was St. Patrick's, where the servant girls went. It was forty-five years ago, and all the servant girls I had ever seen were Irish, so, of course, they went to St. Patrick's. So I knew the Episcopal church as "The Church of Good Society," and the Catholic Church as "The Church of the Servant Girls."

The Catholics of California could hardly understand that I was writing as a Socialist, and that "servant girls" were to me not objects of contempt, but of pity and sympathy; I regarded them as persons who pay their own way in the world by hard labor at long hours, and I esteemed them more highly than their mistresses, who had never done anything useful in their lives, and would think nothing of spending a servant girl's wages on an embroidered handkerchief or a bottle of perfume.

I could go through this anti-Sinclair leaflet, and show how each quotation has been taken out of its context and garbled. Here is one from page 108, which my enemies found significant enough to print in black type: "It is no longer possible to do without Catholics in America; not merely do ditches have to be dug, roads graded, coal mined, and dishes washed, but franchises have to be granted, tariff-schedules adjusted, juries and courts manipulated, police trained and strikes crushed."

How could I explain to the Catholics the class protest which motivates that bitter utterance? The Catholics who have come to America in successive waves, the Germans, the Irish, the Italians, the Poles, the Slovaks, the Hungarians—it is quite true that they have dug the ditches and graded the roads and mined the coal; but have I spurned them for that? Let the literary products of my lifetime be the answer. Let "The Jungle," let "King Coal," answer. For these poor exploited people my heart has bled and the blood has run out through my pen. My only thought has been to save them, and all my scorn has been reserved for those who exploit their labor and use them as tools of corruption. It has been for the Crokers and Murphys of Tammany Hall, the Bradys and Ryans of the traction trust, the Schwabs and other steel kings, men who have purchased legislatures and political machines, made our national capital into a sink of corruption, and used the prelates of the Catholic Church as their pawns.

The poor Catholics of California had nothing to fear from me as Governor. Again and again I told them that I had no program that would interfere with their church or with the practice of its rites. What I wanted to do was to end poverty in California, and the poor Catholics would get their share of the benefit. But the rich Catholics wanted to hold onto their riches—despite the fact that they pretend to believe in the divinity of Jesus, who commanded them to sell all they have and give to the poor. The rich Catholics put up the money to print lying leaflets and make the poor Catholics think of me as a monster; so the poor Catholics will stay poor for another four years, and "The Profits of Religion," written in 1917, has been tragically vindicated in 1934.

CHAPTER XX

Returning to California, I was instructed to get off the train at Glendale, where KNX had set up a microphone on the platform and I was invited to use one of its news periods to tell about Washington and Hyde Park. The whistling of the trains and the cheering of a hundred or two EPIC folks provided picturesque local color over the air.

And then one of our huge mass meetings in the Shrine Auditorium, packed to the top with people anxious to hear the stories about President Roosevelt— which I was not at liberty to tell! But I told them about the Ohio plan, and the District of Columbia plan, and what was being done in Michigan, and in Richmond, Virginia, and other places where the unemployed are having a chance to go to work for their own benefit. It is coming everywhere in America, and the roaring of that crowd revealed the determination that it shall come in California—and without many more years of starvation and the piling up of debts.

The last pages of "Immediate EPIC" were prepared and printed and our people set out to distribute it. There were rumors that we had been changing the Plan, and that the whole EPIC movement was in confusion; "EPIC Chaos" was the title of a column editorial in the San Francisco "News." It was intolerable to our opponents that we should change anything; they wanted us to be the same kind of stupid persons as themselves. But I have specialized all my life in the open mind, and was willing to learn even from our enemies when they had a valid criticism. I used to tell our audiences that when I set out to drive to San Francisco, I did not set the steering-wheel of the car and lock it fast and then start. I kept moving the steering-wheel this way and that—and I would seem quite "unstable" to a person who did not understand that I was keeping on the road.

In the beginning the EPIC Plan had called for a tax of 10 per cent on all land which was held out of use. An elderly woman got up in an audience in Santa Monica and said: "Mr. Sinclair, suppose that a person has worked hard all his life and saved money and bought a lot for a nest-egg; what will you do with that nest-egg?" I answered, "Madam, I am sorry to have to tell you that your nest-egg has gone rotten." The crowd roared, and I got away with that answer; but I realized that the old lady had put a real proposition to me. We had graduated other taxes, but had forgotten to graduate those on idle land. So we modified the plan, to provide that land of less than a thousand dollars valuation held by an individual should be exempt from taxation, and calling for a State building loan fund in order that those who wanted to build homes on their vacant lots might be able to do so.

I am aware of the difficulty in determining what idle land is. It would be necessary to classify all the land in the State, and to set up standards of what constitutes utilization. That would take time and cost money; but surely it is better than our present situation, where a man like Hearst can set aside tens of thousands of acres for a private park while one and a quarter million people are slowly starving; where every city and town in California is ringed around with a belt of lots and acreage deliberately held out of use by speculators hoping for a rise in value. Now is a good time to start, when the speculators have almost given up hope, and when unpaid taxes are piling up—and when tens of thousands of homeless men are wandering the highways. I say that it would be an act of statesmanship to put each idle man on an idle lot and make it possible for him to build a home there. I say that if the property owners of California do not do it, they may live to regret the failure of their brains and human sense.

In the "I, Governor" book we had called for a bond issue of $300,000,000 to cover the cost of equipment to make the unemployed self-supporting. But soon our lawyers began pointing out how many devices our opponents would employ, to keep us from getting and expending any of that money. Also, as time passed, I saw the crisis growing worse; the number of unemployed persons increased from a million to a million and a quarter, and emphasis had to be laid upon steps which could be taken without delay. In the book, page 54, I had mentioned the possibility of starting on a rental basis, and I took to stressing this feature of the Plan.

Of course, our enemies immediately set up a clamor that we had dropped the bond issue, and thus admitted another blunder. This was entirely untrue; for I never failed to specify that after we had made a trial on a rental basis and convinced the taxpayers that the unemployed really could produce goods, we could more easily get the consent of the voters to spend money for a capital investment, and thus put the EPIC system on a permanent and self-sustaining basis. See "Immediate EPIC," pages 27–29.

In the course of the summer President Roosevelt announced a program of social insurance which he said would be one of the tasks of the new Congress. Naturally that made it futile for any State to go ahead with a pension program, and I said that the EPIC movement would wait and see what Congress did before taking up this subject. Again a chorus from the hostile newspapers: "Sinclair drops his pension plans." Oddly enough these same opponents, who insisted that we could not raise fifty dollars a month for the aged persons of California, made political capital out of the fact that I did not favor the Townsend Plan, which proposes to pay to the aged a pension of two hundred dollars a month!

Impossible to imagine a greater instance of hypocrisy than Frank Merriam's coming out for the Townsend Plan. Of course, it cost him nothing; for it is avowedly a Federal plan, and he could grin and leave it to the poor victims to appeal to Roosevelt and to Congress. And, meanwhile he would have the votes!

I, too, needed those votes. How easy for me, when the proposal first came before the public, to say yes, of course, I favored it; pay the old people pensions, pay them anything they want—two hundred a month, or two thousand a month. They have worked hard all their lives, the dear, good old people, and why should they not have comfort and security in their old age? How they would have flocked around me—the million people who have signed Townsend petitions all over the State of California!

But I was not trying to be elected so much as to educate the people. So as soon as the problem was put up to me I said: "The Townsend plan proposes to raise money by a sales tax, and a sales tax is a tax on consumption, which reduces consuming power and makes worse the condition it is supposed to remedy." When the Townsend supporters would get up in our meetings and argue that their inspired physician of Long Beach would solve the problem by compelling the old people to spend their two hundred dollars every month, and thus it was a "revolving" plan, and would promote trade and production, I would reply by pointing out to them that every time the money "revolved," the profit-takers would take a profit on it, and if it "revolved" twelve times a year, they would take twelve profits instead of one. It would simply mean that we speeded up the process whereby all the money in the country falls into a few hands, and is locked up in hiding in the vaults of the Wall Street banks. You cannot stop the collapse of the profit system by making it happen twelve times as fast!

What Acting-Governor Merriam really thinks about old age pensions is proved by his actions. He has been acting for six months, and what has he done? Our law provides a pension for needy persons over seventy years of age, and fewer than twenty thousand persons are getting less than twenty dollars per month each; about eighty thousand more have proved their right to the pension, but there is no money for them. Has Merriam moved a finger to get that money, as ordered by the law of the State? He called a special session of the Legislature to pass certain fiscal measures; but no word about money for old age pensions.

But see what it costs to deal honestly with the people! I have before me a leaflet distributed at a mass meeting of the Townsend people in the Hollywood Bowl on the evening of September 28. It is headed: "What Upton Sinclair Thinks of the Townsend Plan." and it concludes:

The duty of all adherents of the Townsend Plan is very plain: WE MUST REPUDIATE SINCLAIR AT THE POLLS ON NOVEMBER 6TH.

The Townsend Plan cannot be stopped by a man whose vanity causes him to reject all movements or suggestions which he himself did not happen to create.

A VOTE AGAINST SINCLAIR IS A VOTE FOR THE TOWNSEND PLAN.

Acting Governor Merriam got the extra votes which he needed, and now he is Governor-Elect, and the grin is on his face, and on the faces of all the politicians who worked for him, and of all the big business gentlemen who put up his millions of dollars. The poor deluded old people can take their petitions to Congress and to President Roosevelt, and cherish their dream of two hundred dollars a month until they die.

The newspapers said it would be that way with our fifty dollars a month pension. They would challenge me to say where I was going to get that money, and when I answered they did not publish what I said. Impossible for any editor of a commercial newspaper to understand the difference between a profit system in a state of collapse, driving the State and everybody in it to bankruptcy, and a system of production for use in process of growth, providing security and plenty for all. I used to say to our audiences: "It is difficult to get a man to understand something, when his salary depends upon his not understanding it!"

There were and still are a million and a quarter

people in California dependent upon public charity. At fifty cents a day, this represents $228,000,000 a year, which must somehow or other be taken away from those who still have jobs or incomes. It represents a deficit which the State must make up by taxes or bond issues. If we put those people at productive labor and make them self-supporting, we have $228,000,000 which we can use in pensioning the old people.

Among the one and a quarter million idle are some five hundred thousand able-bodied workers. If they were put at work, what would be their productive capacity? Let us assume that they worked very badly, and turned out no more than the amount of wages they used to get in prosperous times, four dollars per day each. That is two million dollars a day; omitting Sundays and holidays, it is $600,000,000 per year. The difference between $228,000,000 loss and $600,000,000 gain is $828,000,000; and there you have the difference between EPIC and not-EPIC to the people of California.

CHAPTER XXI

The next big task we had before us was the Democratic Party Convention, which under the law was to be held in Sacramento on September 20. Delegates to this convention consisted of the party's chosen nominees for State offices and for the Legislature; also of all incumbent Democratic legislators, congressmen, and senators. This made something like one hundred and fifty delegates; as our EPIC ticket had pretty well swept the primaries, we had to plan the proceedings of the convention.

Here began a new chapter in my life: as party leader and manipulator of caucuses. The old party people came to see me—at least those who were not making plans to go over to the enemy. Doctor Malaby came, and brought Milton K. Young; later came William McNichols—these three former candidates pledged their support and made speeches for us during the campaign. Several of the congressional candidates came,

From the San Francisco "News"

and of course there were conferences withour own EPIC nominees.

Our candidate for State senator from Los Angeles County was a lawyer, Culbert L. Olson. He had come fourteen years ago from Utah, where he had been a member of the legislature and had a great deal to do with the framing of that State's labor laws, which the railway brotherhood men tell me are the best in the Union. Mr. Olson had come forward early in the EPIC campaign; he was president of the Los Angeles Democratic Club, and invited me to explain my ideas to this organization. He assured me of his devotion to the idea of production for use and his willingness to go along with our forces; but he did not want to come out definitely as an EPIC man until after the primaries, thinking that he could have more influence over the old line Democrats by following that course.

To this I assented, and as a result the old line Democrats put up no opponent to Olson, and he was now the Democratic nominee. Before leaving for Washington, I had prepared a suggested draft for the party platform and turned it over to Downey, Olson and Otto, and we now had a series of conferences about it.

Another mentor who appeared on the scene was United States Senator William G. McAdoo. We had known him for many years, and also the lady who was his wife, President Wilson's daughter. "Mac" had been abroad during the primary campaign, a prudent course. Now he was prepared to support the party nominee, and I went to visit him at his home, and there met his law partner, Colonel Neblett, a younger man who had just come out very ardently in support of my candidacy. McAdoo made suggestions about the platform, and about how a good Democrat should behave.

Then came George Creel. I had already met him in San Francisco, returning from the East; he and Maurice Harrison, with Downey and Olson, had come to what seemed an agreement. Creel now came to my home for a conference, attended by Olson, Otto, Downey, John Beardsley, John Packard, and others of our people. His physical behavior was symbolic. He took off his coat and hung it over a chair; he took off his tie and hung it over the coat; he rolled up one sleeve and then the other, and sat down and proceeded to go to work.

He admitted quite freely at the outset that all the essentials of the EPIC Plan must be in the party platform, because that was the program for which a majority of the Democrats of the State had voted; but he argued that we should avoid going too greatly into detail and content ourselves with statements of general principles. McAdoo urged the same thing; and it was perfectly satisfactory to me, for I was to be the Governor, and would have charge of the details. Creel had only one peremptory demand to make—that we would have nothing to do with Justus Wardell. I felt quite safe in promising that.

Creel had given a good deal of time to labor matters and he undertook to write the labor planks, in cooperation with the State Federation people in San Francisco. We spent three hours discussing all these matters, and came to complete and cordial agreement. We agreed on Olson for permanent chairman of the Democratic party. I suggested that Creel should act as chairman of the convention, and he promised to consider it.

Next day Otto and I went to McAdoo's office for another conference, and an embarrassing issue came up. McAdoo wanted his law partner, Colonel Neblett, to be State Chairman. He was quite insistent about it and said that his long service to the party entitled him to this. I said it was my understanding that the candidate for Governor was permitted to select the chairman who was to carry on his campaign; and our forces had agreed upon Olson. McAdoo insisted that he had a right to be consulted, and I replied that I supposed I was consulting him when I consulted his candidate Creel. McAdoo replied with some heat that Creel did not speak for him; Creel was his own candidate, and McAdoo had not even known that he was going to be a candidate until after he had announced himself. However, McAdoo had endorsed Creel's candidacy.

I am pretty good at fighting with my pen, but I dislike personal controversies, and took refuge in the suggestion that McAdoo take the matter up with Culbert Olson. Incidentally, I was curious to see what Olson would have to say for himself. The result was a most amusing scene.

Culbert Olson is an extremely fine-looking man, large, grave, and slow of speech. It is easy to interrupt a slow speaker, so Olson has evolved a method of defense—he goes right on with what he has to say, regardless of what the other fellow may be doing or saying. He came up to the office and was introduced to McAdoo, and without any preliminaries McAdoo proceeded to inform him that he wanted Neblett to be State Chairman. Whereupon Olson put his head down and started for "Mac". He informed him that it was not a question for either McAdoo or Olson to decide. It had been decided by EPIC leaders, who represented the EPIC voters, and those persons would never in the world accept Colonel Neblett, who had remained out of our campaign until after he read the election returns. Colonel Neblett stood in the corner and blinked his eyes.

McAdoo stood upon his prerogatives as a senator and elder statesman of the party, and ventured to say that he thought Creel would prefer Neblett to Olson. Said Olson: "I am able to inform you upon the best possible authority that Creel would not wish to have Neblett become State Chairman." McAdoo expressed surprise at this and asked what Creel had said. Olson replied: "I do not care to put myself in the position of a tale-bearer. I simply say that I know from Creel's own lips that he would not accept Neblett."

As a matter of fact I also had heard Creel discuss that subject. He had spoken of both McAdoo and Neblett in bitter terms. He is a reckless slinger of epithets, and the particular epithet he had slung at McAdoo's partner was a dead cockroach."

To complete this story, let me say that Colonel Neblett came up to Sacramento, and we made him a member of the platform committee, and he assisted in framing the platform and in putting it through the convention. A week or two later came the first meeting of the new State Central Committee, which had the selecting of the State Chairman, and it selected Culbert Olson. Shortly after that Colonel Neblett issued a manifesto to the press, denouncing the EPIC program and the EPIC candidate. He said that I was leading the State into Communism, and thereafter he made speeches over the radio, attacking me vehemently in the name of true Democracy!

While I am on the subject of "treasons, strategems

Facing the Redskins—1934

—From *The Kansas City Star*

and spoils", I will tell the story of a Los Angeles Democrat who was secretary or something of a Democratic Club, and published a little weekly paper. Soon after I announced my candidacy he became quite cordial and invited me to address his club. I did so, and there was a huge crowd and every evidence of enthusiasm. The weekly began to boost our cause in a tactful way, publishing nice things about me and telling how I was outdistancing all other candidates.

Then one day the editor asked for an interview, and I stopped in to see him. We sat alone in his office and he revealed to me his idea of his future. He was an engineer and would like to be State Engineer if I was elected. I explained politely the basis on which our campaign was being conducted: no promises were being made. He then went on to say that he would like to be State Chairman of the Democratic party. Since that was purely a political matter, surely I could make promises about it! My answer was that decision would be made in the future by the Democratic action of our workers.

I remember mentioning to our campaign committee this man's interest in our movement, and one of the members said: "I don't think he has a particle of idealism in him." "Maybe not," I replied; "but he has a grand card-file." I thought longingly of that card-file for a month or two; but I heard no more from my friend, and there were no more compliments in his little paper.

I forgot him until I had become the nominee of his party and the campaign had reached its full fury. Then all at once his weekly blossomed out in double size— supporting Merriam! None of the Republican campaign sheets published more vicious personal attacks upon me than this so-called "Democratic" paper. Among other things it printed as a serial a piece of fiction entitled "Thunder Over California." This story also appeared in tabloid form, and hundreds of thousands of copies of it were distributed over the State. It had on the cover a hairy monster supposed to be a Bolshevik. You cannot get the full effect in black and white; you must imagine the monster having bright red lips and a bright red flag and plenty of blood scattered all over the page.

AND HOW I GOT LICKED

It was supposed to be a story of California as it would be in thirty years, after the Communist Upton Sinclair had got through destroying all the homes and nationalizing all the women and children. After the campaign was over I picked up an item of information from the "New Republic": This story had been written for Minnesota, to show the horrors which the Farmer-Labor party was going to perpetrate. It had been rewritten, with changes of names and scenery, to adapt it to California. No doubt it will make its appearance in the other forty-six States as needed.

One more anecdote which ties in with this weekly paper. From the outset of the EPIC campaign there was a young cartoonist who made drawings for our paper. His work was crude, but he had an enormous idea of its importance, and when it was not published he would send it to me, and write me long letters in printed characters, demanding to know why I did not do something about it. Before long he became dissatisfied with Richard Otto, our campaign manager, and served upon me the demand that Otto be deposed in his favor. Then presently he wanted the editor of our paper ousted and himself made editor. In short, there seemed to be nothing this young man could not do and did not clamor to do to make me Governor of California!

He would come to see me and say that he was starving, and once or twice I gave him a few dollars. He came, very early one morning, because he had heard that the "Utopian News" had fired its editor, and wanted me to recommend him for that position. I told him that I could not recommend him for any position, because I did not share his own idea of his abilities.

And then no more, until the last three weeks of the campaign, when money was free in California political life. Lo, and behold—the editor who wanted to be State Engineer and Chairman of the Democratic party, publishing a drawing by the cartoonist who wanted to be editor of the "EPIC News" and manager of the End Poverty League and editor of the "Utopian News", ridiculing the author who wanted to be Governor of California!

I, CANDIDATE FOR GOVERNOR

CHAPTER XXII

The twentieth of September was my fifty-sixth birthday, and the Democratic party of California presented me with a charming gift: the best political platform which I have ever known to be adopted by a party in America.

The law provides that all political conventions shall be held in Sacramento on the same day. Our party being the biggest, and able to make the most noise, we had the large assembly chamber. When I entered at ten o'clock in the morning it was packed to the doors, and the gallery was a mass of EPIC supporters, all prepared to make history. The aisles were full of newsreel cameras and spotlights, and we knew that the eyes of the world were upon us that day. We knew also that the EPIC movement was watching us, for presently there was unfurled over the balcony a huge blue-and-white banner reading:

E P I C
460,000 VOTES
NO COMPROMISE!

You see, the conferences with Creel and McAdoo had been widely exploited, and our enemies had not failed to say that we were abandoning our views and making "deals", as the price of political success. I had kept silent, realizing that our new Democratic friends were in a difficult position; I thought it could do no harm if they saved their faces a little bit. Senator McAdoo, for example, had publicly stated that "The EPIC Plan is one of utter and hopeless impracticability"; and now here he was, a prominent delegate to a convention full of EPIC supporters!

Most of the old-line Democrats were there. Creel was chairman, and with me on one side of him and McAdoo on the other, the kleig lights were turned on and the camera-men snapped away to their hearts' content. All public events in America are now carried on in two sections: the real thing for those present, and a rehearsal or second performance, for the benefit of those who cannot come to the show but must have it brought to them.

The Democrats who disapproved of us were there

Weekly Political Opinions
CALIFORNIA'S ORGAN OF
DEMOCRACY
Los Angeles, Calif.

"Thunder Over California"

By ROBERT C. EMERY
Copyright 1934

CHAPTER ONE

CALIFORNIA! Sunny California! Golden California!
John Hopewell Hart was coming back home to California after a long absence. In a few more hours he would again see the white Orange County farmstead where he was reared. He would again clasp his brother David's hand. Once more he was going to see his only child, a woman she would be now, whose face he had not looked upon since she was a child. And for the first time he was going to see that two-year-old grandson David had written him about.

In such blissful anticipation there was sufficient cause to justify eagerness which made it impossible for the no longer young adventurer to remain placid in his deck chair while the liner warped her way painfully into San Pedro harbor and made him press nervously against the steamer's rail, as if by so doing he could hurry the ship along the last tedious mile of her voyage.

There was more than the fond thoughts of persons and places to draw the traveler back to his homeland. Decades abroad amid strangers and in strange climes had dulled in him the poignancy of longing which most men have for ties of family and place—to a certain extent.

[119]

also, and ready to put up a fight. We could not tell how many there were. "Ham" Cotton, a Federal office holder from Los Angeles, was introduced to me, and said: "I appear to be the only Democrat who is going to fight you." He managed to find others later on— after the Republican purse-strings were loosened up!

The first test came over the appointing of the platform committee. The opposition wanted representation on this committee to be by assembly districts; because this would make a big and unwieldly group, and some of their members would be on it. Our plans called for a committee of eight members to be named by the chairman, and we had an understanding with Creel who the eight were to be. Our proposition was carried by a vote of something like five to one. The convention then adjourned, and the committee retired to a room to perform its labors.

The committee consisted of Creel, Olson, Downey, Otto, Neblett, Frank Hennessy, Judge Carr and myself. We went over the proposed draft sentence by sentence, and everybody had his say, and in the end every decision was unanimous. In three or four hours the committee was ready to report.

Every person in the assembly chamber was on tiptoe with excitement. Curiosity had been worked up for a week or more by reports about compromises and deals; and here at last was to be the answer! How far had Sinclair given way to Creel? How far had Creel given way to Sinclair?

The platform was read by Sheridan Downey in his clear, practiced voice, and everybody in the assembly chamber heard every word of it. It started off with an endorsement of the President's efforts toward the New Deal, and vigorous denunciations of Republican reaction, and of the Rolph and Merriam regimes. Of course that all sounded good to our EPIC people and every sentence was punctuated with cheers.

Then came a demand for repeal of the sales tax on the necessities of life, and the substitution of a state income tax and increase in inheritance taxes. No audience in California had ever failed to applaud these propositions.

And then the paragraphs about unemployment, and what the Democratic party of California purposed to

Balaam Up to Date

do about it. Downey read: "As the greatest possible measure of tax reduction, and also as a means of industrial and social rehabilitation, employment of the unemployed, and of ending poverty in California. . . ."

At that point every EPIC man and woman in that audience leaped up, and the cheering stopped the proceedings of the Republican convention in the senate chamber down the corridor. Such waving of hats and handkerchiefs, such stamping and clapping of hands! Creel had to take a bow, and I had to take a bow, and McAdoo had to appear between us with his arms around us. It was all right; the EPICS and the Democrats had got together, and poverty was going to be ended in California!

At last Sheridan Downey was able to continue: ". . . we pledge ourselves to a policy of putting the unemployed at productive work . . ." The whole thing started over again, and Downey had to wait a while longer before he continued: ". . . enabling them to produce what they themselves are to consume. Such a system will restore to activity our idle and profitless processing plants and factories, and give to the unemployed citizens an opportunity to engage in productive and distributive services for their own exclusive use and benefit.

"Cooperative self-help groups have sprung up all over the state. We propose to put the resources of the state behind these groups and enable them to function and grow."

Of course that was our EPIC Plan, and everybody knew it was our EPIC Plan, and when Creel and Neblett pretend that we withdrew our EPIC Plan, or compromised our EPIC Plan, they are distorting history. Both Creel and Neblett voted for these two paragraphs as members of the platform committee, and they voted for them as delegates to the convention. They knew exactly what they were voting for, and when Neblett afterwards called it Communism, and when Creel afterwards called it SociaLism, they were damning themselves, not me.

The platform goes on to cover every essential point of our Plan to end poverty in California. It calls for "immediate exemption from taxation of $1000 of assessed valuation of homes and farms occupied by their owners, and authorizing the legislature to increase that exemption to $3000 when State revenues permit." It calls for taxing of "large land-holdings held out of productive use", and goes further in calling for the taxing of "natural resources." It proposes an emergency tax measure corresponding to our so-called EPIC tax.

The Central Valley Project is to be completed "under a system of production for use." There are to be "the six-hour day and the five-day week without a corresponding reduction in wages," and "adequate old age pensions . . . as well as for the blind, the disabled, and the widowed mothers of helpless children, also for maternity care." It closes with a paragraph which I wrote, and of which I had repeated the substance in a hundred speeches throughout California:

"Progress versus reaction, public welfare against private greed—this is the issue in the present campaign. We are going forward upon a new road to reorganize our society by peaceful, orderly, constitutional, and Christian methods, and see to it that government of the people by the people and for the people does not perish from California."

Anybody who thinks that platform compromises the EPIC Plan ought to have been present at the convention and seen and heard what the crowd in the gallery thought about it. The men who had unfurled the "NO COMPROMISE" banner joined in the cheering, and everybody there know that we had brought about a marriage of the EPIC movement and the Democratic party; everybody there believed we were going on to triumph.

Mr. Hamilton Cotton and his friends had a bright idea to embarrass us; they wanted to read the original text of the EPIC Plan, and propose that for a platform. But the convention did not want any more discussion; the previous question was moved, and voted by a roll call, and was carried, if I remember correctly, by 113 to 4. The newspapers took this as the vote on the platform, and it was so stated in the press. For the benefit of historians I record that this was the vote on the previous question. The vote on the platform followed immediately afterwards, and was taken without a roll call; there was silence when the "noes" were called for, so the correct statement is that the platform was adopted unanimously.

The Republican convention, meeting in the Senate

chamber, waited to see what we would do. I had no time to look in on them, but others told me that the small chamber was only half full and it was like a funeral; everybody anxious and depressed, and the leaders trying their best to figure out some way to dress up their old reactionary as a progressive. At the last moment they decided to take over our plank for the thirty-hour week. Whenever I think over this campaign in future I shall be able to get a good laugh out of the idea of our forcing the Republican party of California to such a pledge. Of course they won't keep it, but it will give us an opportunity to make them unhappy, and perhaps to recall some of their legislators for broken promises. Already Merriam has found a way to get out of it—he says that the thirty-hour week, like old age and other pensions, is a matter for the Federal government. But he didn't say that in his speech at the convention!

I was called on to address the Democratic convention, and did so for half an hour. I spoke now as a full-fledged Democrat and leader of the party. People said it was a good speech; anyhow it was deeply felt and full of purpose. Creel followed me, and then McAdoo, and everything was harmonious. Afterwards we repaired to a porch outside, and made little one-minute speeches for the newsreel men. In the evening we had a grand banquet for all the EPIC Democrats in Sacramento who could afford a dollar and a quarter; and the candidate for Governor ended a perfect day by being laid up with a touch of ptomaine poisoning!

CHAPTER XXIII

The time for the real fight had now come. Up to the primaries, many Republican papers had "laid off" me; they wanted me to be nominated, figuring that I would be easy to beat. But now the conventions had been held, the platforms were before the people, and the issues were joined. For the remaining six weeks it would be rough and tumble, no quarter asked or given.

There were three antagonists in the ring; and there is something to be said about each of the other two.

AND HOW I GOT LICKED

Raymond L. Haight is a young lawyer of Los Angeles, whose grandfather was once governor of the State. He had been active in attempts at civic clean-up, being the head of an organization known as the "Minute-men." Soon after I announced my candidacy, we had a conference; I wanted him to consider coming into our movement and running for Attorney-general. But his traditions were all Republican, and he had the idea of running for Governor himself. He had been promised the support of "Bob" Shuler, Methodist clergyman of Los Angeles active in politics; and Shuler would not support me.

Haight filed on the Republican ticket, and on that of Shuler's newly organized Commonwealth party. He got some 80,000 votes as a Republican, and a few hundred on the other ticket. Since he had no opposition on the latter, he had a place on the ballot in November.

Haight said to me, in substance: "It must be either you or I. If Merriam carries this election, the cause of civic decency is sunk." He said that he was going to concentrate all his fire on Merriam, and added, with a smile: "Before I get through he won't know that Sinclair is running." This program he carried out to the best of his ability, and earned my respect as an honest and public-spirited man.

On the train going up to the convention, Haight and a friend came into my stateroom and talked things over. Haight by that time had got the Merriam crowd badly frightened, and had a most interesting story to tell about their behavior. Four different times he had been approached by big business men, with arguments that it was his duty to withdraw, to avert the menace of Sinclairism; also with what he regarded as bribes, but which they considered plain common sense. They offered: (1) any of the State's law business he wanted; (2) any State office he wanted; (3) the United States senatorship in the event that a senator died while Merriam was Governor; (4) the governorship after Merriam's four years; and (5) $100,000 cash.

He described one of these scenes: "They told me exactly how old McAdoo was and what diseases he suffered from; they laid him out cold in his coffin, right there before my eyes." When Haight told me this, I quoted: "Again, the devil taketh him up into an exceeding high mountain, and sheweth him all the kingdoms of the world, and the glory of them; and saith unto him, All these things will I give thee, if thou wilt fall down and worship me."

Now for Merriam. Day by a day, while writing this book, I have pondered the question: how much shall I tell about Merriam? All through the campaign I refused to deal in personalities, and when somebody brought me more facts against my rival, I made another speech about Ending Poverty In California. But the fight is over now, and I am writing this book as a permanent record. I ask myself: Why shouldn't the people of California know the kind of man they have got for Governor? Why shouldn't the rest of the world know our California plutocracy?

Frank F. Merriam is nearly seventy-four years old. He was born in the town of Hopkinton, Iowa, and I happen to have a friend from there, so I learned that early in life Merriam deserted his wife and two-months-old boy, and went off with another woman, and was sued for maintenance.

Merriam was State auditor in Iowa, and made a practice of pretending to examine insurance companies, and charging big fees for it. His conduct was investigated by a committee of the State legislature, which made a scathing report, concluding: "The committee has no hesitation, however, in condemning without reservation the practice of Merriam as auditor, and of Beehler, as examiner, in collecting from foreign companies the unwarranted and excessive charges exacted from them as exhibited in this report." Governor Cummins of Iowa commented: "Upon the face of the papers that I have, and upon the information that I have received, it appears that many of these examinations were not in good faith, were without value, and that the farce was enacted for no other purpose than to collect money which had not been earned."

Merriam came to California, and was recognized at once as the kind of man who belongs in our State legislature. He became a member of the Assembly in 1917, and voted against an anti-injunction bill, and voted to weaken workmen's compensation; also against limiting the exorbitant charges of private employment agencies. In the 1919 session he repeated these votes, and added a vote to weaken and destroy the initiative; also against creating a bureau of child hygiene. In the 1921 session he again voted in favor of private employment agencies, and against extending and improving the workmen's compensation act. In 1923 he voted for himself as Speaker and was elected. He appointed unfair committees on insurance and public utilities, and again voted in favor of private employment agencies, and against an anti-blacklist bill, and against improvement in the child labor law, and to re-establish a poll tax; against civil service and to re-establish the spoils system. In 1925 as Speaker he voted to tax publicly owned utilities, and three times against abolishing the poll tax, and voted against increased weekly payments under the workmen's compensation act and against the anti-blacklist bill.

I have selected a few of many items. It is the record of a perfect servant of special privilege. Merriam has always been known as a power trust man, and I was amused to notice that when he promised to further the Central Valley Water and Power project during the campaign, he referred to it as the "Central Valley Water project."

While he was State senator, Merriam became president of the Crescent City Investment Company, which was going to build a wonderful new city in Oregon. Merriam employed a two-term convict as a high pressure salesman, and they sold lots to "come-ons," and Merriam wrote them ardent letters; among other marvels he promised the immediate building of a million dollar hotel. After a thorough investigation of the project, the California Real Estate Department pronounced it "a fraud upon the public," and ordered the company to change its representations; a deputy commissioner later wrote that this was never done. When the company's license was held up, Merriam agreed to return the money of dissatisfied customers; but when some of these customers demanded their money back, Merriam fell silent. Subsequently some of the people sued the company and got judgments. All this story was published in detail in the Sacramento "Bee," but it did not do the slightest harm to Merriam's political career. There is so much graft in California that no one can keep any particular item in mind more than a few days.

I, CANDIDATE FOR GOVERNOR

Merriam became Lieutenant Governor, and presided over the Senate in the same spirit and to the same effect as formerly over the Assembly. When Governor Rolph's health began to fail, he aspired to take his place, and his intrigues were such that Governor Rolph's son came to see me in San Francisco and told me that he held Merriam responsible for his father's death. Merriam's brother, Harry, came several times to our Los Angeles headquarters, and told us that Frank had been the executor of their father's estate, and had cheated Harry out of his share. Harry desired to file a suit against him at the height of the campaign, and would have done so if we had given him encouragement.

Governor Rolph died, and at the height of the primary campaign came the strike against the shipowners in San Francisco. The San Francisco police were not brutal enough, and the shipowners wanted Merriam to call out the militia to break the strike. Merriam at that time was carrying on his campaign for the Republican nomination for Governor, and the week before the militia was called out his headquarters was unable to meet its payroll. Immediately after the militia was called out, a campaign committee account was opened at the Crocker National Bank in San Francisco, the initial deposit being $13,700. Raymond Haight charged over the radio that the shipowners paid to Merriam's headquarters more than $30,000 on this deal. He challenged Merriam to deny it, and Merriam replied with a denial that *he* had ever received any such money. That, of course, didn't meet the issue, and Merriam has never denied the real charge which Haight has again and again repeated.

I personally know a man who claims to have seen these checks. Haight writes me the name of a State official who had the checks in his pocket, and showed them to a friend of Haight's on the street. They were payable to the treasurer of the Merriam campaign; they totaled $30,000, and the man said that $20,000 more was coming. Haight adds: "A Los Angeles shipper advised one of my committeemen in Los Angeles that the contribution of his company for the Merriam campaign, promised in return for the order calling out the militia, was $5,000. I have the names of the companies in-

volved and the name of the man who acted as their representative."

A few days after Merriam became Acting Governor, I happened to be in Sacramento, and paid a call upon him. I had two purposes: first, to ask him to pardon Tom Mooney, and second, to ask him to help the unemployed. I told him what I had seen of distress all over the State; how in fifty different meetings I had called for a show of hands, and an average of thirty per cent of those in every crowd reported themselves out of work; how, two or three days previously, I had met a group of three hundred gaunt and haggard men in San Luis Obispo, who told me that all local aid had been cut off, and they did not know where they were going to get food for their families the next day. I offered Merriam the EPIC Plan freely, asking him to put the idle men at co-operative work.

He smiled; his face is like a mask, because of an incessant smile. He thanked me, and shook my hand cordially. One of the legislative representatives of the railway brotherhoods told me that when Merriam was presiding over the State, he met him seven times in one morning, and Merriam shook hands with him every time. Said the labor man: "I don't know if he was showing me special courtesy, or if he makes a practice of shaking hands with everybody every time he passes him."

Next day Merriam announced in the press that unemployment is a Federal problem. He has said the same thing about old age pensions, and now about the thirty-hour week. He tried to put off the relief problem also, but Federal Administrator Harry Hopkins threatened publicly to cut off Federal money, and so forced Merriam to call a special session of the legislature, right in the middle of the political campaign. When Merriam tried to get the handling of the new relief funds for his gang, Hopkins sent his agent to run the legislature and rewrite the bill.

One last word: in order for "The Profits of Religion" to be completely vindicated, it is necessary that such a man should be a Sunday school teacher in a Presbyterian church. Merriam is.

AND HOW I GOT LICKED

CHAPTER XXIV

I was half ill for a week after the convention; but campaign schedules take no account of health. Two of our biggest meetings came at once—in the San Francisco Auditorium and in the Oakland Auditorium. Our Oakland meeting always meant a dinner in advance; for our manager, Frank Lukey, used me as a bait to make the EPIC workers go out and sell tickets for the big event. Only those who sold ten dollars' worth of tickets were privileged to buy a ticket to the meal! We had three or four such events at Oakland, and never less than two hundred diners. Not even on account of ptomaine poisoning could I miss such an event. If I did, the story would start that the candidate was sickly, old, and decrepit, unfitted for the exacting post of Governor.

I think that on the whole I did pretty well. I carried on a campaign of fourteen months and spoke a couple of hundred times, and only missed three or four dates. But that didn't stop the stories about my health.

In a weekly paper of Los Angeles, "Independent Review," I learned that the EPIC candidate was an invalid, and "lays around in the sunshine most of the time." Not being a hen, I have never done any laying. It so happens that I like to lie in the sunshine and read. I do that kind of lying—and leave the other kind to the newspapers.

One of the San Francisco papers discovered a most ingenious form of lying during this visit. In telling the story, I apologize again for so many personal details. It was not I who made them an issue in the campaign.

This time the matter has to do with the homes I have lived in, and what they cost, and why I moved out of them. It started with the Los Angeles "Times," fountain-head of so much unloveliness in California life. "The evil that men do lives after them," said Shakespeare, and few men have left more after them than the old man who begot the "Times."

My reactionary friend, Harry Carr, is one of the editors and owners of this paper, and early in the campaign he stated that I was making $100,000 out of the EPIC movement. I thought I would settle that once for all, so I addressed a long letter to Harry, giving him the financial history of my entire life. Having learned that the "Times" was photographing the houses I have lived in, I gave Harry full particulars: and if you are curious, read "The Lie Factory Starts," which you may purchase for twenty cents.

I will be as brief as possible. My wife bought some cheap lots in a working-class neighborhood in Pasadena, and bought some old houses, one by one, and had them moved onto the lots and joined together. Thus she made the home in which we lived for a matter of fifteen years. But two years ago I found myself tied up with "Thunder Over Mexico," and having to go over to Hollywood nearly every day; then, as we had no money to finish the picture, I had to work for one of the studios, which meant going to Culver City every day, a matter of forty or fifty miles through traffic. I found it wearing, and went over to Hollywood to find a house to rent, and discovered that Beverly Hills was full of beautiful mansions, half of them for sale for the mortgage. We could assume one of these mortgages, and the interest on it would be less than the rent of a house; so we assumed a mortgage—and we still have it, because nobody else will assume it!

We moved to Beverly Hills, and my secretary rented a cottage near by, and there the End Poverty movement was born, as I have previously told. After three or four months, it had to move downtown; and as I had finished with the motion picture business, there was no longer any reason for my staying in Beverly Hills. Our home there had become a conference place for the campaign; the house in Pasadena seemed a refuge in which to be quiet, so one day, without telling anybody, we put a few clothes into our car and ran away to hide. There were only a few pieces of furniture left in the old house; but the phone didn't ring, and that made it heaven.

Such was the situation when the Los Angeles "Times" unearthed the scandal. You can see what a find it was for them: Upton Sinclair had been living in a Beverly Hills mansion, but now wanted to pose as a Democrat and friend of the common man, so he had moved to a dilapidated old house in Pasadena. More "Times" photographers appeared. They asked to take me sitting in a rocking-chair on my front porch; and being a candidate, I said: As you please.

I, CANDIDATE FOR GOVERNOR

The Beverly Hills place presents a convincing appearance of aristocracy; it is all out in front, and its two stories loom up most impressively. The Pasadena house, on the other hand, is long and rambling, made of five old one-story cottages strung together. You can't get more than one of the five into a photograph, so it looks extremely humble.

But even that wasn't bad enough for the "Times." They went over and took the little cottage in which my secretary had lived; and to make it look worse they got a big ash can and set it out on the sidewalk, turned over on its side! They printed three photos, six columns wide, with a four-column head: "Ex-Socialist leaves Palatial Residence for Ballot Battle." Also they ran a column story with separate headlines, "EPIC LEADER SHIFTS HOME—Sinclair Deserts Mansion—Candidate Now Receiving Followers in Modest Pasadena House—Records Disclose Valuable Real Estate Holdings in Wife's Name." (Records of the Mortgages Not Mentioned!)

This juicy scandal went all over the State. The San Francisco "Chronicle" published it two or three days after the convention. But they were not satisfied with what the "Times" had done; they added a little fancy work of their own. They cut me and my rocking chair out of the Pasadena picture, and superimposed it upon my secretary's cottage with the turned-over ash-can; they told the people of San Francisco Flint was where I was living, in my efforts to pose as a Democrat and friend of the common man!

The editor of the "Chronicle," Mr. Chester H. Rowell, is a well-known California publicist. Early in the course of our End Poverty movement I had paid him a courtesy call and invited him to discuss our program on a public platform. He answered tactfully that in debate with a man who had a positive program, one without dogmatic views was at a disadvantage. He promised to think it over and let me hear from him, but never did.

Now, when the rule of big business in California was threatened, it appeared that Mr. Rowell had developed dogmatic views. His paper became, next to the "Times," our bitterest opponent. As a satire on our Utopian promises, its cartoonist invented a "bird of

AND HOW I GOT LICKED

Paradise" with the head of the Democratic donkey, and each day the "Chronicle" had an article, illustrated by this artist, pointing out to some new group of Californians just how I was going to ruin them.

We had our big meeting at the Civic Auditorium, with fifteen thousand cheering people packed inside; and how I did scald the "Chronicle" for that faked photograph! I described details to my auditors, and at every detail there was a new roar. I advised them to call up the "Chronicle" and say what they thought, and I learned next day that something like a thousand had followed my advice.

I wanted to stop the business of faking photographs, and thought it a good occasion for a libel suit. But my friend, John Beardsley, who was taking care of me on this trip, is a lawyer who does not believe in seeking trouble; he went to see Chester Rowell, and put the facts before him, and heard the excuse of the editor who had doctored the photograph—he had not wanted to take the space for three pictures and decided to combine the features of my secretary's home and my own! The "Chronicle" agreed to print the three with a statement of the real facts.

At this time there came certain menacing developments, the meaning of which we did not know, and may never know. There were strange men hanging around the place, and I was being followed; our telephone wires were tapped, and friends came to us with warnings of this and that—gangsters from the East, utterances by some of our enemies, "a little German frightfulness," and so on. I very soon made up my mind that there was no use paying any attention to this; if physical harm were done to me it would help our cause, and I thought our enemies must know that. I wrote a statement to our EPIC workers—"Last Will and Testament"—telling them how they were to carry on if anything happened to me; and then I wanted to go my way as usual.

But my wife wouldn't have it that way. She wanted a husband, not the memory of a martyr. She dragged me away to rest for a few days at the home of a friend. I had some radio talks to write, and a magazine article; I could do it just as well at the beach. But then headquarters called up; the correspondent of a New York paper was in town for a day, and it was very important. I agreed to see this man, after getting his pledge that he would not reveal where I was staying. He came one evening; and the very next morning came the "Times" photographers, taking pictures of this new house—and the "Times" published it with appropriate comments— how many luxurious mansions the "Socialist-Democrat" had at his disposal!

One more detail, and I am through with the subject of houses. While we were living in Beverly Hills, my wife tried to sell the Pasadena property, hoping to pay off the mortgages on both. She put an advertisement in the "Times," and paid the "Times" ten or twenty dollars; and how did the "Times" show its appreciation? Incredible as it may sound, on the day before election they dug up that old advertisement from their files, and made it the basis of a story with a two-column head. Of course, my wife, in her advertisement, had set forth the charms of her property; and the "Times" used this to prove how very wealthy she was—again not mentioning the mortgages! Not merely was she wealthy, but she had tried to conceal the fact by using a box number in her advertisement!

Did that keep anybody from voting for Upton Sinclair for Governor of California? I am sure I don't know; something did, and that may have helped. Certainly the "Times" thought it would help; so on the day before election the "Times" turned against the principles for which it has stood since old General Otis begot it. The "Times" repudiated the virtue of thrift! The "Times" repudiated the virtue of accumulating wealth! The "Times" repudiated the virtue of trading in California real estate! The "Times" repudiated the most exalted of all possible California virtues—that of advertising in the "Times"!

CHAPTER XXV

So far I had managed to get through this campaign without making any very serious blunder; unless, to be sure, you count the writing of "The Profits of Religion,"

MANSION TO COTTAGE ☆☆ **TO CAMPAIGN**

UPTON SINCLAIR and pictorial view of his evolution from Socialist to Democrat. Camera shows the "then and now" of candidate's shifts in homes. Sinclair occupied a veritable palace when he was a mere author and socialist. Today, as chief of California Democracy, he lives in a modest cottage.

FAKE PHOTO FROM SAN FRANCISCO "CHRONICLE"

seventeen years back. But now you are to have the pleasure—or the pain, as the case may be—of seeing me "put my foot in it." If I were asked about one thing which may have cost me the election, it would be the story which follows.

I came home a week after the Democratic convention. I had had no rest in the interim, and was still feeling the effects of the ptomaine poisoning. I arrived on the morning train from San Francisco, and learned that headquarters had made an appointment for me to receive the press at eleven o'clock. My wife saw my condition and begged me to rest. There had developed between her and the "boys" at headquarters a little war. Each of those boys, of course, wanted what he wanted; the one in charge of meetings wanted to make speaking dates; the one in charge of radio wanted to make radio dates; the publicity man wanted to arrange press interviews, newsreels, photographs to be taken at all hours of the day or night, emergency receptions for magazine writers, and correspondents from London or Paris. When all these things were added up, they made a formidable program; and my wife kept asking, what would be the use of electing a Governor and having a corpse?

That morning a dozen reporters arrived. My wife begged me to cut it short, and kept sending me little notes to the effect that I was making it too long. But I am so wrapped up in the EPIC message, I would sit up all night explaining it to anybody who wanted to hear. What more natural than to explain it to a group of nice, friendly young men, some one of whom might possibly be able to get a little of it into a paper?

That is the way I have always felt about reporters. They had been personally decent to me through the campaign; we had joked and "kidded" one another. "What good is your EPIC Plan to me?" said one. "I'm not unemployed." Said I: "You go back and tell your boss what you think of him, and you'll be eligible under the EPIC Plan." So it went.

I failed to allow for the change that had now taken place. The war had begun, and any reporter who was decent to me would lose his job. As a matter of fact I learned later that the Los Angeles "Times" had three men continually on the assignment of trying to get something "on" me. I learned that some of the men who were contacting me at this time were getting fifty dollars a week each from Merriam headquarters, just to keep them in the proper frame of mind.

They asked me every question they could think of about the EPIC Plan, and I answered freely and humanly. One said: "Suppose your Plan goes into effect, won't it cause a great many unemployed to come to California from other States?" I answered with a laugh: "I told Mr. Hopkins, the Federal Relief Administrator, that if I am elected, half the unemployed of the United States will come to California, and he will have to make plans to take care of them."

I went on to discuss this subject. "Of course," I said, "I was making Mr. Hopkins a sales talk. But he recognizes the situation: the unemployed come to California every fall, because it is less easy to freeze to death here. The Federal Government is taking care of them where they are, and it will have to take care of them in California. Mr. Hopkins knows that."

Someone asked if there was any way they could be kept out of California; and I said the only way was to keep the people of California so poor that those in other States would not envy their condition. In fact, they have to be kept a little poorer, because California is a pleasanter place to live in. Such was the program actually favored by our big business masters, I added.

My wife interrupted the session, and the reporters took their departure. One of them happens to be a friend of mine, and he told me afterwards what happened: how three or four of them walked away together, and my friend said: "I think the highlight of the interview was what he said about turning the EPIC clubs into production-for-use groups immediately after election." But the reporter for the Los Angeles "Times" said: "I think the important thing was what he said about half the unemployed coming to California." "But you know he didn't mean that," said my friend. The "Times" man answered: "Maybe he didn't mean it, but he said it, and it's what my paper wants."

So next morning the "Times" came out with a front page story: "HEAVY RUSH OF IDLE SEEN BY SINCLAIR—Transient Flood Expected—Democratic Candidate Cites Prospect in Event of His Winning Election. By a 'Times' Staff Correspondent. Pasa-

I, CANDIDATE FOR GOVERNOR

dena, Sept. 26.—'If I'm elected Governor, I expect one-half the unemployed in the United States will hop the first freight for California,' Upton Sinclair, Socialist-Democratic gubernatorial candidate said here today."

Next the "Times" had a two-column editorial, dealing with the ruin which the EPIC Plan was going to bring to California, according to Sinclair's own admission. There were estimated to be 10,000,000 unemployed in the United States, said the "Times"—the first occasion on which that admission had ever appeared in its columns. One-half of 10,000,000 was 5,000,000—the arithmetic was unexceptionable, and the "Times" proceeded to discuss in all seriousness the problem of those 5,000,000 people, what should they eat, what should they drink, and wherewithal should they be clothed?

I saw, of course, what I had done. Speaking over the radio that night, I told the story, explaining that I had been speaking playfully. The San Francisco "Chronicle" discussed my answer and condemned it, saying that I was "jesting with human misery."

The story had gone all over the State, as far as the telegraph could carry it. There was no end to it; there never would be any end to it, so long as our opponents controlled press and radio. It was a perfect illustration of Mark Twain's saying that "a lie can travel half way round the earth while the truth is putting on its boots." The statement was reproduced in millions of leaflets; presently it was painted upon two thousand billboards—I know the number, for a reason which I will mention later. In large blue lettering on a white background stood out these words:

"IF I AM ELECTED GOVERNOR, I expect one-half the unemployed in the U. S. will hop the first freight to California." UPTON SINCLAIR, Sept. 26, 1934. MORE COMPETITION FOR YOUR JOB.

In the last week of the campaign I traveled North on a speaking trip, and I think I must have seen five hundred of these billboards. It was literally true that one could not enter any town in California by any road without seeing one of them; one could-not leave by any road without seeing another.

The cartoonists rang endless changes upon the theme. They showed the State of California as a beautiful Spanish home with the American flag flying over it, an endless stream of bums going in at one door and a stream of business men, professional men, farmers, and honest workers coming out at the other. They showed the States of Florida, Arizona, and Nevada holding out welcoming arms to our desirable citizens. They showed the typical comic-page bums reclining on the ground, debating the problem of whether Florida or California offered the better attraction—and, of course, deciding in favor of the "EPIC paradise."

The photographers went out to collect evidence, and show the unemployed already heeding Sinclair's call. Nowadays you cannot find a freight-train in the United States without a number of youths and men riding in the empty gondolas; it has got to be such a plague that the railroads have given up, and no longer attempt to drive them off. They are always coming into California and always going out. So it was easy for the newspapers to get pictures, and put under them captions about "the Sinclair immigration."

Also the auto caravans. At the border our State officials, part of the Merriam machine, gave out alarming reports as to the sudden increase in auto immigration; and of course the newspapers got pictures of the most dilapidated cars, with broken furniture and crates full of chickens and babies tied on to the runningboards. They showed an elderly bearded hermit traveling with a stick, and leading a donkey-cart. They even showed baby-carriages loaded with household goods.

The newsreel cameras got these "immigrants" to talk, and say why they had come to California; of course, for two-bits any one of them would say that he had read about Sinclair offering everybody jobs without work. If he didn't say it convincingly enough, the studios had plenty of actors who were used to saying whatever they were told; the wardrobes were full of hobo costumes, and the make-up experts know how to put a week's growth of whiskers on anybody's face. Presently the Los Angeles "Herald-Express" came out with a picture of nearly half a page, showing a group of hoboes in front of a freight-car; it was most striking and realistic—except that the movie fans recognized Dorothy Wilson, Frankie Darrow, and others of their favorites! It was a "still" from "Wild Boys of the Road," presented as a real picture of what Sinclair had done!

Were the people fooled by all this? Of course they were fooled. I can answer, because a friend of mine was discussing the campaign with a woman, who said that I would ruin the State of California if I was elected. "He says himself that he's going to bring half the unemployed of the United States to California." "Do you believe he really intends that?" asked my friend, and the woman answered: "Of course he intends it. He has put it up on billboards. You can see it all over town—his name is signed to it!"

This propaganda lasted until election day, and then it was folded up and put away until next time. The Los Angeles "Times" waited eleven days after the election before it ventured to reveal the truth. On Saturday, November 17, appeared a leading editorial, of which I quote the first three paragraphs:

"INDIGENT JOY-RIDING

"The extent to which Western States and particularly California are being loaded up with indigent itinerants through the operations of the 'auto-caravan' method of certain automobile dealers in having cars, new and used, driven from eastern points for sale here, is little realized by the general public.

"So far this year, with a month and a half yet to go, 12,000 cars carrying 20,000 persons have been brought here for re-sale, most of them to Southern California—and on the arrival of the cars the drivers have been dropped jobless, onto the charity rolls, frequently without receiving any wages.

"At least one murder, several suicides and a material amount of other crime has been traced directly to auto-caravan drivers in Los Angeles alone."

As I am reading page proofs of this book I receive a circular sent out by Rev. Martin Luther Thomas, one of the clergymen who attacked me in the "Times." He now tells his flock that "God spoke" to him, and told him "what to do in the recent state election." After reading this book wouldn't you say it was the Prince of Lies who whispered to the "Times" and its preachers?

Bids For The Winter Tourist Trade

From the Chicago Daily "News"

I, CANDIDATE FOR GOVERNOR

CHAPTER XXVI

One more story, to finish the record of what the Los Angeles "Times" did in its crusade to Extend Poverty In California. This is the story of the "boxes."

A "box," in newspaper parlance, is reading matter set apart, with a border around it to make it more conspicuous. The "Times" began taking extracts from my books and putting them into boxes. It started this immediately after the Democratic convention, and kept it up every day for six weeks. There was always one box on the front page, and sometimes another on a later page.

My friends all found this a wonderful thing; they said it was the most interesting reading matter ever seen in the "Times." But then, most of my friends are educated persons, while the majority of Californians are less so. For my part, reading these boxes day after day, I made up my mind that the election was lost. I said: "It is impossible that the voters will elect a man who has written that!"

I was told they had a dozen men searching the libraries and reading every word I had ever published. They brought up many things which I myself had entirely forgotten. They had plenty of time to prepare, having known several months back that I was going to be the Democratic candidate. They had a staff of political chemists at work, preparing poisons to be let loose in the California atmosphere on every one of a hundred mornings. They passed this poison on to other newspapers all over the State, whether freely or for sale I do not know.

There was a series of articles about my very offensive personality. I have talked a lot about myself, and have changed my mind frequently—unlike the "Times," which is fixed in its hate of every progressive idea. There was a series of articles describing my life, and of course making everything I had ever done appear odious. There was a series of reviews of my books, picking out features that would offend various groups in California. There was a series of articles to show how EPIC was identical with Bolshevism, which has been destroying civilization in Russia for the past seventeen years—but never seems to finish! There was a history of "socialistic" experiments, beginning some millions of years ago with the ants and the bees, and coming down through Plato and the Incas to Brook Farm and Llano, California. There were columns of opinions of the California press about me—they had no difficulty in finding a plenty, because every daily newspaper in the State was fighting EPIC, with the exception of one small country daily, and one tabloid, the "Illustrated Daily News" of Los Angeles, which remained neutral.

So far as the "boxes" were concerned, it was not merely a question of reading my books and finding the alarming passages; it was a question of studying sentence by sentence and line by line, to find how something could be made to mean the opposite of what it really meant. They would leave out words from the middle of a sentence; or they would begin a sentence after its real beginning, or end before its real ending. And when I complained about this garbling of my books, the "Times" denied that it was garbling anything, and printed photographs of three pages which were not garbled; that proved its case! After I had wasted hundreds of dollars of precious radio time in pointing out instances of garbling, the "Times" blandly stated in an editorial that I accused it of garbling my books but never cited any cases!

I will now cite a few; and if there is ever such a thing as a court of justice in this world, let it judge between us.

I begin with the most obvious kind of lying—the taking of passages from works of fiction, and attributing to Upton Sinclair the opinions of imaginary characters. Thus in "Love's Pilgrimage," page 650, a fictional character writes a letter about his marital difficulties; and on October 9 the "Times" printed an extract from it, headed: "Sinclair On Marriage." In the novel, "100%," page 310, a perfectly odious character, the wife of a spy, learns that her husband has been invited by a great society lady, president of the Daughters of the American Revolution, to address some disabled war veterans. "Gladys made a wry face, because the lecture was to be delivered before a lot of good-for-nothing soldiers in some hall, while it had been her hope that it was to be delivered to the Daughters themselves and in Mrs. Warring Sammye's home." The "Times" (Oct.

12) kept its readers from understanding that sentence by stopping at the word "hall," and substituting a period for a comma. It then put over the passage the heading: "Sinclair On Disabled War Veterans."

In explaining this to audiences I used an illustration. Lady Macbeth has incited her husband to commit a murder, and his hands are covered with blood, and she is ridiculing his fears. "A little water will wash that out," she says; and the "Times" takes that and put it in a box and heads it: "Shakespeare Justifies Murder."

Joking to an audience about this performance, I said: "I don't know what there is left for them to bring up, unless it is the nationalizing of women." Maybe my remark was passed onto the "Times"; a day or two later, October 3, there appeared a box headed: "Nationalizing Children." This was a quotation from "The Industrial Republic," a book twenty-five years out of print and therefore not available to readers of the "Times" It was a discussion of cooperative care of children, such as we had at Helicon Hall, and such as we are now familiar with under the name of the day nursery or creche.

I have shown you Justus Wardell garbling a passage from "Letters to Judd." The "Times" quoted that same passage, but did an even more ingenious form of garbling. As published in the "Times," September 28, the passage read: "We are moving toward a new American revolution . . . . We have got to get rid of the capitalist system. It is close to breaking down," and so on. What did the four dots signify? Well, they signified a whole paragraph, telling about Samuel Adams and Patrick Henry and George Washington and Thomas Jefferson, and quoting a couple of sentences from Abraham Lincoln. I am trying to be as brief as possible so I give merely the first thirteen words of what the "Times" omitted: "That does not mean riot and tumult, as our enemies try to represent."

And here is one from the "Times" of October 6, headed: "Sinclair On the Public." "Fifteen years ago there was a strong movement for social justice in Oregon, led by reformers who fondly imagined that if you gave the people the powers of direct legislation they would have the intelligence to protect their own interests. We now see that the hope was delusive; the people have not the intelligence to help themselves. . . .

That is the way the "Times" printed it. Of course the "Times" wanted the people to think that I was expressing contempt for the people. It did not want to let the people know that I was trying to help them, and so it garbled the last sentence. In "The Goose-Step," page 169, the word "themselves" is not followed by a period. It is followed by a comma, with the further words, "and the interlocking directorate is vigorously occupied to see that they do not get this intelligence." (By the term, "interlocking directorate," the book means those big business masters who control our universities.)

Let us leave the field of politics and enter the more dangerous one of religion. On October 7, the "Times" ran a box headed: "Sinclair On Christ." It was quoted from "The Profits of Religion," pages 97–98. The opening sentence, as quoted by the "Times," was: "Let us realize at the outset that they (the clergy) do their preaching in the name of a proletarian rebel, who was crucified as a common criminal because, as they said, 'He stirreth up the people.' An embarrassing 'Savior' for the Church of Good Society, you might imagine; but they manage to fix him up and make him respectable. . . ."

This represents still another kind of garbling, even worse than taking out a comma and putting in a period. The words, "the clergy," were put in by the "Times," and they constituted a falsehood. The opening sentence, cut out by the "Times," reads: "There remains to say a few words as to the intellectual functions of *the Fifth Avenue clergy*."

I wonder what the "Times" would say if I applied its methods to the Bible, and make a box reading: "Bible Justifies Suicide." The text would read: "And Judas went and hanged himself. . . . Go thou and do likewise."

One curious thing I noted and commented upon frequently to my audiences. These hired liars quoted from a dozen of my books, and from many articles and letters in obscure Socialist papers, published in Kansas, and in New York, and even in Moscow; they wrote about everything I had ever done, and everything I had ever written. But one thing they omitted—one book they never quoted, although it is one of my best-sellers, and one of my best known and most significant. I never saw a box in the "Times" from "The Brass Check," my exposure of American journalism!

How the audiences would roar when I mentioned that! Now I will give the reader of the present book a polite smile, by making up a little box of my own:

SINCLAIR ON THE "TIMES"

"This paper, founded by Harrison Gray Otis, one of the most corrupt and most violent old men that ever appeared in American public life, has continued for thirty years to rave at every conceivable social reform, with complete disregard for truth, and with abusiveness which seems almost insane."—"The Brass Check," page 202.

That was Sinclair on the "Times" in 1919; and here is the "Times" on Sinclair in 1934:

"What is eating at the heart of America is a maggot-like horde of Reds who have scuttled to his support."

CHAPTER XXVII

I have shown the attacks made upon my religious ideas all through the campaign. There is only one subject more dangerous than religion, and that is sex. Tens of thousands of good, earnest ladies in California voted for Merriam because they had been made to believe that Upton Sinclair was a free-lover.

In the novel, "Love's Pilgrimage," written in 1910, the idealistic young hero, twenty-two years of age, discovers that his wife is in love with another man, and he considers it his duty to step out of the way. He writes a letter to the other man, explaining his attitude, and in the course of it the solemn young jackass states as follows (page 650): "The crux of the whole difficulty I imagine must lie in what you say about your profound belief in the sanctity of the institution of marriage. That is, of course, a large question to attempt to discuss in a letter. I can only say that I once had such a belief, and that as a result of my studies I have it no longer."

It wasn't enough for the Los Angeles "Times" to put

The Fourth Horseman!

HOLD that pose, Mussolini, Hitler and Stalin! Here comes another man on horseback, another dictator!

His mount is more imaginary than real. There is more of it in his mind than under his body, but such as it is he hopes it will carry him into your dictatorial company.

It is only Upton's hobbyhorse, but if it cannot make the grade and keep in line it might be able to follow. Sinclair ought to be able to follow Stalin—in fact he has been following him all through his campaign for Governor.

He has no chance of being elected Governor and therefore no chance of becoming dictator of California, but he would have to become the latter to carry out his EPIC or rather IPECAC policy.

From the Los Angeles "Examiner"

that in a box in the year 1934. The cartoonists took it up, and portrayed me as a bespectacled creature with long pointed fingernails like the devil, enunciating the following words: "The sanctity of marriage . . . I have had such a belief . . . I have it no longer." One of my pointed fingernails is directed toward the picture of a happy family with a child climbing upon its father's back.

Most of the garbling on this subject was done from the "Book of Life," and so I discuss the ideas of that book. Part III, known as "The Book of Love," contains one hundred pages; it was published twelve years ago, and I had pretty well forgotten its contents. I run through it, and am disposed to be somewhat proud of myself, and to say that I would rather be the author of those hundred pages than be the Governor of a State in which men such as the editors of the Los Angeles "Times" hold and exercise power.

These pages discuss every detail of a complex subject, the sex relationship of human beings. They carefully make every qualification, they cover every contingency, and leave no room for any sort of misunderstanding. Any person who reads those hundred pages will know exactly what I think about love, the kinds to which I permit the name, as well as the kinds to which I deny it; about marriage, divorce, celibacy, prostitution—everything.

What are these ideas? I believe in and defend monogamous love, permanent love, love which involves the whole being, body, mind and soul. It is *love within marriage.* The only exceptions are when the marriage laws are such as to block the way of true love; then I advocate changing the laws. It so happens that the laws of California on the subject of marriage are liberal. Therefore, so far as concerns the State of California, I am writing "within the law."

Among those who read the book when it first came out was Professor Robert Herrick, for thirty years a teacher of English at the University of Chicago, and one of our best-known novelists. He wrote: "I find it an extraordinarily sensible and useful book, and gave it to my son to take away with him, as stating certain matters of special importance to youth more sanely than any book I know." May Sinclair, the English novelist, wrote: "I read it with intense interest and admiration and agreement. You have written the best and sanest things about love."

In discussing the subject of the sex relationship and its rights and wrongs, I used two words, "love" and "lust," and made precise and careful definitions. I quote:

"That purely physical sex desire I will indicate in our future discussions by the only convenient word that I can find, which is lust. The word has religious implications, so I explain that I use it in my own meaning, as above. There is a great deal of what the churches call lust, which I call true and honest love; on the other hand, in Christian churches today, there are celebrated innumerable marriages between innocent young girls and mature men of property, which I describe as legalized and consecrated lust.

"We are now in position to make fundamental distinction. I assert the proposition that there does not exist, in any man, at any time of his life, or in any condition of his health, a necessity for yielding to the impulses of lust; and I say that no man can yield to them without degrading his nature and injuring himself, not merely morally, but mentally, and in the long run physically. I assert that it is the duty of every man, at all times and under all circumstances, to resist the impulses of lust, to suppress and destroy them in his nature, by whatever expenditure of will power and moral effort may be required."

So much for "lust"; and now for "love." I quote again:

"Personally I am prepared to go as far as the extreme sex-radical in the defense of love and the right to love. I believe that love is the most precious of all the gifts of life. I accept its sanctions and its authority. I believe that it is to be cherished and obeyed, and not to be run away from or strangled in the heart. I believe that it is the voice of nature speaking in the depths of us, and speaking from a wisdom deeper than we have attained, or may attain for many centuries to come. And when I say love, I do not mean merely affection. I do not mean merely the habit of living in the same home, which is the basis of marriage as Blatchford describes it. What I mean is the love of the poets and the dreamers, the 'young love' which is thrill and ecstasy, a glorification and a transfiguration of the whole life. I say that, far from giving up this love for marriage, it is the true purpose of marriage to preserve this love and perpetuate it."

Naturally, the garblers would not overlook that paragraph. On November 1, a few days before the election, the Los Angeles "Times" printed one of its "boxes," with two sentences taken from that paragraph. The heading, "Sinclair and Sex," was in itself a falsification, for "sex" to the average person means lust, not love, whereas I had explicitly stated that I meant love, not lust. And what did the "Times" quote under that heading? Two sentences, as follows: "Personally I am prepared to go as far as the extreme sex radical in the defense of love and the right to love . . . And when I say love I do not mean mere affection." That, and no more!

Of course the pamphleteers took up that garbling. Here is a four-page leaflet entitled: "Upton Sinclair Discusses the Home, the Institution of Marriage and Advocates Free Love." This leaflet is published by Berenice H. Johnson, clubwoman and Women's Christian Temperance Union worker, who has conducted a "Current Events Class" for some twenty years in Los Angeles. I do not know whether she ever read my "Book of Life"; my guess is that she just took the passages which the "Times" and other garblers provided. She quotes the fictional passage from "Love's Pilgrimage," and a number of passages from the "Book of Love." Here is one of them, which she judges so helpful to her cause that she has the printer put lines underneath it: "*I do not say that I believe, I say I know, that free and happy love, guided by wisdom and sound knowledge, is not merely, conducive to health, but is in the long run necessary to health.*"

I am so depraved that I have to study that passage carefully to find out what is wrong with it. Presumably the lady allows that there is to be *some* love in the world. Is it to be love of sick people, or of healthy people? Is it to be guided by wisdom and sound knowledge, or by ignorance and delusion? Is it to be sad love, accompanied by weeping? Or can the trouble lie in the little word "free"? Does Mrs. Johnson favor

MARRIAGE SCORNED

"... THE SANCTITY OF MARRIAGE ... I HAVE HAD SUCH A BELIEF ... I HAVE IT NO LONGER"

See Page 650 "Love's Pilgrimage" by UPTON SINCLAIR

slave love? Does she want young girls to be sold by their parents to middle-aged men who are "eligible"— that is who have money; and then, having been lawfully contracted for, must they keep the bargain the rest of their lives—or may they seek a divorce if they are too unhappy?

Another passage quotes page 6 of the "Book of Life," part III: "The sex arrangement under which we live in modern society is not monogamous love, but marriage-plus-prostitution. It is obvious that our present-day religious creeds, ethical ideals, legal codes, and social rewards and punishments have been powerless to pro-tect marriage, or to make it the rule in sex relationship."

Of course, that is a question of facts. The sheltered lady who issued this leaflet may just possibly not know everything about the vice districts of Los Angeles and Hollywood, the conditions in department stores and offices—or even the divorce statistics of the State of California.

Having quoted the garbled passages from the Los Angeles "Times," and several of her own, Mrs. Johnson calls upon the readers of her leaflet to vote for Governor Merriam as the only way of saving California. She says: "And now Upton Sinclair calls upon decent, self-respecting men and women—whose votes he now knows are as useful to him as the votes of Communists and Free-lovers—to make him Governor of a Christian State."

I am known to be a person who practices what he preaches, so of course it was inevitable that the circula-tion of such statements should start nasty stories about my private life. As early as July the San Rafael "Inde-pendent" told its readers about Helicon Hall. "Once he tried to lead civilization out of the darkness by gath-ering up a flock of artists, writers, food-faddists and ordinary run of the mill nuts, placing them on a large farm and forcing them to eat nothing but vegetables." The end was told: "What with violent quarrels among the enlightened and some rather distressing amatory monkeyshines, the scheme failed." I wrote to the edi-tor, calling his attention to the falsity of all these state-ments; but no correction was ever printed.

It was not long before there were "free love" whispers

all over the place. My wife's friend who told her about the society folk throwing pillows at one another, also told her that she, the friend, was said to be in love with Upton Sinclair. This lady has a perfectly good husband, but that didn't stop the story. Another friend, considerably older than I and several times a grandmother, was reputed to be among my mistresses—for no other reason than that my wife and I occasionally have dinner with her and her family. I wonder how many thousands of women in Pasadena voted against me for that reason? And how many on account of the following:

At our home in Pasadena there is a house which I use as an office. To this office come every day two elderly ladies who open my mail and answer it and fill the orders for books. Both these ladies are churchgoers and both deeply conscientious. Also there live in the house my wife's sister and her fourteen-year-old daughter. In the last weeks of the campaign, this little girl came to my wife and said: "Aunt Mary Craig, what is a harem?" My wife, who was reared in Mississippi, is a little shy of answering the questions of young girls, so she said: "A harem was something that used to be but isn't any more." "Yes," said the niece, "but what was it when it used to be?" My wife said: "Why do you want to know?" The child replied, "Well, the girls at school are saying that Uncle Upton has a harem up here, and I wondered what it was."

In order to make the record complete, let me state what my practice is. Twenty-one-and-a-half years ago I was married to a lady who believes in love as I have defined it in my book. For that period of time she has been my friend and partner, and has shared my victories and defeats. When it has been the latter, she has told me the causes with the utmost frankness. She takes care of me after the manner of a tigress with one solitary cub; and if there should ever come along a female creature having the idea that I don't believe in marriage—well, somehow the female creatures understand the situation, and they just don't come along.

I, CANDIDATE FOR GOVERNOR

CHAPTER XXVIII

When I first came to California, nineteen years ago, I met Harry Carr, of the Los Angeles "Times". Discussing journalism, he remarked to me: "Sinclair, it has been so long since I have written anything I believed that I wouldn't know the feeling." I quoted that in "The Brass Check," but without Harry's name. Recently I met him at a friend's home, and he said that I had named him in "The Brass Check." I told him no, it was just that the cap fitted, and he had put it on.

There are hundreds of Harry Carrs in California journalism. There are thousands like him in another profession, that of advertising and publicity, where, of course, the concept of believing what one writes is unknown. It is interesting to note that when our big business men wanted to smash EPIC, the groups they relied upon were these two; also, of course, a few lawyers, who are hired to represent either side of any cause. It is notable that they used very few politicians. Merriam and his crowd are all right to manage the business of the State of California, and spend the money of the taxpayers; but when there is serious work to be done, and the plutocracy wants to be sure of getting its money's worth, they put their own people on the job.

The publicity was handled by a national advertising agency, Lord and Thomas. The Los Angeles manager talked quite freely to a friend of mine, about how it felt to be doing a piece of dirty work. After he had spent a day revising copy for billboards and newspaper ads, and selecting garbled extracts from the books of Upton Sinclair, he would drive home, and see a home-made sign for the Ending of Poverty In California, painted on a strip of cotton cloth and set up between two sticks; he would feel ashamed, because these amateurs were getting so much the better of him. "It was the swellest amateur job ever done in America," said this expert.

He told furthermore the attitude of the staff toward the man they were making Governor of their State. They left out his picture almost entirely, because they decided that nobody wanted him. They wrote able speeches for him, and he did not have sense enough to deliver them. While at their work they referred to him by four-letter words of Anglo-Saxon origin, which custom has decreed shall not be printed. "Hold your nose and vote for Merriam," was a general saying in California.

Another person to whom part of the job was entrusted was a young lawyer named Albert Parker, son of a Los Angeles bookseller, and connected with the ultra-plutocratic law firm of O'Melveny, Tuller and Myers. He wrote a letter to a friend, telling a little of what he was doing; I shall print this letter before long, and tell how it came into our possession. Suffice it for the moment that young Parker became secretary of the "United for California League," and raised more than a million dollars to "beat Sinclair", and circulated six million leaflets, and put up two thousand billboards.

I have an assortment of these leaflets before me. "The Proof That Upton Sinclair Preaches Revolution and Communism" contains all the rubbish from "The Red Network," and the garbled passages from Justus Wardell and the "Times", and some new ones.

Immediately after the Communist revolution in Russia, I wrote in "The Brass Check", page 385: "Let me make clear at the outset my point of view, oft repeated. I am not a Bolshevik, and have never been a Bolshevik. I understand that a Bolshevik is one who repudiates political action, etc." The argument continues for a half a page, explaining the idea I have held to all my life, that in countries where the people have universal suffrage and democratic institutions, they can bring about the changes they wish peaceably and by majority consent, and they should do so, and there is no excuse for doing otherwise. Every book, pamphlet, and article I have written on the subject in my entire lifetime reiterates that point of view, and it is known to be my point of view by every student. No one could get any other impression from reading anything of mine, and no one could make it appear otherwise except by lying.

What was Mr. Albert Parker doing when he printed in his leaflet the following words from "The Way Out", page 43: ". . . you will bring on a Russian revolution, and councils of workers and farmers will build a new industrial state without any assistance. That is the final goal in any case, and the only question is the quickest and easiest way to reach it." Here, you see, are dots at the beginning of a sentence. Why those dots? Why not the words for which the dots stand? If some of my words are worth printing, why are others not worth it? Is it because there are too many of them? Not so; in this case there are only six. Why did young Mr. Parker cut out six words, and put three dots in their place? You will understand the moment I tell you what the words are: **"If you behave like a tsar."** Put those words where they belong, and see how different the sentence becomes!

"The Way Out" is a series of letters addressed to a young man exactly such as Mr. Parker; a member of the privileged classes, secure in his power—and in the position of a child using a can of nitroglycerine for a baseball. I am trying to appeal to his reason; also to his heart and conscience. I am showing him exactly how social changes, made necessary by the invention of new machinery, can be brought about peaceably, and without waste and bloodshed. Immediately following the sentences which Mr. Parker quoted, page 43 is one more sentence, completing the paragraph. Why did he leave out that sentence? Read the first thirteen words of it, and you will see. "I am pleading that we should travel by the road of mutual understanding."

I wonder—does that young lawyer feel any shame for the work he did in this campaign? I wonder also— is the achievement going to help him to a great career in California? Will our big business men honor him as their savior? Or will they look upon him as English gentlemen did on Benedict Arnold, living in London after the American revolution? Or will he perhaps go out like Judas Iscariot, and hang himself from a tree?

Other reasons for young Mr. Parker's hanging himself are entitled: "What Sinclair's EPIC Means to You"; "Upton Sinclair on the Legion, the A. E. F., the R. O. T. C., and the Boy Scouts"; "Upton Sinclair Reviews the University of California and U. C. L. A.: 'The University of the Black Hand'"; "Upton Sinclair's Attitude on Christianity"; "Upton Sinclair's Opinion of Christian Science"; "Upton Sinclair on the Catholic Church"; and the one from which I have previously quoted: "SINCLAIR, Defiler of all Churches and All Christian Institutions."

The only good thing I can think of to say for this

young lawyer is that he had so much company. I think of one of the most ferocious of my traducers, a certain Mr. Hobday, who used to talk every night over the radio on behalf of his "Constitution Society." I say talk; but when Mr. Hobday got really going on Sinclair as a RED menace—and especially when he got to asking for money—his voice would rise to a sort of chanted shriek. I have seen a roomful of auditors sit gazing at one another. One woman cried: "It can't be **real!**" But it was.

Equally real was the Hollywood movie actor whom this "Constitution Society" put on, to impersonate a quavering pitiful old man, who told the radio audience how he had attended one of our meetings at the Shrine Auditorium, and stood near me, and I had picked his pocket and stolen his purse! For purposes such as that the society expended, so I am told, $105 per night.

Also the Reverend Martin Luther Thomas, a prize-fighter turned preacher, to whom God gave personal instructions. He had a church and a radio hour, and night after night he raved at me, and read more and more horrifying affidavits, challenging me to put him in jail if they were not true. Affidavits that I had trampled on the American flag at San Pedro on the occasion, which you may read about in "The Goslings," when I was arrested for attempting to read the Constitution of the United States, while standing on private property with the written permission of the owner! Affidavits from men who heard me curse the Constitution and the flag! Affidavits from men who had heard me say, when forty-eight sailors of the battleship Mississippi had been killed by a gun explosion, that I wished it had been forty-eight hundred! And me the descendant of a long line of naval ancestors, from Virginia and back in England! I was told that "Spouting Thomas", as our people called him, was going to read an affidavit that I had caused the Preparedness Day explosion in San Francisco. Maybe he did, and nobody told me about it. I couldn't listen to all the oratory; I had to do some of my own!

From Norman Thomas I learn of something else that I missed. Writing in the "New Leader", Thomas states: "Actually a radio play was put on in which Sinclair's name was connected in one way or another with the assassination of McKinley." As it happens, when McKinley died, I was just out of Columbia University, and thought he was a great President!

CHAPTER XXIX

The little book, "I, Governor of California," proved an almost perfect piece of prophesy, up to the day of the election. Among other things I told how our movement would cut the two old parties in half, and bring about a new alignment of rights and lefts, the reactionaries and the progressives. This happened, and the people of California now have the names of those leaders who are ready for social change, and of those who mean to oppose it. Republicans of social vision came either to EPIC or to Haight; while the Democrats who are Democrats for plunder all joined the Merriam camp.

It took no genius to foretell this; I had watched the same thing all my early life in New York. In my campaign I spoke of "Democrats who feed out of the Republican trough", and the audiences made plain that they "got" me. In San Francisco the Democratic machine was so mixed up with the Republican that you could hardly distinguish them.

Take, for example, Judge Matt Sullivan, formerly of our supreme court bench, and one of the men who has labored hardest to keep Tom Mooney in jail. "Matt" is a Democrat, and a law partner of Theodore Roche, Governor Rolph's attorney; there you see the two machines working in the same office. "Matt" proved one of my fiercest opponents; he became chairman of the "Democratic Merriam for Governor Campaign Committee", and compiled a collection of all the lies ever told about me. "Is he not in fact a dyed-in-the-red Communist? Here is his Communistic record. Let him answer for himself. Sinclair would Sovietize the United States. He would Russianize California and inflict on our people the curse of Communism."

It happens that Senator Hiram Johnson is also a member of that firm, so I suppose that accounts in part

SINCLAIR

DYNAMITER
OF
ALL CHURCHES
AND
ALL CHRISTIAN INSTITUTIONS

ACTIVE OFFICIAL
OF
COMMUNIST ORGANIZATIONS

COMMUNIST WRITER

COMMUNIST AGITATOR

THE MAN WHO SAID THE
P. T. A.
HAS BEEN TAKEN OVER BY THE

BLACK HAND

Issued by
California Democratic Governor's League
M. J. Brown, Secy., 2000 Holly Drive, Los Angeles

The Proof That

Upton Sinclair

Preaches

Revolution
—and—
Communism

●

His Record and Activities in Behalf of Communism

●

Additional copies may be secured from
UNITED FOR CALIFORNIA LEAGUE
A Non-Partisan Organization
Robert M. Clarke, *Chairman*   Albert Parker, *Secretary*
411 W FIFTH ST.   ●   LOS ANGELES

COVERS OF TWO CAMPAIGN PAMPHLETS

for the silence which Hiram maintained all through the campaign. Several months before the primaries I called on the Senator, who is listed among the "New Dealers." He was friendly, and we talked things out; he said he was taking no part in primary contests, but to come around if I got the nomination, and we would "see about it." When I called on Roosevelt, he told me to be sure to see Hiram, and "tell Hiram I said for him to see you." I wired this to the Senator, but thereafter, whenever I was in San Francisco, he was out of it.

The retiring State Chairman of the Democratic party was Maurice Harrison, a corporation lawyer of San Francisco. He supported Creel, and I am told was Creel's principal backer. My nomination put him in an awkward position, since he enjoys an income of a hundred thousand dollars a year from the Crocker National Bank and other corporations which were putting up money to defeat me. He played his part at the convention, and soon afterwards announced that there were some of my plans which he could not endorse, and he therefore retired from the campaign. He did not call me an atheist or a Communist.

Mr. "Ham" Cotton, head of the P. W. A. in Los Angeles, on the night of the primary election "conceded the rape of California Democracy by Upton Sinclair." He went home from the convention, and proceeded to organize the "American Democracy of California," in support of Merriam. I have before me a leaflet containing their "Statement of Principles", and I note that there are nine; the first and the eighth pledge support to the principles of Democracy, and all the other seven denounce Upton Sinclair. It is generally reported in Los Angeles that Mr. Cotton received $3,000 a week for his services in electing Merriam. He opened many spacious offices, all over our part of the State. Every single one that I saw was in a closed bank!

Also, there was the "League of Loyal Democrats," organized by a lawyer of Los Angeles with a once-honored name, William Jennings Bryan, Jr. When I was a youth, the "Great Commoner" was my father's beau ideal. "You shall not press a crown of thorns upon the brow of labor; you shall not crucify mankind upon a cross of gold." The Great Commoner built up a fortune, and left it to his children, and now his son wished to protect it from income and other wicked taxes. Mr. Bryan described his plan "to build a sane Democracy for the future." The report is that he expects Merriam to make him a judge.

And then Ole Hansen, hero of the Seattle general strike; the Great Ole, who transformed himself into a real estate speculator, and then back into a crusader against Communism. Ole started the "Save Our State League," and a paper, the "Save Our State News." On my copy one of our supporters has written: "They have flooded Riverside with these lies." And what are the lies? Well, most everything I have listed in this book; those about my being a Communist and a "Red official"; those about my being an atheist; those about half the unemployed coming to California; those about my being against old age pensions. On the back page are the pictures of my wife's homes—Ole calls them mine— and also the cottage of my secretary. Explaining them he says: "Sinclair is no modest man! Sinclair is a hypocrite," etc. Across the front page is an eight column "streamer": "SINCLAIR EXPOSED." And what is the exposure? It is explained in a box:

"COMMUNISTS WANT SINCLAIR ELECTED

"As proof that the Communists and other forms of REDS want Sinclair to be elected Governor, is the photostatic copy of RED literature that was distributed to many young REDS in California recently. The RED flag of Communism is self explanatory."

And then what? Why, that fake Communist circular which we had nailed so many times; which we had exposed in the "EPIC News", and a full account of which, with a facsimile, had been published in Prof. Moley's magazine, "Today." Of course Ole knew that no Communists had issued that circular; he knew that Creel headquarters had issued it, and that it was a fake. But then so is Ole.

And here are the "Progressive Friends of California," with a paper, the "California American." Across the top you read: "Merriam Hi-Wage Plan Routs Epic 'Poor Farm' Idea." And inside you read: "Sinclair Plan Would Take Over Children—California Women Aroused by Radical Attack on Homes.—Would Take Tots From Mothers."

I, CANDIDATE FOR GOVERNOR

At risk of boring you, I could go on and tell about scores of other organizations. Here is the "California Real Estate Association," with a poster: "Please post in a conspicuous place: PROPERTY OWNERS BEWARE." And here is our old friend the "Better American Federation," with a pamphlet asking: "CAN THE LEOPARD CHANGE HIS SPOTS?" Of course I am the leopard, and the spots are RED. Here is the "California Laymen's League Against Religious Intolerance," which proposes to prove its tolerance by punishing me for not liking big business control of the church.

Here is the "California Democratic Governor's League"; the "Progressive League for Merriam"; the "Veterans' Non-Partisan League—one for nearly every group. Here is the "T. P. U.—The People United", of Berkeley, and the "Anti-Communist Society" of San Jose. Here is a swarm of organizations in San Francisco: the "Non-Sectarian Voters' League" and the "Young Liberal League" supporting the Old Illiberal. Here is the "California League Against Sinclairisim," with a string of publications, repeating the same old lies. I am tired of writing about them, and I am sure you must be tired of reading. One leaflet is headed: "HAS CALIFORNIA GONE CRAZY?" and you will agree that is a good note on which to close.

I wish there had been more humor, so that I could lighten up the story. They tried it a few times, but it was pretty sickly. The Haight people got out a paper called "EBIC Snooze: Expose Bunk In California." They had a spider in place of our EPIC Bee, and the motto: "I Induce, I Pretend." I search in vain for anything good enough to quote. Here is a four page leaflet headed: "N. U. T. S.—National Union of Technocrats and Socialists. F. B. O. S.—Free Beer On Sundays. The Platform of Ulysses Stupnale, The Pied Piper of Pasadena"—and so on. Somewhat better was the "Sin-LIAR Dollar." We got a lot of these from Merriam headquarters, and I autographed them and we were going to sell them at meetings; but our lawyers were afraid we might be breaking some law!

Mr. Irwin Cobb is a humorist, and you might have expected something lively when he entered the campaign via the radio. But something happened to Mr. Cobb—he forgot his powers of laughter, and sounded

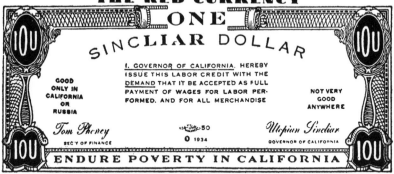

like the president of the Chamber of Commerce, as he set out to denounce a fellow-author for daring to interfere in politics. "Mr. Sinclair, this mad, well-intentioned but misguided, dancing dervish advocate of Communism expects and invites the unemployed to come to California."

CHAPTER XXX

One of the great institutions of Southern California is the movies, and I now have to tell what **they** did to "stop Sinclair."

I have had dealings with the movies since their infancy. Twenty years ago the late Augustus Thomas made a really honest version of "The Jungle". That caused me to have hopes, but they were quickly dashed. I sold to a movie concern a story telling about a self-confident young rich man who made a wager that he could go out as a hobo and get a quick start in life. When I next heard of that story, it had to do with a lost will. Soon after the War, my old friend, Ben Hampton, historian of the industry, undertook to make a picture of "The Moneychangers", which tells how the elder J. P. Morgan caused the panic of 1907. When I went to see it, it was a story of the drug traffic in Chinatown!

I don't think I am egotistical in saying that I have offered to the motion picture studios some good opportunities. "King Coal", "Jimmie Higgins", ""100%", "They Call Me Carpenter", "Boston"—all these are motion picture scenarios ready made. There is only one thing wrong with them, they indict the profit system. "Oil" has been read by every concern in the business— I suppose a dozen agents have set out full of confidence to handle it, and never have they reported but one thing: "Magnificent, but dangerous."

That I know what I am talking about was proved when I happened to write on a subject that did not involve the profit system. Several concerns were bidding for "The Wet Parade" before the book was out. Metro Goldwyn-Mayer paid $20,000 for it, and they spent half a million and made an excellent picture, following my story closely.

Now I loomed on the horizon, no longer a mere writer, but proposing to apply my rejected scenarios! While I was in New York some reporter asked: "What are you going to do with the unemployed motion picture actors?" I answered: "Why should not the State of California rent one of the idle studios and let the unemployed actors make a few pictures of their own?" That word was flashed to Hollywood, and the war was on.

Louis B. Mayer, president of Metro-Goldwyn-Mayer, was vacationing in Europe when he got this dreadful news, and he dropped everything and came home to take charge of the campaign to "stop Sinclair". You see, he is chairman of the State Committee of the Republican party, so he had a double responsibility.

Also Mr. Hearst was summoned from his vacation. Mr. Hearst belongs in the movie section on account of Miss Marion Davies. Hearst had been staying at Bad Nauheim, and Marion, through a coincidence, was there also. They were hobnobbing with Hanfstaengl, Nazi agent to the United States. You see, Hearst wants to know how the Reds are to be put down in America; so "Huffy", as they call him, flew with Hearst to interview Hitler.

As soon as Hearst learned of my nomination, he gave out an interview comparing me with the Pied Piper of Hamelin; and then he and Marion came back to New York and gave another interview, and from there to California, where he called me "an unbalanced and unscrupulous political speculator." His newspapers began a campaign of editorials and cartoons denouncing me as a Communist. I didn't see any denouncing me as a free-lover, and a menace to the purity and sanctity of the American home.

The first threat of the movie magnates was to move to Florida. Warner Brothers said they would go—and proceeded to start the construction of two or three new soundstages in Hollywood. Joseph Schenck of United Artists travelled to Florida to inspect locations, and the Florida legislature announced its intention to exempt motion picture studios from all taxes, and a mob of new "come-ons rushed to buy lots.

Of course this talk of moving was the veriest bunk. It would cost a billion dollars to move, and the British would grab the business meanwhile. Where would they get their mountains, and their eucalyptus trees, which represent the foliage of North and South America, Europe, Asia, Africa, and Australia? Above all, what would they do about the mosquitoes? I have lived in Florida, and I said to my audiences: "Right in the middle of a scene, one would bite the lady star on the nose and cost them fifty thousand dollars."

But that didn't keep them from building up the terror. Orders for an assessment came; and in Hollywood an assessment means that the check is written for you, and you sign it. In this case it was for one day's pay of everybody in all the studios—except the big "execs." The total amount raised was close to half a million. There was a little rebellion, but I didn't hear about it in any paper in California. I had to go to the London "News-Chronicle" to learn that Jean Harlow and James Cagney were among the protestants. From the same paper I learn that Katherine Hepburn was threatened with dismissal if she supported Upton Sinclair.

I am happy to say that a few Hollywood writers showed political independence. Frank Scully got up a committee in my support, and it was joined by Dorothy Parker, Morris Ryskind, Gene Fowler, Lewis Browne, and Jim Tully.

The release of the picture made by King Vidor, "Our Daily Bread," was held up in California, because this picture deals with the affairs of a Cooperative, and they were afraid this might help EPIC.

Also they started in making newsreels. Will Hays sent a representative to attend to this. They invented a character called "the Inquiring Reporter". He was supposed to be traveling around California, interviewing people on the campaign. They were supposed to be real people, but of course they were actors. On November 4, the New York "Times" published a two-column story from their Hollywood press correspondent, from which I quote:

FILMS AND POLITICS
Hollywood Masses the Full Power of Her Resources to Fight Sinclair

"The city of Los Angeles has turned into a huge movie set where many newsreel pictures are made every day, depicting the feelings of the people against Mr. Sinclair. Equipment from one of the major studios, as well as some of its second-rate players, may be seen at various street intersections or out in the residential neighborhood, 'shooting' the melodrama and unconscious comedy of the campaign. Their product can be seen in leading motion-picture houses in practically every city of the State.

"In one of the 'melodramas' recently filmed and shown here in Los Angeles, an interviewer approaches a demure old lady, sitting on her front porch and rocking away in her rocking chair.

"'For whom are you voting, Mother?' asks the interviewer.

"'I am voting for Governor Merriam,' the old lady answers in a faltering voice.

"'Why, Mother?'

"'Because I want to save my little home. It is all I have left in this world.'

"In another recent newsreel there is shown a shaggy man with bristling Russian whiskers and a menacing look in his eye.

"'For whom are you voting?' asks the interviewer.

"'Vy, I am foting for Seenclair.'

"'Why are you voting for Mr. Sinclair?'

"'Vell, his system worked vell in Russia, vy can't it vork here?"

"All these 'releases' are presented as newsreels.

"Another 'newsreel' has been made of Oscar Rankin, a colored prizefighter and preacher who is quite a favorite with his race in Los Angeles county. Asked why he was voting for Governor Merriam, he answered that he likes to preach and play the piano and he wants to keep a church to preach in and a piano to play.

"Merriam supporters always are depicted as the more worthwhile element of the community, as popular favorites or as substantial business men. Sinclair supporters are invariably pictured as the riff-raff. Low paid 'bit' players are said to take the leading roles in most of these 'newsreels', particularly where dialogue is required. People conversant with movie personnel claim to have recognized in them certain aspirants to stardom."

One more little story from the New York "Times":

"At another studio an official called in his scenario writers to give them a bit of 'advice' on how to vote. 'After all,' he is reputed to have told his writers, 'what does Sinclair know about anything? He's just a writer'."

Hitherto the movies have maintained that they could not do any kind of "educational" work; their audiences demanded entertainment, and they could have nothing to do with "propaganda." But now, you see, that pretense has been cast aside. They have made propaganda, and they have won a great victory with it, and are tremendously swelled up about it. You may be sure that never again will there be an election in California in which the great "Louie Bee" will not make his power felt; and just as you saw the story of "Thunder Over California" being imported from Minnesota, so will you see the "Inquiring Reporter" arriving in Minnesota, Mississippi, Washington, or wherever big business desires to ridicule the efforts of the disinherited to help themselves at the ballot-box.

Listen to the lords of the screen world vaunting themselves: The front page of the "Hollywood Reporter" eleven days prior to the election.

"When the picture business gets aroused, it becomes AROUSED, and, boy, how they go to it!

"This campaign against Upton Sinclair has been and is DYNAMITE. It is the most effective piece of political humdingery that has ever been effected, and this is said in full recognition of the antics of that master-machine that used to be Tammany. Politicians in every part of this land (and they are all vitally interested in the California election) are standing by in amazement as a result of the bombast that has been set off under the rocking chair of Mr. Sinclair.

"Never before in the history of the picture business has the screen been used in direct support of a candidate. Maybe an isolated exhibitor here and there has run a slide or two, favoring a friend, but never has there been a concerted action on the part of all theatres in a community to defeat a nominee.

"And this activity may reach much farther than the ultimate defeat of Mr. Sinclair. It will undoubtedly give the big wigs in Washington and politicians all over the country an idea of the real POWER that is in the

THAT'S THE QUESTION

From the Sacramento "Union"

hands of the picture industry. Maybe our business will be pampered a bit, instead of being pushed around as it has been since it became big business.

"Before Louis Mayer, Irving Thalberg, Charlie Pettijohn (a good old Democrat under ordinary conditions) and Carey Wilson stepped into this political battle here, the whole Republican party seemed to have been sunk by the insane promises of Mr. Sinclair. With that group in the war, and it has been a WAR, things took a different turn. Gov. Merriam's party here in the South had a HEAD, something that was missing before. It received the finances it so direly needed AND the whole picture business got behind the shove.

"Sinclair is not defeated yet, but indications point to it, and California should stand up and sing hosannas for their greatest State industry, MOTION PICTURES, and that same industry should, for itself, point to its work whenever some of that screwy legislation come up in the various State Legislatures during the next few months.

CHAPTER XXXI

In September, when I came from the East, everybody was saying we had the election "in the bag". Even our enemies conceded it; newspaper correspondents expressed their surprise at how leading business men gave up, saying there was no way to "stop Sinclair." All our friends took to calling me "Governor". But I said, "Wait, the fight hasn't begun yet."

I knew, because I had been through it before. Ten years ago I had done what I could to help make LaFollette President. I had written about it in the book, "I, Governor". Imagining myself addressing the EPIC workers, I told them (page 43):

"In August and September we thought we had the victory. Everywhere we went the people were with us. But in the last three weeks of the campaign the enemy turned loose their heavy artillery. I was living in Pasadena at the time, and I watched the thing with the feeling of a man bound hand and foot and witnessing a murder. It was a murder not of flesh and blood, but of truth and decency. Meetings were held in every neighborhood, and leaflets and campaign papers were distributed from house to house, and seldom in my life have I seen such a mass of lies as were turned loose against LaFollette and his supporters and their program. We were helpless, because we had no money, we had no campaign papers, we had only a few speakers and only a few meeting places. The radio was new in those days, but it was booming lies all over the country, and we had no means to buy our share of time.

"I warn you that the same thing is coming this October. The fear of our enemies is great and their money support is ample. All we can do is to educate the people in advance; explain to them every detail of our plan and warn them as to what the enemy will do and say. We have to answer every lie before it is invented. We have to make the people understand our present social system, in which a privileged few control the sources of wealth and exploit the labor of the many. Those few control all the channels of publicity and information, and the crisis which we Americans confront at the present day is precisely this, that the people, who are supposed to use their votes to protect themselves, are kept in ignorance and do not know how to make use of their rights."

That was pretty accurate prophecy. But I did not get much happiness out of seeing it come true. The truth was, my mind was torn fairly in half. I saw the viciousness of the fight, I saw the turmoil and confusion in the State, the hatefulness of our enemies, and the mess they had made of public affairs. I would say: "Let this cup pass from me". Then I would see our people in bitter need, I would see their fine devotion, the state of exaltation in which they were working. I would say once more: "All right. I will do my part."

The real shock came at the beginning of October; the letting loose of those blasts against the "Profits of Religion", the mailing out of the millions of leaflets— the whole campaign of terror. One could feel it in the air; one saw people begin to tremble and run. I began to hear of attacks upon me in the churches, and the reaction of the church people. Our precinct workers began to report real opposition for the first time.

I, CANDIDATE FOR GOVERNOR

Those whom they approached no longer wanted to hear about how to end poverty; they wanted to argue that Upton Sinclair was an atheist and enemy of the Lord Jesus.

SERA workers would come in to report how they had been fired for talking Sinclair, or even for refusing to wear a Merriam button. They would tell how Merriam headquarters were offering the SERA workers three dollars a day to go out and canvass. They would tell how big department stores, like the May Company of Los Angeles, had summoned their workers to a meeting and commanded them to wear Merriam buttons, telling them that if Sinclair were elected the store would immediately close. Form letters were presented to them which they were required to copy and send to relatives and friends.

That went on all through the last weeks of the campaign; it had been ordered by the Chambers of Commerce and the Merchants' and Manufacturers' Association. Nearly every bank in the State sent a circular to its stockholders, warning them of the ruin which EPIC would mean. The big life insurance companies and innumerable business concerns did the same. Here, for example, is a circular sent out by the Pacific Portland Cement Company from its San Francisco office, October 26:

"To Our Stockholders In California: It seems evident from Upton Sinclair's own words that if he should be elected Governor of this State, the business of this company and the value of your stock therein would be seriously imperiled."

Here is one to the stockholders of El Pajaro Theatre Co., of Watsonville, telling that the EPIC Plan will "TAX CORPORATIONS in an AMOUNT THAT WILL EQUAL THEIR INCOMES"—an utterly false statement.

During the latter part of the campaign people sent me scores of such circulars. You found them on your table in the dining car, on your bureau in the hotel, in your seat in the street-car.

Hear a disinterested witness on the subject, Dr. Hubert C. Herring, a Congregational clergyman, who wrote to the "Christian Century":

"They are waging a campaign of fear. It is clear

that many employers are doing their level best to coerce the votes of their workers. They are freely saying that there will be no jobs if Sinclair is elected. They are saying that the election of Sinclair will be followed by the flight of capital from California, the failure of savings banks, the destruction of life insurance values. The little merchants are being told that Sinclair's socialistic schemes will ruin them. Teachers are warned that their salaries will not be paid. Ministers are being cornered and made to declare where they stand. It is hard to get many men and women to talk. Some say that they are for Merriam, confessing only to their intimates that they will vote for Upton Sinclair. I opened the subject with scores of porters, taxi drivers, waiters, hotel clerks and idlers on street corners. Men without jobs spoke their mind—usually for Sinclair. Men with jobs hedged, talked with a fine show of impartiality, said nothing.

Immediately after the primary election, California stocks and bonds took a tumble—$50,000,000 lost to California, said the newspapers. How were the people to know that the big insiders manipulate the prices of stocks and bonds, and drive them wherever they please? When they get them low enough, they buy and make another clean-up. Said the market-letter of C. A. Henshaw of San Francisco, Oct. 27: "Wall Street is capitalizing the Sinclair campaign to depress the stock market."

Then came word about business concerns closed down. If they didn't close down, the papers said they were closed down; for example, the Chrysler plant was turning off a thousand workers because Sinclair was certain to be elected. The vice-president of the Chrysler plant tells a friend of mine that no such statement was ever authorized; the plant was employing only a hundred or so persons at the time. They tried their best to get a correction published in the newspapers, but in vain.

All kinds of new devices were invented in those last desperate weeks. Persons who owned lots would receive a call from a would-be purchaser. He would inspect the property. Yes, he liked it, he was planning on building a home, but perhaps he had better wait until after the election. If Sinclair were elected, of course nobody would be able to build a home. If Merriam were elected, he would come back and buy the lot.

The "EPIC News" published on the front page a story about the Pacific Mutual Life Insurance Company calling in its employees and coercing them to vote for Merriam. Our lawyers committee gave us the law of the State of California: "Every person who by force, threats, menaces, bribery, or any corrupt means, either directly or indirectly, attempts to influence any elector in giving his vote . . . shall be guilty of a felony."

Thereafter I used to read that law to our audiences. I remember saying to the big crowd in the San Francisco Auditorium: "If any employer orders you how to vote, bring me the evidence, and when I am elected I will send that man to San Quentin to take Tom Mooney's place." I do not think I ever heard louder noise inside a building.

There was nobody too high or too low to feel the pressure. Society ladies told my wife that they had to withdraw from the campaign because of the fury of their relatives. One said, quite seriously: "They get so wild they throw pillows at one another." I suppose that they were showing their good breeding by not throwing dinner plates and vases. Even the children took up the quarrel; thirteen-year-old "Jick" Packard, son of a lawyer of Pasadena, was beaten by his playmates because he dared to wear a Sinclair button. I was told of another family—I won't name it !—where two small brothers began fighting each other, one for Merriam and the other for Sinclair.

I am told that in these campaigns the most effective work is done by whispers; and the things they were whispering about me! The things I was going to do to the people of California! Take all the babies away from the mothers, and all the wives from the husbands! Socialize all the doctors, discharge all the civil service employees, and cut the appropriations of the State university in half. "Mrs. Sinclair," said an anxious man who appeared on our front porch, "I must ask you one question—what is your husband going to do to the poultrymen?"

The oddest things happened. For example, an elderly lady, a high school teacher, had taught my son, and had lived next door to us for a year or so. On

Just When It Was Starting Up, Too!

From sheer force of a lifelong habit of tilting at every-body and everything, Don Quixote Sinclair spurs his steed and sets his EPIC lance in a mad rush against the sign of industrial revival in California.

Instead of encouraging industry, he would destroy it by his Socialist plan and his open invitation to all the unemployed of America to come marching over the California border. Stop that crazy knight with your ballots on Tuesday,

From the Los Angeles "Examiner"

[177]

account of her knowledge of our family life she ventured to write a letter to a local newspaper, bearing testimony to the fact that I am a mild-mannered gentleman devoted to a noble-minded wife. A few days later this lady received a call from a reporter of the Los Angeles "Times". The "Times" had a story which they intended to publish about her unless she would retract her endorsement of me. The man gave her the story to read. It was to the effect that I had been living in California under an assumed name and that I was the lady's brother. Apparently the worst charge they could bring against a high school teacher was that she was the sister of Upton Sinclair!

This lady became so incensed that she took out of the bank some of her slender savings and paid for a month's rent of a headquarters. Whereupon one of the most wealthy real estate agents in that city went to the school board to demand that they cancel the pension of this lady. He accused her of having said, "To hell with the Constitution." To appreciate this story, you would have to know that retired teacher of literature, so frail—she cannot weigh more than a hundred pounds—her hair snow-white, her blue eyes so gentle, her soul fairly trembling with conscientiousness and loving-kindness. Never had she dreamed that this world could turn into such a madhouse!

The election has been over three weeks as I write this, and I go for a walk, and a newsboy stops me. "You are Mr. Sinclair?" he says. "I want to tell you something. A lady was talking to me on this corner yesterday, and I was telling her about the campaign. A man heard a few words, and he turned and yelled at me: 'You're a Red, and you ought to be stopped from selling papers.' I heard that he called up the 'Herald' and reported me, and tried to get me turned off. I know that lady, and she will tell you I wasn't talking no Red talk—I was just telling her about EPIC."

AND HOW I GOT LICKED

CHAPTER XXXII

What was the attitude of the churches toward this campaign of terror waged against the Ending of Poverty In California? I quote again Dr. Hubert C. Herring:

"They are fighting for God in California. That is the record as it appears upon the billboards, in the pamphlets passed out to all comers, and in the outcry of news columns and editorials. God has new allies. The Southern Pacific railroad believes in Him; so do the utility interests, the banks, the insurance companies, the Los Angeles "Times", the San Francisco "Chronicle", and a host of other corporations which have hitherto been carelessly dismissed as soulless. California is experiencing a revival of religion. . . . They are carrying this campaign of fear into the churches. Timid women thrust well marked leaflets into my hands, with tearful injunctions that I should read and ponder."

I am happy to say that there are a number of clergymen in California who were not party to all this. Early in the campaign I spoke in many churches. The First Methodist Church of Hollywood gave me a great reception. So did the Grace Methodist Church of Los Angeles. Dr. Ashleigh of the First Unitarian Church of Hollywood formed EPIC Club No. 1 in his home. Dr. Ernest Caldecott, Unitarian; Dr. Allan Hunter, Congregationalist; and A. A. Heist and Gross W. Alexander, two Methodist clergymen, were tireless supporters—I am told that the latter's trustees are trying to remove him as punishment for his EPIC crimes.

Our movement was introduced to the cities of Oakland, Berkeley, and Sacramento in churches. I pay tribute to these brave clergymen and wish there had been more of them. I know of one Catholic priest, Father Philip, from up in the country where they make wine. He came to one or two of my meetings and stood by us to the end.

"Bob" Shuler is one of the best-known pastors in Los Angeles. He supported Raymond Haight, and disapproved of production for use as being "Socialistic"; but he did me the honor of reading the "Profits of Religion", and then he told the truth about it over the radio. He said in substance: "It is not true that Sinclair defames Jesus; he defends him. The things that he says about the churches are terrible, but they are all true." Shuler has since been put off the air.

On the other hand, there were the great rich churches, the big city churches, with the moneychangers in the front pews. Those clergymen had one sure way to fame, and that was to denounce Upton Sinclair; their sermons would then get the headlines on the religious page of the "Times" on Monday morning. They came out for Merriam by the column, and they saved the State of California from atheism, Communism, and free love. In my home city of Pasadena is a very fashionable Episcopal rector whom I have met two or three times at civic affairs. Friends tell me that when he preached against me he "fairly raved."

George H. Shoaf wrote in the "American Guardian":

"Ministers of the Gospel who, until recently, were open in their advocacy of Sinclair, have had their voices silenced by wealthy and influential members of their congregations. Fully 90% of all property in California is mortgaged to the banks and mortgage companies, most of this property being mortgaged for more than it is worth. The church members who control their respective ministers were simply informed by their creditors, on pain of foreclosure, that they must keep their ministers and congregations in line for Merriam for Governor. In large measure it is being done. All corporation employees have been notified that under no circumstances will Sinclair be tolerated as Governor of California.

"Merriam headquarters in Los Angeles is alive with action. 'Foghorn' Murphey, a notorious underworld character; Bob Gans, king of the slot machine fraternity; Guy McAfee, chief gambling concessionaire in Los Angeles, and other underworld celebrities, rub shoulders in perfect comradeship with Rev. Gustav Briegleb, pastor of St. Paul's Cathedral; Rev. Martin Luther Thomas, pastor of Metropolitan Federated Church; Rev. Stewart P. MacLennan, pastor of the Presbyterian Church of Hollywood, and other high Protestant and Catholic dignitaries, as all of them take orders from and do the work of professional politicians employed by the forces of special privilege.

AND HOW I GOT LICKED

I have told how the society folk got to arguing and threw pillows at one another. The clergy took to throwing epithets in the papers. The Methodists appointed a committee to investigate and ascertain whether I was an atheist; this committee endorsed me, and then other clergymen arose and denounced them. It proved all over again what a mistake Jesus made when he got mixed up in politics.

No account of the church situation would be complete if it left out Sister Aimee. Early in the campaign a friend of mine who is in touch with Angelus Temple had a bright idea; he would get Sister Aimee to debate EPIC with me. He inquired and found that Mrs. McPherson was very friendly toward the idea of Ending Poverty In California. Many of her followers were poor, and this had a tendency to reduce the collections; so the debate with me was to be a "frame-up"—Sister Aimee was going to pretend to debate, and be converted, and then her fifty thousand followers would all vote for EPIC.

Some of our people thought it would be beneath my dignity to appear in Angelus Temple; but I insisted that I would talk wherever there was an audience. I kept waiting for Sister Aimee to set the date of that event, but somehow it never came off. Later on I learned that the bankers had found out what was in the air, and they had put the screws on, threatening to foreclose Sister Aimee's mortgage. Then the next thing I knew, Sister Aimee had run away to the mountains. In the last couple of weeks of the campaign I learned that the bankers had put the screws on still harder, and she had come back and taken somebody's money to stage a pageant for an anti-Sinclair meeting in the Shrine Auditorium. All kinds of church people came, and various clergymen denounced me, and Sister Aimee's pageant showed the skulking Communists pulling down the pillars of the Constitution.

The same thing that was done in the churches was done in the universities. There were several professors who promised us help at the beginning, and those professors were warned. There were several others who owed us help, but did not pay their debts; they apologized, saying frankly they didn't dare. One brave man came to our headquarters and put in his summer vacation in charge of our speakers bureau. He used a pen name, in order, as he said, to protect the university. I am told that he is now in peril of his job.

At the University of California in Los Angeles there was a group of students who were keen for EPIC, and who persisted in talking politics. The provost of this university, Dr. Moore, is an elderly gentleman, pitifully out of touch with modern affairs. Instead, he is in touch with our Red-baiting Chief of Police, and believes everything he is told about the spread of Communism. This old gentleman let himself be persuaded to get up a Red scare in the University, just at the proper moment to affect the election. He expelled five students, charging them with being tools of the Communists. Soon after the election the President of the University came down from Berkeley and reinstated all of the students and apologized to them. Nobody has apologized to me!

The same thing happened to those few newspapers which failed to obey orders. The Norton chain of eight neighborhood papers in San Francisco came out early in support of EPIC. The next time I was in town the publisher came to me and apologized; his advertising had been cut to such an extent that he could not go on. Down in Southern California the publisher of the Beverly Hills "Bulletin" stuck it out in spite of all the advertisers. Then the landlord gave him notice to quit on the first of November—five days before the election. The "Illustrated Daily News" of Los Angeles persisted in its policy of printing the news and not taking sides editorially. For that offense it lost two of its biggest advertising accounts. One editor of the Los Angeles "Times" was fired because he said he was going to vote for Sinclair. Another lost his job for a still stranger reason—he was friendly with a young lady connected with the American Civil Liberties Union!

On the other hand, what did those papers get which fought us? I wish that I could tell you. It would be interesting to know the reward of the "Downtown Shopping News" of Los Angeles. This is an advertising sheet, the means whereby the dwellers in the suburbs are brought to the center of the city to spend their money. It contains sixteen pages of department store advertising, and twice every week it is thrown on the

Where Have We Heard That Voice Before?

From the Los Angeles "Times"

front porches of 400,000 homes in and around Los Angeles. It had hitherto never had anything to do with politics, or in fact with any sort of idea. But in the last three or four weeks of the campaign it suddenly blossomed out with terrible stories on half of its front page:

PAYROLLS MENACED;
PROTECT YOUR JOBS!

"Upton Sinclair says: 'If I am elected I expect half the unemployed in the United States to hop the first freights for California.'

"Such an influx would create an impossible relief burden; business could not maintain its payrolls, and those now employed would lose their jobs or divide the paychecks with the newcomers."

Each week it played upon that theme; closing down of factories, the end of all business, the loss of jobs, starvation for the poor. "All paychecks stop when business fails. Sinclair the wrecker. Sinclair's cure-all is business poison." This paper of course reaches a stratum of the people which no one else could reach: women who never read anything but the "pulps" and the "ads". I look to see what they are interested in. "We have given over thirty thousand genuine Eugene Permanent Waves, $1.95 complete, no extras. Genuine Eugene Spiral or Eugene Top with ringlette. Croquignole ends." Here is a second beauty shop that does even better: "Our Feature Oil Wave. Remember we have given over a million Permanents on the Pacific Coast. One Dollar complete. This price includes your shampoo, finger wave and our special rinse." No, I am afraid EPIC lost the beauty parlor vote. Two days after we lost it, the newspapers of Los Angeles published a statement by Dr. J. L. Pomeroy, County Health Officer, to the effect that "Malnutrition among children in impoverished homes in the county is becoming increasingly evident. He attributed this condition directly to the rapid decline in the rate of milk consumption by these children during the last few years." Dr. Pomeroy went on to explain that SERA was providing 37,195 families with only $4.03 each, and that isn't enough to buy milk for children.

AND HOW I GOT LICKED

CHAPTER XXXIII

For some time it has been the rule in California that persons applying for SERA relief must be registered voters. So men and women would go and register, giving any sort of address, making up one if they had none. Thus it came about that when sample ballots were mailed to the voters, great numbers came back in the mail, marked "moved," or "unknown," or "no such address."

There began suddenly a concerted clamor about registration frauds; wholesale efforts on the part of the EPIC people to pack the Great Register of Voters! Of course, those who made the charges well knew what had happened; they knew that those who had registered from these addresses had not been thinking about voting, but about getting something to eat. But most of them, being poor, were Sinclair supporters; so here was one more campaign cry.

As a matter of fact, the charge was doubly dishonest, for the reason that under our laws a person does not lose his residence until he physically acquires another. All these homeless men who are wandering the highways still have the right to vote in California, if they ever had it. They could come back and vote from their last home, or they could vote by mail. But most of them don't know the law, and the people who were out to "stop Sinclair" didn't tell them. There is a general sentiment among our ruling classes that it is dangerous for so many unemployed to have a vote; one of the first aims of would-be Fascists is to get it away from them.

So, under the stress of the campaign, a brilliant idea occurred to a group of lawyers in Los Angeles. The plot was hatched in the offices of our tiptop plutocratic law firm, O'Melveny, Tuller & Myers. I have mentioned this firm before, and promised to tell about it. Early in the spring, when our headquarters had to move to a downtown address, we had great difficulty in finding a place; nobody would take our money. Finally, we leased a fine property through an agent; but when the owner learned about it, the lease was cancelled. The owner was Mr. O'Melveny.

Then came the primary election, and that fake Communist circular printed by the Creel headquarters. We learned that the scheme had been conceived in the offices of the same firm, by a young lawyer named Albert Parker. This "tip" was given to us in confidence by a man employed in the office, who was outraged by what he saw. Late in October this young man, Edmund M. Smith, came to us with a strange story. Albert Parker had written to a friend in New York a letter telling what he and his associates were doing to beat Sinclair, and it was so close to a criminal conspiracy that Smith had gone to O'Melveny and resigned his position, and brought a copy of that letter to the Sinclair headquarters.

I read the letter over the radio, and it was printed in the "EPIC News," and made such a sensation that the opposition press was forced to pay attention to it. Mr. Parker never denied the genuineness of the letter. It so happens that I know some of his friends, and some friends of the Tuller family, and learned amusing things about what happened when that bombshell burst in the midst of the power trust's leading law firm. Here is the Parker letter:

October 20, 1934.

Eli Whitney Debevoise,
 Messrs. Debevoise, Stevenson & Plimpton,
  20 Exchange Place,
   New York, N. Y.
Dear Whitney:
 I have been most dilatory writing you, but I think you must realize that we are engaged in a very bitter contest and my office mail must simply be permitted to go to the Devil. However, I am writing you at the earliest opportunity to express to you my fervent gratitude for one of the several suggestions which you made in your letter of October 10. This is the suggestion relating to secret indictments. To show you how fruitful your idea was I am enclosing a clipping taken from a headline in one of our newspapers. The District Attorney was delighted with the suggestion (for which you may be sure I gave you full credit), and adopted it at once.
 We are convinced that there are at least 150,000 false registrants in Los Angeles county, and we are proceeding against them in three ways:

AND HOW I GOT LICKED

(1) We are challenging them at the polls through the media of Deputy Sheriffs and other peace officers.

(2) We are bringing the secret indictments which you suggested in sufficient numbers to terrify many people from coming near the polls.

(3) We are bringing a series of actions in which I am drafting the complaint and order to show cause for the purpose of enjoining the false registrants from voting and having their names stricken from the Great Register of Voters. In this first action we named approximately 25,000 defendants. Of course, personal service was out of the question, but we have considerable authority supporting service by publication and posting under false circumstances.

In addition to this false registration work I have been acting as secretary of the United for California League, which is a non-partisan organization, designed principally to raise money to support every organization which is combatting the election of Upton Sinclair. By the time of the election we will have raised nearly $1,000,000 in the State of California. We have to date distributed some 6,000,000 pamphlets, of which I am enclosing a few specimens. We have also caused to be erected some 2,000 billboards, upon which we are displaying suitable anti-Sinclair publicity.

Altogether it has been a lot of fun, and I think it will be very successful, for I honestly believe that Mr. Sinclair will not be merely defeated but demolished on November 6.

With best regards to Francis and many other friends in New York, I am,

Yours very sincerely,

A. P.: L. K.

This legal procedure to which Parker refers was the boldest move ever made towards Fascism in the United States. The proposal was that 24,136 persons, alleged by their political enemies to be illegally registered, were to have their names stricken from the list of voters, unless they individually and personally appeared in court and proved their right to vote. The only notice to these persons was by the mailing of a postcard, and the publishing of the names in a paper of very small circulation. I saw the paper, and the names, set in small type, filled eight full-sized newspaper pages.

The power trust attorneys found a Red-baiting judge who was willing to sanction this racket. To make it look more respectable, they came to court in company with a Democratic lawyer, none other than my venerable opponent, Isidore Dockweiler, attorney for the Southern Pacific Railroad. But the animus of the procedure was indiscreetly revealed by Mr. Walter K. Tuller in the elevator, on his way up to the courtroom. One of our lawyers overheard him say that this was the only way the Democratic ticket could be beaten in November. Judge Collier sustained the procedure, and the authorities announced that a second order was being prepared, disfranchising 30,000 more persons; the total was expected to reach 150,000 in Los Angeles county.

The man who did most of the work of stopping that racket was a lawyer of Pasadena, John C. Packard. He had been a member of the national executive committee of the Socialist party, but disapproving of the recent resolution adopted by that party, he withdrew and became one of our EPIC workers. In company with several colleagues, he took the matter to San Francisco, and persuaded the Supreme Court to deal with it at once. Attorney-General Webb appeared and argued for the procedure, and stated that if it was sustained he was prepared to file suits all over the State, affecting more than 200,000 voters. Supporting him appeared ten or a dozen of our highest-priced corporation lawyers.

There is probably no more reactionary body of judges in this country than the Supreme Court of the State of California; but this scheme was too raw even for them. A week before the election they issued an order forbidding Judge Collier and the Los Angeles Superior Court to proceed in the case of any defendants save those who had been personally served with notice or who had voluntarily appeared. Justice Langdon added an opinion, from which I quote:

"It is perfectly clear now that the action below is a sham proceeding and a perversion of court process, absolutely void, and it can now have no effect other than to intimidate and prevent eligible voters from going to the polls.

"It outrages every principle of justice and fair play. In brief, it attempts, in a personal action in the Superior Court, to abrogate and cut off the constitutional right to vote of more than 24,000 defendants, without personal service of any kind upon the said defendants, and upon a purported service by publication of this mass of names, without addresses and not even in alphabetical order, on a single occasion, in a newspaper of some 1,500 circulation.

WHAT THE COMMUNISTS REALLY THOUGHT ABOUT EPIC
From the "Daily Worker", New York

I, CANDIDATE FOR GOVERNOR

That settled the matter for the present, and the unemployed still have the right to vote in California. But don't overlook the crucial fact, that the power trust lawyers who lost that court case, won the election. The men who engineered the "sham proceeding and perversion of court process," and got themselves denounced in those scathing words by a Justice of the Supreme Court, are still part of the ruling gang of the State of California.

Also, you may be amused by one or two human touches in connection with this skirmish. Mrs. Walter K. Tuller is a friend of a friend of ours; and when the decision was announced, Mrs. Tuller was outraged, and told several persons that the Supreme Court of the State of California had gone Communist! However, Mrs. Tuller was probably not inconsolable; for the Republican boss of our State told a friend of mine that Walter K. Tuller got $10,000 for his services in "stopping Sinclair."

CHAPTER XXXIV

All through the campaign, everybody was always taking straw polls. We used to get several every day; so did Haight, and I suppose so did Merriam. It is an odd fact, that whoever took the poll usually found his candidate in the lead. Our people used to be cheered by the results of a poll taken by radio KNX; it showed that I was beating Merriam by 5 to 1. But, having spoken several times over that radio, I felt that the poll was "loaded."

Then came the "Literary Digest" poll, the result of mailing some half million double postcards to voters in California. From the beginning it was pretty nearly uniform throughout the State; it gave Merriam about 62 per cent of the vote, and me about 25 per cent. That settled it for me; I became fixed in my belief that we were beaten. I told my wife to dismiss all her terrors from mind; the wolves were not going to have a chance to tear her husband. I only told three or four friends how I felt, because the reaction was so painful. They were all fixed in the certainty of victory, and could not face any other thought. "Hush! Hush! Don't let anybody hear you say that!"

AND HOW I GOT LICKED

From that time on I lived a strange kind of double life; I went through the last two weeks like a man acting in a play. The meetings had been scheduled, the radio time paid for, and I had to go through with it. But I never did commit the insincerity of saying that I expected to win. I would say: "Whatever happens, we are educating the people, and California political life will never be the same again."

An odd idea occurred to me late in October, that of writing two magazine articles, one entitled, "If I Win," and the other, "If I Lose," and having them published in parallel columns, just at election time. I thought of that on a Saturday, and I wired my friend, Fulton Oursler, editor of "Liberty." I dictated the two articles on Sunday morning, and took them with me and revised them on a motor trip to San Francisco, and when I arrived on Monday morning, I found a telegram from Oursler, saying that he was holding the presses, and for me to put the two articles on the wire at once. That is the way they do things in American journalism! The two articles appeared in the issue which was supposed to be on the news-stands the day after election; in California they delivered it on election day, close to half a million copies.

About a month prior to the election, I had written what I called a "Proclamation," supposed to be issued in the event of our victory. It was a call to action to the EPIC movement. I would not be inaugurated for some sixty days, and in that period half a million idle workers would lose something like $120,000,000 of possible production. In order to save as much of that as possible, I called for our political movement to be converted at once into an organ of the people's economic action. Each of our 2,000 clubs were to set to work to get the necessary information as to idle land and factories; to list the experts who were ready to go to work; to ascertain just what could be grown on the land and produced in the factories, on what terms these could be rented, where the seed could be got and the raw materials purchased. I named executive committees of the CAL (California Authority for Land), the CAP (California Authority for Production, and the CAB (California Authority for Barter). Our Research Associates were to become a central clearing-house for information—so on through an elaborate program, minutely worked out.

I, CANDIDATE FOR GOVERNOR

All my spare time went to this; and while the capitalist press of California was telling the people that I had no idea how to bring about the EPIC plan, and didn't really believe it could be done!

It was my idea to publish this "Proclamation" in the "EPIC News" at once, in order to make the program real to our workers. I gave it to some of our group to study. John Packard, life-long Socialist, was delighted; his dream had suddenly come to life. But others of our committee were dubious. Dick Otto, the campaign manager, insisted that all our workers were straining to the last gasp, fairly staggering to the goal. What would be the effect of suddenly opening up a new vista of toil and sacrifice?

We argued it out, and the consensus seemed to be against me, so I gave up. But I still feel that if that "Proclamation" had been given out, it might have turned the tide, just at the critical moment. I will print it as an appendix to this book, and you can make your own guess as to what it would have done.

This question has been asked me a hundred times: Did I really believe that I could do the job? The truth is that a doubt of it never crossed my mind. I have spent my whole life studying the idea of production for use. It is to me as obvious as arithmetic, as certain as sunrise. If you give hungry men tools and access to land, they will grow food; if you give them access to factories, they will turn out goods. Who but a lunatic—or a hireling—would question it? Of course, there will be difficulties, discords and blunderings. Such things can never be escaped in human affairs. But the people will go to work, and a stream of wealth will pour out.

What kind of a Governor would I have made? Well, I am aware of deficiencies for the role; among the chief of them being acute boredom at the thought. But I was prepared to go through with it; to give four years of my life to helping the people of one State to peace and security. I was going to put my own tastes and desires aside, and work at the job with the same concentration which has brought this present book into existence, down to this word, in twenty-two days. I once wrote a three-act play in three days and a half; I wrote "Boston," one of the longest novels, in less than a year.

AND HOW I GOT LICKED

I was going to be Governor of California at the same tempo. Many friends were surprised by the vigor of our campaign, and I expected to surprise them once more.

To return to our story: the "Literary Digest" poll proved to be badly off. Instead of getting 62 per cent of the total vote, Merriam got less than 47; instead of getting 25 per cent of the total, I got over 38. How this blunder came about, I do not know, and the "Digest" has not referred to the embarrassing subject. I will tell them a few things that came to us: first, the Merriam people were paying 25 cents each for "Digest" ballots; second, a postmaster listed the names of all those in his town to whom the ballots were sent, and gave the names to our people, who checked by the voting lists, and found that 75 per cent were registered Republicans; third, one superintendent of a great plant had 200 "Digest" ballots to distribute among his people. I don't know what precaution the "Digest" takes to keep its ballots from being forged, but anyone reading this story will agree that the bright young men of the "United for California League" were quite capable of conceiving the idea.

The error did us irreparable harm. It encouraged our enemies, it weakened our friends, and it shifted the betting odds; in short, it started a chain of unfavorable events. Many people were waiting to know which band wagon to climb onto—and now they knew. Some of these people occupied important positions. I have good reason to believe that it was the "Literary Digest" poll which started the bad news out of Washington.

Our enemies there were powerful and active. "Ham" Cotton, head of the Public Works Administration in California, was continually sending emissaries, and every item of scandal about the "Socialist interloper" was made use of. You may be sure that the leaflets full of garbled quotations reached Washington officials, as well as California voters. What would be the effect of the Catholic quotations on my friend "Call-Me-Jim" Farley? I am told that the effect was most distressing. I am sure that Jim has no time to read books, or to search out garbled texts. He is a man of old-fashioned economic beliefs, following reluctantly in the footsteps of his venturesome Chief.

The Postmaster General, in his capacity as Chairman of the Democratic National Committee, had written one of our followers a letter, containing this sentence: "By electing Hon. Upton Sinclair, your popular Democratic candidate for Governor, California will have a combination of leaders in Washington and Sacramento who can cooperate in the best interests of the people of the State and of the nation." Of course, there was glee in EPIC headquarters when that letter arrived, and it was put on the front page of our paper.

But then came the "Digest" poll, and the weather changed suddenly. There came stories out of Washington to the effect that the letter had been mailed through an accident; it was one of those blunders which stenographers commit whenever their chiefs alter their minds suddenly; it was a mere form letter, and signed with a rubber stamp. The stories became more detailed each day. I don't know that my friend Jim inspired them, but I do know that he left them uncontradicted, and the effect was that of a severe snub by the Administration. Our enemies made the most of it.

Let me make clear my own position. I am not blaming Farley. I am recording history, in a vein of amiable tolerance. I had never done anything for him. To be sure, I had brought some 350,000 new members into his party; but I had done that for my own cause. I had acted as a free lance, and without asking his approval. If I got myself into a mess, it wasn't up to him to get me out. He hadn't written "The Profits of Religion," and it wasn't up to him to pay the price. The Honorable James A. Farley is a practical politician, and the proof is the fact that he is now sitting on the top of the world, while I am off in my garden, writing a book to tell "How I Got Licked."

CHAPTER XXXV

I am telling how, early in October, it became evident that Upton Sinclair was not going to be the next Governor of California; and how suddenly the political weather changed in Washington and New York.

AND HOW I GOT LICKED

Professor Raymond Moley came out with a denunciation of the EPIC Plan and its candidate. In a two-page editorial in his magazine, "Today," he told the public that I was to be classified with Hoover, and also with Rousseau; I wanted to carry America "back to nature." This, of course, was front page stuff for the California press. "Brain Trust Head Condemns EPIC"!

It was not possible for any one to misunderstand my thought more completely than did this professor-editor. There is no one in America who believes in the machine technique more heartily than I. My effort is to adjust all the rest of our culture to it. As for barter, which the professor accused me of favoring, I proposed it only as an emergency expedient; our people in California had no money, and how were they to get goods? Any way that would get them goods was a good way, in my opinion. If the professor would show us a way—fine! But the professor didn't show us anything. He just called on the people of California to repudiate me; and when I asked him to state what he thought of Frank Merriam's qualifications as Governor of California, he ignored the question.

Well, he had his way, and the people have Merriam. It is rumored that Raymond Moley is top-dog in Washington just now, and has the President's ear. If that be true, it is a tragedy, for he revealed himself in our California crisis as both ignorant and dogmatic. Grim events will judge between us, whether or not it is "a blessed retreat" to give the idle workers of America a chance to produce the necessities of their own lives!

And then, still more dramatic and more damaging, the defection of George Creel. George had left for the East immediately after the Democratic convention; telling me that he was "broke" and had to do some writing. I heard no more from him, until I read a news story to the effect that he was dissatisfied with my attitude to the Democratic platform. I at once sent him a telegram, assuring him that I had been talking the platform up and down the State, and was standing by it loyally. The truth was, I was going farther than any candidate I ever heard of; I not merely asked everybody to vote the ticket straight, I asked that nobody should vote for me who was not willing to vote for all the other Democratic candidates.

I, CANDIDATE FOR GOVERNOR

Of course, the talk about my disloyalty to the platform was just camouflage. It was perfectly clear what had happened; so long as he thought I was going to be elected, Creel was willing to swallow EPIC, sugarcoated; but when he read the "Literary Digest" poll, he decided that the ship was sinking. He had been in New York, looking for magazine contracts—and what had he found? Knowing the game, I can come pretty near to telling. George had one big story; and its price depended upon one thing, the attitude he took. If he wrote about California politics as a supporter of Sinclair, it was a story for the "Nation" or the "New Republic," worth, say, $100; if he wrote it in ridicule of Sinclair, it was a story for the "Saturday Evening Post," worth $5,000.

George wrote me a blistering letter; or rather he told the newspapers he had written it—I never saw a copy, but read the news on the front page: "CREEL SPURNS SINCLAIR." It made a front page story in every newspaper in the State; and Creel, who is a master propagandist, gave it point by going to see the President a day or two before he gave it out.

The ground of his attack was that I had broken faith with him and the Democratic party. He specified one offense, that I had issued my pamphlet, "Immediate EPIC," after having accepted and pledged support to the Democratic platform. My answer was to give the dates. The serial publication of "Immediate EPIC" had begun on August 4, which was three and a half weeks before the primary election. The manuscript of the book had been delivered to the printer September 4, and the first copies had been ready about a week later. Creel's conference with me had taken place on September 16, and the Democratic convention had taken place on the 20th. When Creel was in my home, the copies of "Immediate EPIC" were lying on the table, and if I failed to give him one, it was an oversight.

A curious incident: in the latter part of October, while I was in San Francisco, I received from an EPIC sympathizer a proof of the "Saturday Evening Post" to be published a month later, containing an article by George Creel entitled, "Utopia Unlimited," ridiculing the EPIC plan, the Townsend Plan, and the Utopian Society. So I saw what Creel's price had been. The

And No Way to Turn Back

article contained the same false statement as his public letter—that I had published "Immediate EPIC" after the Democratic convention. I at once wired the "Post," asking them if they would correct this statement. In reply they wired, asking me to tell them by what means I had obtained a proof of their article a month in advance. To this I replied: "You answer my question, and then perhaps I will answer yours." They went ahead and published the false statement, and so far have failed to correct it.

A month after the election, I received from Creel a four-page letter, dealing with this incident. It is characteristically full of bad words. The EPIC Plan is "an unconscionable vote-catching device," "wishful imaginings, medicine show hokum, Socialistic babble, and high dope content." I am "dishonest, imbecilic, a catspaw of the reactionaries, an instrument of confusion, and a gigolo of politics." Creel says that the publication date of "Immediate EPIC" does not matter; it was my duty to withdraw that book as soon as the Democratic platform was adopted, and my continuing to talk about EPIC was "a plain breach of faith."

I put this question to four lawyers, Culbert L. Olson, John Beardsley, John C. Packard and Sheridan Downey, who attended the various conferences with Creel. Did I ever make any agreement that the EPIC Plan was to be scrapped?

Senator Olson writes: "Mr. Creel stated at this conference, as he had also stated at a conference with yourself, Mr. Downey, me and others at San Francisco a few days before, that he realized the platform must contain all essential principles of your EPIC program, leaving the practical details of carrying those principles into effect for discussion by the candidates."

John Beardsley writes: "There was no agreement with Mr. Creel that the EPIC Plan was to be scrapped." Beardsley points out that Creel, in my home, and again in Sacramento, demanded a plank in the platform repudiating Socialism, and that this was refused. Beardsley says: "I objected strenuously, saying that I could not coincide with their apparent attempt to make a hypocrite of Upton Sinclair."

John C. Packard writes: "It is very difficult for me to understand Mr. Creel's accusation. I was present

Not Interested!

during your entire conference, and at that time no promise or suggestion of promise was made in reference to the EPIC Plan. At the later conferences with Mr. Creel the platform was discussed more in detail. You were not present; but even at that time no suggestion was made that the original EPIC Plan should not be advocated in the campaign."

Sheridan Downey telegraphs: "At conference you mention it was stated by you and agreed by all present that production for use plank should be in Democratic platform. That you were not to waive EPIC principles, but were to consent to other liberal planks. This understanding was embodied in Democratic platform, and further agreed to at time of convention."

Here is the testimony of four well-known lawyers, men accustomed to making agreements and to stating facts. To these I add Richard S. Otto, campaign manager and president of the End Poverty League. He says: "Most certainly, we were never asked by George Creel to drop EPIC. If any such thing had ever been proposed I should have fought it bitterly, and I should certainly never have forgotten it."

This, I think, should settle the question of who broke faith. I have not answered Creel's letter, and am pleased by the thought that I need have no further dealings with such a man. I am told that he is thinking of running for Mayor of San Francisco this spring. My guess is that there are 100,000 Democrats in that city who will take pleasure in telling him at the ballot box what they think of him.

CHAPTER XXXVI

At my conference with President Roosevelt at Hyde Park on September 5, he had volunteered the statement that it was his intention, on or about the 25th of October, to come out "in favor of production for use"; and I had remarked that if he did that, it would elect me. He was to give his talk to the people in two sections; the first, near the end of September, came on schedule, so naturally my wife and I, with half a dozen friends to whom I had entrusted the secret, were "on pins and needles," waiting for the second talk. A week ahead, the announcement was made that on October 23rd the President was going to broadcast on the subject of relief; so, of course, we all made up our minds that this was the expected speech.

On the 23rd of October I happened to be in San Francisco, due to address the Independent League of Women Voters in the St. Francis Hotel at 1 o'clock in the afternoon, and to speak in the Civic Auditorium in the evening. Speaking to the ladies, the question was sprung on me, what was the attitude of the Administration towards my program. Perhaps I committed an indiscretion, and deserved punishment—I will tell you what happened, and you may judge for yourself.

Bear in mind that I had kept this state secret in my mind for exactly seven weeks. In the meantime, I had read literally hundreds of deliberate falsehoods about my attitude to the Administration and the Administration's attitude to me. I had seen the Merriam Democrats—"Flag" Democrats, "Loyal" Democrats, "American" Democrats, they called themselves—going the limit in deliberate mendacity. I had just been traduced by Creel in a front page letter; also, I thought that something not quite fair had been done to us in the name of Farley. I had learned that to the newspaper men the President had spoken favorably of the Ohio Plan, and had compared it to the EPIC Plan; but no word of this had reached California.

Now, at last, the President was going to speak; he was coming out "in favor of production for use." Bear in mind my certainty in the matter; it no more occurred to me to doubt what he was going to say, than to doubt that the sun was going to set at the same hour. Bear in mind also that the question was sprung on me suddenly. Fully three-quarters of those leisure-class ladies were for Merriam, and they were taking advantage of the practice I had begun a year ago, of answering questions wherever I spoke. I was standing at the speaker's table, with my watch before me, so that I would not overstay my time. I looked at the watch: in four hours the secret was to be out; so what harm could a hint do?

I said: "The President is scheduled to speak over the

radio in four hours from now, and if he says what he told me he was going to say, I expect to be elected."

An hour or two later the San Francisco "News" was on the street with a front page story to the effect that I had said the President was going to come out *in favor of my candidacy.* Of course, I hadn't said that. You see, the identical trick I have already explained in connection with Father Coughlin, and again with Secretary Ickes. They made me say more than I had said; then their reporters went to the White House, and telegraphed back a story that the White House denied that the President was coming out in support of the candidacy of Upton Sinclair. Once more I was repudiated!

Of course, I was in distress, and telegraphed the President, pointing out the trick which had been played on me. Also, I called up the "News" and protested. I talked with Paul Edwards, the editor, a man whom I know well enough to call by his first name. I know several of the staff that well; the "News" is supposed to be a liberal paper—but, of course, all that meant nothing in this crisis. California capitalism was threatened, and the "News" was just one more capitalist paper.

There is a law supposed to prevail in American journalism, and never broken. All newspapermen will tell you about it. When you tell a newspaperman something "off the record," he respects your confidence and does not publish it. Maybe so; but does he tell some other man on his staff, and let that man publish it? I don't know; I merely record the events. I said over the telephone: "Paul, in order that you may know just how great a wrong the 'News' has done me, I will tell you, strictly off the record, what the President actually told me he was going to say." He accepted the "off the record" agreement, and I then told him. Next day the "News" did not print any correction of its false story about me, but two staff men on the paper published, over their signatures, what I had revealed to Paul Edwards. One wrote that it was beginning to be rumored that I said the President had told me he was going to speak for production for use; the other, the political man, wrote that one of our workers, Captain January, had stated to him that that was what the President had told me. January assured me that he made no such statement, and I have a perfect reason for believing him—he did not know the fact.

Somewhere around 6 o'clock the President gave his speech. Our friends got a radio in our hotel room, and we sat and waited for the priceless words. The fable about the mountain in labor and the little mouse coming forth must have been written in anticipation of our painful experience. The President spoke in connection with some drive for charity funds, and read a five-minute sermon on the beauty of giving and the sacredness of the emotion of pity. The speech might have been written for him by Bishop Manning or Helen Gould. He stopped, and the rest of the half hour was padded out by an orchestra.

Of course, I was dished. No use to say a word more; the newspapers had me in their jaws, and would shake me as a terrier shakes a rat. I had to take it. "Let them have it as they please—geese are swans and swans are geese."

I went to the Civic Auditorium, packed with 15,000 or 20,000 people, and I told them how to End Poverty in California. That is my life, and my justification. The future, if it remembers me at all, may forgive blunders caused by a too impetuous desire to stop the starving of men and women, and especially of little children, in a world which has learned to produce more than it can consume.

What is my attitude to this matter, now that the campaign is over?

The "New Republic" wrote editorially that nothing Roosevelt had done as President reflected less credit upon him than his treatment of Upton Sinclair. I find that most of our EPIC people feel such bitterness; but I argue that this is not justified. In the first place, the President had made no promise to me; he had made a simple declaration of intention, and he had a right to change his mind. I had done nothing for him; and he had an election to win, and power to hold. I was an unknown quantity, and how could he tell what I might spring next—or what might be sprung on me? He told me how, when he was a young man, his mother had read "The Jungle" to him at the breakfast table; but assuredly his mother had never read "The Profits of Religion" to him; and if somebody brought him one of those leaflets from California, full of garbled quotations, might he not reasonably decide that I was a dangerous partner on the political trapeze-ring?

I was taking a gamble with the State of Califor... but F. D. R. had the whole country on his hands—forty-eight problems to my one. He had $900,000,000 of notes to sell right away in Wall Street; and a convention of the American Bankers' Association coming on, and the task of bringing those reluctant gentlemen into his New Deal. He got them in, and hopes to keep them there; he still believes that the profit system can keep going for a while—at least until he can get a group of new administrators trained, to run the huge machine that is going to be required.

The important question is not what Franklin D. Roosevelt did to Upton Sinclair, but what he is going to do to the people of this country. With no personal bitterness whatever, I tell him that he cannot go on much longer traveling on two divergent paths. He has to choose between EPIC and Hoover.

CHAPTER XXXVII

The day after my San Francisco adventures I had a speaking date in Chico, and on the way I stopped in Sacramento, and learned that Raymond Haight was there and wanted to talk with me. We spent an hour alone in his hotel room, and threshed out our problems as friendly enemies. Haight had taken a post-card poll, getting the names from the voters' list in Los Angeles and the telephone book in San Francisco. He had a thousand answers, and his poll showed not merely whom the voters favored as between Merriam, Haight and myself, but also how they would vote as between Sinclair and Merriam, and between Haight and Merriam. From this it appeared that if Haight withdrew, most of his vote would go to Merriam, but if I withdrew, most of my vote would go to Haight. So he put it up to me as a duty to withdraw, and avoid turning the State of California over to a reactionary for the next four years.

UPPIE AND DOWNEY

I, CANDIDATE FOR GOVERNOR

I was willing to consider any proposition that was not dishonest, and I told Haight I would think it over. It wasn't merely my campaign; it had been made by an army of men and women, and I would have to consult others. Driving on to Chico, I put the proposition up to the two friends who were with me, and I saw from their indignation how any such action on my part would be misunderstood. To the very last hour our EPIC followers would believe that we had had the victory in our hands, and that I had sold them out. I asked others, and got the same reaction. Our people would simply not think about defeat; they could not make the idea real to themselves.

The news of the conference with Haight leaked out almost immediately. I learned afterward that the reporters had worked a familiar device; they called up Haight and told him that I had given out a statement—and so he gave out a statement. There was nothing for me to do then but to say that I would not withdraw. I said it at our big mass meeting at Oakland on the following evening.

Home again the next day—we learned to drive 400 miles in a day without thinking anything about it. Put a pillow under your back and slide down in the seat and think about your next radio talk or your editorial in the "EPIC News." Stop and get the papers in the next town, and see what new falsehoods they had printed about you, and then practice self-control. I had read the world's best literature, and my mind was stored with consolations.

> How happy is he born and taught
> That serveth not another's will,
> Whose armour is his honest thought
> And simple truth his utmost skill.

More radio dates in Los Angeles, and a series of final meetings. We had taken the Philharmonic Auditorium every noon for two weeks, and every day it was packed. I appreciated these crowds, because I had been in the Philharmonic Auditorium for scores of lectures and concerts, and never before had seen it really filled. Now thousands were turned away.

I had been listening to the men of God over the radio; to "Spouting Thomas" and to Sister Aimee's pageant against Communism, and to someone quoting the words of Jesus, thinking they were mine. Not all the philosophy, not all the beautiful poetry in the world, could keep me from being annoyed by such lies. Awake in the small hours one morning, I composed a poem on the subject, and read it to one of the audiences at the Philharmonic, and also published it in the "EPIC News." The "New Republic" printed it, not as a poem but as an editorial—a comment, possibly, on its literary quality. Anyhow, the crowd liked it, and it has its place in this record, as showing how it feels to be lied about in the name of God.

POLITICAL PRAYER
(A Candidate's Answer to the Charge of Atheism)

O God my Father, and God, my Friend,
And God, my Guide to Poverty's End:
Hear in our homes the children cry,
See in our streets the hungry die;
While hushed machines and idle acres
Await the greed of profit-takers.
Send us Thy prophets as of yore
To smite the starvers of the poor.
Light in our hearts the cleansing fires
And save us from the purchased liars.
Lend us Thy voice to pray them down;
Send us Thy saints to rule the town;
Wash from our streets the bloody stain
And let Thy justice live again:
O God, our Father, and God, our Friend,
And God, our Guide to Poverty's End.
Amen.

The fury of these last days of the campaign was indescribable. Strangers commented on it with dismay. Nobody in Los Angeles was talking anything but "Sinclairism," and nobody talked calmly. Max Stern reported to the San Francisco "News":

"Los Angeles, Nov. 2.—A reign of unreason bordering on hysteria has this sprawling city in its grip as the nation's ugliest campaign approaches zero hour. The 'stop Sinclair' movement has become a phobia, lacking humor, fairness and even a sense of reality. Here one feels himself dwelling in a beleagured town with the enemy pounding at the gates. Convinced that this is not politics, but war, the defenders excuse their excesses on the ground that in war all's fair.

"For years this city of the Angels has waxed on propaganda. Today all its native arts of make-believe are being invoked to two ends. One is to paint Upton Sinclair as a Communist menace, the other to camouflage Acting Governor Frank Merriam as a progressive, strong, and capable Governor-to-be.

"Yesterday there rained upon the city's downtown thousands of lurid leaflets in red and black, picturing a hideous Russian figure waving a red flag over the state's hills and valleys. It was called 'Thunder Over California.'

"Also, there appeared a cleverly-worded appeal by a non-existent 'New Citizen's Cooperative Relief Committee' for donations of clothing, food, room space and spending money for the 1,500,000 new citizens expected to arrive in response to the Sinclair pledge to end poverty."

George H. Shoaf wrote to the "American Guardian":

"Without doubt this political contest has been the bitterest and possibly the most corrupt that has occurred in our so-called American democracy. George D. Brewer, who helped put over the Non-Partisan League in North Dakota many years ago, recently stated that the bitterness of the North Dakota campaign was nothing comparable to that which he was experiencing in his present effort to elect Upton Sinclair Governor of California."

I tried to keep out of the way of it as much as I could. I had made up my mind that I was beaten, and I taught myself to take it with a smile. This was the first skirmish, and we were in for a long war; I must save my health and my courage.

I have explained before how I was torn in half. I longed to be free from all this turmoil and hate, this life of being pulled and hauled about; but also I wanted to help all these people who had trusted me, and I wanted to show that organized mendacity could not rule the world forever. Which did I want most? Of course, it didn't matter which I wanted; the thing was too big for me to control. I would take what came.

So I would go on my next speaking date. I had come to refer to myself as a talking robot. My friends would put me in a car and take me somewhere; they would press a button, and I would say my say; when I got through they would wrap me up in an overcoat and carry me out again, and put me in a car and take me home. Such is the life of a candidate.

There were many meetings I shall never forget. One of them was on the last Saturday night in the Olympic Auditorium, a huge prize fight arena, packed to the doors. We had simultaneous meetings in Bakersfield, Fresno, Sacramento and San Francisco, all on a state-wide radio hook-up. Our radio man, Gus Ingles, had planned that artistic masterpiece. Everything that was said in Los Angeles was listened to by all the other audiences. We sang the "Star-Spangled Banner," and raised the flag with the spotlight turned on it; that was our answer to the charge that we were Communists. Then I read the twenty-third Psalm, "The Lord is my shepherd," an answer to the charge that I was an atheist. Then I called, "Take it away, Bakersfield," and lo, there was the Bakersfield audience cheering, and presently we heard the Bakersfield orator greeting us. Then it was Fresno, and the Fresno crowd; then the Sacramento crowd, and finally Sheridan Downey greeting us from San Francisco. All that took about fifteen minutes, and I had fifteen more in which to tell those five audiences how this was just one skirmish and our EPIC movement was enlisted for the war; also how we were going to change the slogan, "End Poverty in California," and make it mean, "End Poverty in Civilization."

CHAPTER XXXVIII

I owe a tribute of thanks to friends all over the country who gave us their help in the EPIC campaign. A little money kept trickling in from outside, and every dollar helped to keep us alive. A few even came from abroad, but none from Russia, be it stated! The Rt. Hon. Charles Trevelyan, formerly parliamentary secretary of education, sent the End Poverty League a ten-pound note, with a beautiful letter. The British press manifested great interest in our movement; Harold Lasky wrote an intelligent appraisal in the "Daily Herald." Many clippings came from Australia and New Zealand; also from the Scandinavian countries, and far-off Iceland cabled to know the election results. From Naples came a cablegram saying that the Cumean Sibyl predicted victory. Perhaps she will explain what she meant!

Early in the year a group of intellectuals had signed a manifesto in favor of our EPIC movement. There was doubt in our campaign committee as to the wisdom of quoting outside opinions; Californians might resent it as meddling. But we printed this endorsement and the enemy press left it strictly alone.

The signers were: Lewis Browne, Porter Emerson Browne, Stuart Chase, Clarence S. Darrow, Jerome Davis, William C. DeMille, Theodore Dreiser, Morris L. Ernst, John Farrar, Dorothy Canfield Fisher, Arthur Garfield Hays, Horace M. Kallen, Archibald MacLeish, Stanley M. Rinehart, Margaret Sanger, Oswald Garrison Villard, Helen Woodward and W. E. Woodward.

My friend Mencken indulged in his customary "kidding." Mencken claims that I have believed more things than any other man in the world; and by listing a number of perfectly obvious things which I believe, and some others which I used to believe, and some which all intelligent men except Mencken believe, he managed to compile quite a list. His article was taken up and featured by the reactionary press of California. In a second article Mencken declared that California political affairs were so rotten that he would vote for me anyhow; but I never saw that in any California newspaper!

When I was in New York, Heywood Broun told me that he might come out to write up the last three weeks of the campaign. He asked to come, but the Scripps-Howard people preferred a sporting chap by the name of Westbrook Pegler, whom they had recently turned into a columnist. Their reason for preferring him is obvious. Broun's magnificent articles exposing the California reactionaries were appearing in the New York "World-Telegram," but were not wanted in California. Pegler, on the other hand, is one of those bright Broadway lads who take nothing seriously, unless it be the cut of their trousers and color of their ties.

I, CANDIDATE FOR GOVERNOR

During my last day in San Francisco, Pegler called up and asked to see me. It was just after I had got the solar plexus blow of President Roosevelt's speech, and a couple of hours before I was to go upon the platform before fifteen or twenty thousand people in the Civic Auditorium. I was having supper in my room with three or four of our friends. I said for him to come up.

He came: a handsome young fellow of the demi-monde type, his trousers creased to a knife-edge and his tie brightly striped. We treated him as a rational being, and patiently explained our plans for Ending Poverty in California. He persisted in pinning me down on the question as to whether I had ever succeeded in any enterprise in my life. I tried to answer according to his own point of view; I had started from zero, and by my own unaided efforts had made myself the most widely-read of living writers; in many European countries I was more widely read than any native writer in that country; I had been that in Germany until Hitler burned my books. I invited Mr. Pegler to come over to the Auditorium and see what the crowd thought about me; but he had a dinner engagement, and no time for political meetings.

He went away and wrote up the scene—me and my friends in the hotel room. He continued to write about us—I didn't have time to read it all, but my clipping bureau kept sending it; I believe he stayed with us every day for a couple of weeks. Of course, he made me into a "guy," and my friends the same.

For example, Hjalmar Rutzebeck, author of "Alaska Man's Luck," one of the grandest true stories ever penned. Whether deliberately or just out of carelessness, Pegler transformed him into Mr. Utzebeck, which, of course, finished him right there. My friend "Hans" is a grandson of all the Vikings, and could have taken Pegler in his mighty arms and broken him backwards if he had wanted to. But he didn't want to, because he is a soul all wrapped up in the idea of cooperation. For a year or two he gave his unremitting labor to the UXA, the marvelous cooperative of the Oakland unemployed. Then he was taken on by Subsistence Homesteads, and sent to the far South to explain cooperative production. Now he was helping with

EPIC, and body-guarding me about the streets of San Francisco, and had just handed me an outline of a project for the organization of our EPIC system, the result of a year's study. And here was this sporting man from Broadway making him into a "guy."

The telephone rang next day. Pegler wanted a few items of information, and to another of my friends, a business man forcibly retired by the depression, he said: "That was a swell bunch of fellows I met last night, and I wish I was so situated that I could write what I really think about them." Well, it is a mystery to me what the Scripps-Howard newspapers can pay to a man that is more valuable to him than his own self-respect. On the perfectly tailored coat front of Mr. Westbrook Pegler I pin a large and shiny brass check, and bid him wear it for the rest of his days.

I have said much against the newspapers. I ought in fairness to record that the magazines of the United States showed themselves entirely independent of the California plutocracy. They gave the news about the EPIC movement. They gave it fairly and intelligently, and they gave it to the whole country.

Three or four days before the primary election the "Literary Digest" appeared on the news stands with my portrait on the front cover and an excellent account of the EPIC plan inside. It was a terrible thing for the Creel people, and they got busy forthwith, and the "Literary Digest" disappeared off the stands. Apparently every copy of it was bought up; our people were offering as high as 50 cents for one.

But that was the last of that. Three weeks or so later came "Liberty" with an article from my pen, telling what I intended to do if elected. The announcement of this article occupied the front cover of "Liberty," and they sent half a million copies into California. Those copies were bought up—but by the public!

After that came a flood of publications. The "Nation" and the "New Republic" had several articles and editorials. Moley's magazine, "Today," had an article describing our movement, in the same issue which contained Moley's attack upon us. The editorial took the front page in the newspapers, but I never saw the article mentioned.

"Collier's" published a long account of our movement

by Walter Davenport. He described one of our EPIC meetings, and it wasn't ours at all, but a meeting of the Utopian Society in the Hollywood Bowl. Our meetings didn't have all those picturesque features. But I forgave Mr. Davenport because he finished the article with a page or so telling the aims of EPIC. "Esquire" published a clever article by Frank Scully, and followed it after the election by a tribute from Theodore Dreiser. The "Literary Digest gave me a thousand words, in which to explain my purposes, and so did Macfadden in his new magazine, "Macfadden's Weekly." My old physical culture friend stated that the EPIC Plan was very bad, but that I would make a good Governor; I thought the voters would find that somewhat difficult to figure out. "Real America" had an article, and "Common Sense," edited by Alfred Bingham, interpreted our movement month after month to its readers. "Unity" and the "Christian Century" also defended us gallantly.

Of course, there was one magazine which is never carried along by any Red tide; the grandmother of all Tories, the "Saturday Evening Post," denounced us in editorials and ridiculed us cleverly in cartoons. I have already told about the George Creel article, "Utopia Unlimited"; but that didn't appear until the fight was over.

The great newspapers of the country also reported the battle, mostly according to their prejudices. The New York "Times" gets its California stories from George P. West of the San Francisco "News" and Chapin Hall of the Los Angeles "Times." West, who used to be a civil liberties man, has become a tired liberal, and talked to me sadly about his lack of faith, and the inevitability of Fascism in America. In his writings he did his best to equal the Los Angeles "Times" in depreciation of our movement; but Chapin Hall ran clean away from him in the last couple of weeks, when he sent to the New York "Times" a story about the Communists supporting us in California. What do you think was his sole bit of evidence? That fake Communist circular which had been got out by Creel headquarters two months back, and was now reproduced on the front page of "Ham" Cotton's newspaper! Not merely had this wretched piece of trickery been exposed in the "EPIC News," but a facsimile of it had been reproduced in "Today" of October 6th, with a statement of its fraudulent nature. "All the News That's Fit to Print," says the majestic New York "Times."

I note a humbler "Times," of Modoc County, California. The editor writes: "I was offered a substantial sum to swing the editorial column of my newspaper behind Merriam, but declined."

CHAPTER XXXIX

Once more we move into the region of high state affairs. I have to tell a series of events which occurred in the last days of the campaign.

The story begins some months back with a gentleman of Los Angeles who is active in many affairs. I had met him in connection with some motion picture matters two or three years ago. He is free-spoken and easy to know, and we took a liking to each other. Now he turned up in the campaign. He gave us advice. He invited us to his home to dinner, and told me a lot of entertaining gossip about the big fellows, what they were doing, and saying and planning.

Then one day he called up and said that I ought to meet A. P. Giannini, head of the Bank of America, California's biggest banking chain, with some eight hundred branches. "A. P." was the only Roosevelt supporter among the big bankers, and if he knew me and understood me he might come out in my favor. It so happened that President Roosevelt had mentioned "A. P." to me, so I had him in mind, and said I would be pleased to meet him. But it was after I had come back from the Democratic convention, where I had got a touch of ptomaine poisoning. I went away for a few days' recuperation, and when I returned "A. P." had left Los Angeles, and we did not meet.

Nine days before the end of the campaign came my friend X again. "A. P." was in Washington, and had been with the President, and had talked about California affairs. X had just talked with him over the telephone, and "A. P." was very favorably disposed toward me. Would not I come up to X's home and from there talk with "A. P." over the phone?

We were, of course, in desperate need of funds in these last days. Our frail political ship had been all but foundered by the masses of falsehood poured over it by newspapers and radio and pamphlets. We owed the printer, we owed for this, and that. Everybody agreed that by heroic labors we had succeeded in turning the tide against us; it was now flowing in our favor, and with a little money to pay our bills we might actually be able to win.

So here was I in the hillside mansion of my friend X, who had tried to get us three hundred thousand dollars. His proposition now was that the biggest banker in California was willing to put ten thousand dollars into our campaign. Said X: "He is sick of the corruption in the affairs of this State, and he doesn't want Merriam to be Governor. He wants to hear just one thing, if you are elected you will appoint an honest man as bank examiner."

I answered: "That's all right; but does he expect to name that honest man?"

"Maybe that's what he wants," replied X, "but if he assumes that and later on finds that he was mistaken, that will be his hard luck. In politics you don't have to be too particular about letting other people make mistakes."

That was all right with me; I had my hands full with looking after my own mistakes. I told my friend I was perfectly willing to tell Giannini that I would appoint an honest man as bank examiner. I would go further and say that I would appoint an honest man to every office in my gift. I would say that to any man, whether a banker or a bootblack.

My friend turned to the telephone and put in a call for A. P. Giannini. This is one of the magical privileges which the rich have prepared for themselves; they can talk with anybody in any part of the civilized world in a minute or two. You don't even have to hang up the receiver and wait to be called, as you used to. It takes only a few seconds more to get someone at a hotel in Washington than it does at the Biltmore or the Ambassador in Los Angeles; and you hear just as

The Sunset State ❋ Look Who's in the Way! ❋ By Harry Murphy

clearly—impossible to tell the difference. But you have to have the price!

There I was talking with "A. P." I told him that the President had spoken of him. I told him that if I were elected, the first thing I intended to do was to appoint qualified men to public office, and that would include the bank examiner. He replied that we ought to have the support of the Administration; somebody ought to come out to California by airplane immediately and speak for us. He said that the man to do it was J. F. T. O'Connor, Comptroller of the Currency, a Californian, and a recognized emissary of the Administration. I should call McIntyre, the President's secretary, at once, and serve a demand for "Jefty," as they call him, to leave by airplane that afternoon. All that in the name of a great banker!

It was, if I remember correctly, Sunday noon, nine days before the election. Mr. McIntyre was not in, but would be back shortly. He was reported to be at this place and at that. We had possibly half a dozen messages; he would call us back, and so on. I had lunch at my friend X's home, waiting for the call. Finally it came. McIntyre told me that it would be perfectly all right for O'Connor to come, but that it would have to be a personal matter, and I would have to ask it from him.

"That is a good sign," said my friend X, and he talked again with "A. P.", and "A. P." thought it was a good sign. "A. P." had talked with "Jefty," and I should now ask "Jefty." So there began another spell of telegraphing and telephoning. First, "Jefty" accepted my invitation—he would come that day. Then he telegraphed that he had changed his mind; there were too many factions in the Democratic party of California. I spoke with him again over the telephone, and told him: "There are no factions in the Democratic party of California. There are only Democrats and Republicans." "Jefty" laughed and got my point. Finally he said that he would take the plane and see me in Los Angeles on the following morning.

So there was another big sensation in the California campaign. How it leaked I have no idea. Very certainly I didn't say a word. But the newspapers learned that "Jefty" had started, and they reported that he was coming on behalf of the Administration, to ask me to withdraw in favor of Raymond Haight. Where had that come from? "Jefty" stated most emphatically that he had never made any such statement.

He arrived, and my friend went to see him in his hotel, and brought him to his home, where we talked for two hours. He proved to be a mild and unassuming person, frank about everything except California politics. I supplied the frankness about that. I told what I had hoped for from the President, and the many falsehoods our enemies were printing; then I left it for "Jefty" to make his decision. He said that he would consult others.

I learned afterwards that he spent two hours with Haight and two with Merriam—exact impartiality. I assume that he also spent some time with "Ham" Cotton, head of the Public Works Administration in Los Angeles, and principal distributor of Federal patronage next to Senator McAdoo—who, by the way, had gone to Mexico, and then to Washington, keeping out of the campaign.

As to what happened behind the scenes, your guess is as good as mine. All I know is what I read in the papers. "Jefty" told the reporters that he had come out on personal business. He told them he had not yet made up his mind whom he was going to vote for. If he finally made up his mind he never told me. He didn't come out for me, he didn't come out for Haight, and he didn't come out for Merriam. The lies which the "Ham" Cotton crowd had been circulating stood uncontradicted. A. P. Giannini didn't contribute ten thousand dollars, nor yet ten cents, to the expenses of the End Poverty League; and so he is not going to get an honest man appointed bank examiner of the State of California. But a few days later it was reported that J. F. T. O'Connor was offered the job of manager of the Federal Reserve Bank in San Francisco, at $24,000 a year, or twice what he had been getting.

On the night before election I had three radio talks. Over a state-wide hook-up at 7:30 I told the people, as I had told them several hundred times before, that it was up to them. I was a believer in Democracy, in the right of the people to decide their own destiny; if they hadn't suffered enough, it was their God-given right to suffer more; all they had to do was to elect Merriam and he would see to it. I told them that the depression was going right on, until we had replaced the broken-down system of production for profit by an ordered system of production for use. I told them that regardless of what might be the outcome of tomorrow's verdict, we who understood the causes of the crisis were going on to educate the people, and sooner or later they would act in their own interests.

At nine or thereabouts I had fifteen minutes over KNX, and Governor Merriam was to follow me over the same station at the next period. I was allowed to speak extemporaneously, and I played a mean trick on the old gentleman. I told the audience all the things they were not going to hear him say. He wasn't going to tell them how he would deal with the problem of unemployment, and he wasn't going to tell them how he would meet the State's deficit. I told them the empty platitudes they would hear—and I learned afterwards from people in the studio that I had got under the old gentleman's skin, for everything I said about his prepared speech was correct. I had another period at eleven o'clock, and for the benefit of whatever voters had stayed up that late, I pointed out how my opponent had backed me up.

CHAPTER XL

Election day. My wife and I cast our votes in the morning, and I obliged the cameramen and newsreel operators—although feeling certain in my own mind that those shots would never be used.

The rest of the day we stayed at home, expecting to rest; but the telephone kept ringing, with messages from headquarters and other places, where members of our lawyers' committee were carrying on the fight against frauds at the polls. This is an aspect of the campaign which I have not discussed. We knew what was being prepared. We knew that every agency of corruption and intimidation in California had been mar-shalling its forces for that day. We knew that our voters had been listed for challenge, and that threats against them had caused thousands who were ignorant of their rights to decide that the safest course was to stay at home.

We knew also of the plans for the stuffing of ballot boxes and the turning in of false returns. A series of incidents had occurred, connected with a proposal to bring from New York a group of men who were familiar with these arts. Some of our friends had worked in New York, and explained our purposes; the upshot being that this particular gang decided not to take the Los Angeles money. I was confirmed in my conclusion that I would rather deal with gamblers and the underworld than with the big business crowd which rules our State.

I had the consciousness of having done my best, and was prepared to take serenely what I knew was coming. I expected a worse defeat than I got—having relied too much upon the "Literary Digest." A few friends came to our home that evening and we listened over the radio. In the first precinct that reported, soon after the polls closed, Merriam was leading me by four to one, and I thought it was going to be that way straight through. But soon it became evident that we had got an enormous vote, and for a while there seemed a possibility that when the industrial districts of Los Angeles were heard from, we might get out in front.

I won't reveal the names of our friends or how they behaved. Suffice it to say, that my wife and I were the least unhappy persons in that company, and we were in the strange position where it didn't seem decent to say how we felt. If we smiled at the funeral, what would the other mourners think? But in my heart were things such as this: I can drive my own car again! I can go and take my walks! I can sleep with my windows open!

Presently we had to bundle into our cars and make a tour of the radio stations. The National Broadcasting Company had prepared a miracle; at ten-thirty I was to have five minutes in which to tell the audiences of ninety-two stations how I felt about being defeated for Governor of California. The alleged Federal regulations were forgotten; I didn't have to "file copy," and was free to say what I pleased. Half an hour later the same privilege was extended by the Columbia chain, sixty-seven stations, if I remember. And then, at eleven-fifteen, KNX turned over its fifty thousand watts for me to use as long as I pleased.

At the first of these stations Governor Merriam preceded me. We were supposed to speak from the same room, but this honor I refused. I have never cultivated the arts of pretense, and I didn't care to exchange courtesies with such a man. I meant to speak out of my heart that night.

I was told afterwards that many people considered that I showed myself "a poor sport," "a bad loser," and so on. I was prepared for that. I was not playing a game, and there was no "sport" about it; I was voicing the anguish of a million suffering people in California. I was fighting for their rights, and making no truce with their enemies. The election had been won by a campaign of character assassination, and Merriam had permitted that campaign, and now was profiting by it.

I owed him no favors, and showed him none. I conceded that the election had been stolen, and that we would try to prove the theft. I said that the EPIC movement was going right on. We would show the people how Merriam failed to carry out his campaign promises, and in six months we would start a movement to recall him. We would make our preparations to spread our End Poverty League over the entire United States, and we would not quit until every man and woman in our country who needed work had been given the right to work and enjoy the product.

People who heard me said that I was menacing that night; one said that I "roared." Maybe so. I have told in these pages what I had endured for six months or more. I felt that a crime had been committed, not against me, but against the people. It was their rage that I was voicing, not my own. The ruling classes of America were listening to me—certainly the ruling classes of California were, and I told them: "We will hang the threat of a recall as a sword over Merriam's head." Maybe that accounts for the fact that the new Governor-elect has not yet forgotten his campaign promises, a whole month afterward!

I had no chance to visit any of our headquarters that night, but I was told of dreadful scenes. Men and women broke down and wept when the certainty of our defeat became apparent. I know of women who cried the whole night through, and doubtless there were thousands. I know of one suicide, and at least one other attempt. The million-and-a-quarter hungry and desolate people had been hoping for deliverance, and suddenly their hopes were dashed.

My friend Lewis Browne was present in the studios of KNX and listened to me "roar." He followed me, and spoke his thoughts, brave fellow that he is. He, too, was deeply moved, and was amused afterwards to hear from his friends that he had "talked like a revolutionist." This broad-minded scholar and wit, who writes histories of the world's religions and biographies of its philosophers and poets, and who lectures to the students of U. C. L. A. under the auspices of Red-baiting provost—well, Lewis's words were not preserved, and perhaps I shouldn't tell on him! Instead, I will tell on his wife, Myna, an artist, who selected the cartoons which accompany this narrative. There were several hundred of them, and I told her to take the meanest, but she couldn't bear to!

To finish the story of the election and its results: The official figures show that Merriam received 1,138,000, I received 879,000, and Haight 302,000. It thus appears that Merriam is a minority Governor by a small margin. He and his masters will not fail to make note of that fact.

A day or so after the election, the Pasadena "Post" stated editorially that I had charged frauds on election night without having had any opportunity to know whether or not any frauds had been committed. Of course, the editors of the Pasadena "Post" didn't mind making charges against me without having had any opportunity to know what I had known. I had been getting reports all day long from people who themselves had been witnesses to the frauds. A few days after the election there was put into my hands a stack of affidavits from the victims and witnesses of frauds. There were reports not only from Los Angeles County, but from all over the State. An official of San Francisco remarked blandly in my hearing that no frauds had been committed in that city; whereupon Ralph Wakefield, our San Francisco manager, replied. "We have one precinct in San Francisco in which three votes were counted for Sinclair, and we have so far the affidavits of forty registered voters in that precinct who voted for Sinclair."

Edmund M. Smith took this evidence to Washington, and laid it before Senator Norris, Chairman of the Senate Committee on Elections. Inasmuch as a senator and congressmen were candidates at this election, the frauds become a Federal matter. Mr. Smith reports that Senator Norris was deeply interested, and advised that the matter be put before the local grand jury; if that body refuses to take adequate action, Senator Norris's committee will take it up. We plan to follow this course of procedure; but we bear in mind that even if the grand jury acts, the matter will rest in the hands of a district attorney who is a friend of all the racketeers, and is himself just now under indictment for perjury.

We elected Culbert L. Olson, State Senator from Los Angeles County, and we elected most of our assemblymen from Los Angeles County, and others from various places. Altogether, we shall have nearly thirty EPIC men in the assembly. It is impossible to tell exactly, because some are Democrats whom we endorsed, and we cannot tell in advance whether they will "stick"; but certainly we have enough to constitute a powerful bloc in the next legislature. We shall bring our measures forward and force them to a vote, and keep our plan to End Poverty before the people of California. The political life of this State is going to be different from now on; the reactionaries will not take everything for granted!

CHAPTER XLI

I have finished the story of the campaign, and now have to comment on its significance to the people of California and the rest of the country.

The victory of Merriam was not a victory for reaction. One of our achievements during the campaign was that we forced the old gentleman completely out of his lifelong position. Before the fight was over he

had announced himself as "heartily in accord with President Roosevelt's policies." He proved it in a genuine and touching way—by dumping onto Roosevelt's shoulders all the gravest of his problems—old age pensions, unemployment insurance, relief for the destitute, and the thirty-hour week.

This sudden conversion of a Republican of the school of Mark Hanna to the most alarming of brain-trust ideas suggests a curious problem. You will recall J. F. T. O'Connor, Comptroller of the Currency, coming out from Washington and having a two-hour conference with Merriam. You may be sure that "Ham" Cotton had conferences with Merriam, and that the Cotton emissaries to Washington carried proposals from Merriam.

Let me make plain: I am not suggesting that President Roosevelt had any part in such a deal. He leaves political matters very largely to Jim Farley and his lieutenants; and in dealing with State political machines these gentlemen have to take things as they find them, and do their best to get what the Administration needs. If the Republican Governor of a key state like California were to agree to come out for the New Deal, and to distribute a reasonable amount of patronage to the Democrats who had supported him, it might then become possible for Federal funds to be entrusted to the handling of so friendly and obliging a statesman. I have shown how such arrangements were made between the Democratic and Republican machines in New York. Why should not the same bipartisan alliance be extended to national affairs? In England they have a dignified name for it, a "coalition government," and its purpose is to put down labor and Socialism. Why should the method not be applied to California, to keep the Governorship from falling into the hands of an "atheist and agent of Moscow?"

We shall be able to tell about this after Merriam has made some of his appointments. We shall be able to judge his new progressivism when the legislature meets and we read his message. So far the signs all point towards the "left."

The Governor-elect waited only two or three days after the election before taking over the EPIC Plan. He announced in a speech that the unemployed must have work, and that, much opposed as he was to the idea of letting them produce for barter, he would adopt it as a matter of temporary necessity. He reiterated his promise for a thirty-hour week, and incredible as it may seem, he broached a State income tax. The State Controller had just announced that the State's deficit was going to amount to $65,000,000 by the first of July; and Merriam, God help him, has to deal with that problem. Up to election night he kept mum; but once elected, he announced we might have to have a State income tax!

That was more than the Los Angeles "Times" could endure, and it gave its new Governor-elect a slap on the wrist: "California is at the cross-roads; her troubles did not end with the defeat of Sinclair. If California continues sane; if she uses the most effective means of defense against the infiltration of mass-insanity; then California may become a focal point from which sanity will spread outward. But this cannot happen if our leaders try to palliate lunacy by adopting some of the folly of the lunatics." Reading that, you can see why I don't feel so cast down over the results of the election!

The developments from Washington have been even more cheering. I told of President Roosevelt's statement that he intended to come out in favor of production for use, and how on October 23 I waited in San Francisco for his speech and did not hear it. At that time the President and his friend, Professor Moley, were interviewing bankers and big business men, and reports in the newspapers were all to the "right." But now the election is over, and the people who are visiting the President are Hopkins and Ickes and Tugwell; they are discussing the problem of relief, and a sudden silence falls upon the great press of California—not one word do we get! But the New York papers reach us four days late—and what is this leaking out? It appears that Mr. Hopkins has a plan which he calls EPIA, and it means "End Poverty in America." Well, well, well!

Mr. Hopkins, reports the New York "Times" of December 2, 1934, does not believe in the "dole." Unlike other Washington officials, he calls it that, and rejects it in favor of what he calls "work relief." Being a tactful and clever man, Mr. Hopkins some time ago set out very quietly to apply his plans on a small scale. He now proposes to apply them to the extent of eight or nine billion dollars, and proposes the slogan, End Poverty in America.

What is this program? The New York "Times" tells us as follows:

"An expansion of the subsistence homesteads and rural rehabilitation programs to include as many families as need such accommodations or are in a position to accept them.

"A large-scale removal of families from sub-marginal (unprofitable) land to home sites where they can live on a more civilized scale.

"Federal advances of funds to both categories to equip their homesteads with tools, livestock, etc.

"An expansion of the program already in progress on an experimental scale to give factory work to the idle, through what the FERA softly calls 'canning centers,' 'needlecraft centers,' or the like.

"A large-scale low-cost housing program to shelter those unable for one reason or another to move to subsistence homesteads, since it appears there is no purpose entirely to depopulate the large cities.

"A social insurance program to give security in the future."

And the "Times" account makes comment:

"All this has a strangely familiar ring to those who can recall the dear, dead days before November 8, when EPIC was a word to make capitalists crawl under the bed. Upton Sinclair proposed to have the State of California take over idle farms and put jobless populations to work on them. He proposed to have the State commandeer idle factories and make jobs for unemployed city workers. In each case the owners would receive a fair rental and the products would be sold at cost, distributed under State supervision. Mr. Hopkins' plan differs from Mr. Sinclair's in detail, but not in principle."

Nearly sixteen months ago, starting our campaign to End Poverty in California, I stated to audiences in substance:

"It doesn't make much difference whom you elect as Governor of California, production for use by the unemployed is coming, because there is no other way to save our State from bankruptcy. It doesn't make much difference what President Roosevelt's ideas may be, or what he may be planning; he will establish production for use for the unemployed, because there is no other way to save our nation from bankruptcy. Four-fifths of our people cannot much longer carry one-fifth upon their backs, and when we have tired of keeping people in idleness, there is nothing we can do about it but give them access to land and machinery, and let them go to work and produce for themselves."

The purpose for which I entered the campaign was to open people's minds to that reality; and if I have been able to do that, it matters nothing to me whether the job is done by a reactionary Republican Governor, or by a progressive Democratic President, or by a bipartisan alliance. What do I care if they pay me the compliment of adopting my slogan, as the genial Harry Hopkins has done, or if they declare it a purely temporary expedient, having no relation whatever to the "lunacy" of Upton Sinclair? You may be sure that every one of the 879,000 persons in California who voted for EPIC will recognize our plan, regardless of Merriam's label; even some of those who voted for Merriam may recognize it!

On the evening that Merriam made his speech, saying that the unemployed would have to be allowed to go to work in a barter system, a friend in our home sat down heavily upon the bed and broke it down. So next morning he drove over to the lumber yard to buy a bed slat. He found the man in charge of the yard in excited controversy with two or three others. "What's the matter?" said my friend, as he got out of his car, and the answer was: "It's this blankety-blank Merriam. They persuaded me this fellow Sinclair was a Communist, and they got me to vote for Merriam, and look here now, he's gone and adopted the other fellow's whole program!"

CHAPTER XLII

The day after election I went down to headquarters and there was a meeting of over a hundred of our active workers. I had never attended a more enthusiastic gathering during the campaign. Everybody agreed that we had won a victory and that we were going on.

Next day I wrote an editorial for the new issue of the "EPIC News," suggesting our program for the future. I pointed out that "Abraham Lincoln's movement to end slavery in America was started in 1854, and lost the election in 1856, and won in 1860." I pointed out that under the law we had the right to recall Merriam and any other elected officials—any time six months after they took office. I pointed out what we could do with the initiative. I suggested four immediate measures: the thirty-hour week; repeal of the sales tax on the necessities of life; a state income tax, identical in rate with the Federal tax, but taking precedence over the Federal tax as the law permits; and a measure providing that 50 per cent of all sums appropriated for relief shall be expended for the rental or purchase of land and machinery to enable the unemployed to go to work and produce for themselves. If these four measures are rejected by the legislature, I feel quite certain that they can be carried by popular vote.

I pointed out also that we can make a start at production for use, independently of Merriam and his machine. "There are $25,000,000 in Washington available for land colonies, and our committee will proceed immediately to find out upon what terms we can get our share of this money. Also, the Federal relief authorities are granting funds for cooperative production, and our people must form self-help groups along the line of the Ohio Plan and get to work immediately."

This statement went into detail as to various plans and measures. Having completed it, I thought I had done my duty, and announced my retirement to write this book. I had my telephone number changed, and kept the new one secret. I told my secretaries to open my letters, and answer them as best they could—every mail was bringing ten pounds of letters to my home; to say nothing of the mail pouring into headquarters and the endless stream of people who wanted to see me. I padlocked the garden gate, and brought a stenographer inside, and set to work.

I stayed there for thirty days, and this is what happened during the interim:

First, the personal irritations which had been pent

From the San Francisco "News"

up during the campaign broke loose at headquarters. The editor of the "EPIC News," who had had from the beginning the unquestioned right to publish what he pleased, now decided that he must have control also of the business end of the paper. The business manager of the paper backed him up, and the Board of Directors of the End Poverty League removed the business manager; whereupon he and the editor rushed downstairs and summoned all the headquarters workers to a tumultuous mass meeting, and turned our internal troubles over to the enemy press. Both sides began waking me up late at night and early in the morning with special delivery letters and telegrams.

I had mailed out a circular announcing my book, and offering the serial rights to every daily newspaper in the United States. Acceptances were coming in by telegraph, and the publication date of the first installment was only a week away. So I had to write the book, whether I wanted to or not; and I wanted to!

The next thing I learned was that our newly appointed State Chairman of the Democratic party had advised all EPIC clubs to change their name to Democratic. Some of our EPIC clubs had done so, and others declared that they would go out of existence first. There came another flood of telegrams and special delivery letters, demanding to know my wishes.

Then our Democratic friends, anticipating the meeting of the legislature a month hence, prepared the draft of an initiative measure to put the unemployed at productive work. The End Poverty League was working on a similar project. The Democrats had theirs printed, and sent out to all the EPIC clubs for them to obtain signatures; whereupon the EPIC groups sent me letters, pointing out flaws in a number of the provisions in this document, and asking me to telegraph them whether or not it had my endorsement.

I continued work upon the book; while my wife argued with people who wanted me to endorse motion picture schemes, and lend my name to a gambling game! I told her to drive them away; and the next thing I knew, a Pasadena newspaper published the story that Upton Sinclair's wife was keeping him incommunicado and withholding his mail!

This book is written not merely for our workers in

California, but for people all over the United States who wish to understand our movement. Its value lies in its timeliness; and there are sixty newspapers scattered over the United States and Canada demanding their daily installments as per contract. These include some of the biggest papers in the country, reaching millions of potential converts of EPIC. The New York "Evening Post," Philadelphia "Record," Boston "Post," Toronto "Star," St. Louis "Times-Star," and in California, the San Francisco "Chronicle," Oakland "Tribune" and "Illustrated Daily News" of Los Angeles are telling the world of our campaign. Our friends ought to understand the strain I am under; but I find most people have the idea that writing is a form of recreation. They don't realize that libel suits are in the offing, and that enemies are watching for one inaccurate statement.

As soon as I finish the writing, I have proofs to read, and the cartoons to fit in, and all the details of publication, both here and in New York. After that I hope to make arrangements for a lecture tour, to explain EPIC to people outside California. Also there is the matter of my health; I have been working too hard, and before long must have some time to rest.

I have been working to end poverty for the last thirty years, and I am not going to quit while I live; but I have to use my own judgment as to how hard I can work, and through what channels I can accomplish most. I may do it by writing a play, or a novel, or a motion picture. I shall continue writing for the "EPIC News," and helping to guide the movement. But our clubs are well established, and we have tested leaders, and the movement will not suffer if I take a vacation.

I am fortunate in being able to put this burden off on the shoulders of Richard S. Otto, president of the End Poverty League, a man of single-hearted devotion, a veritable slave to our great ideal. I have watched him now for fifteen months, and have never seen him shirk, or go off on tangents, or on self-advertising adventures. Every day he goes to the office early, and stays till late, and brings home a portfolio of letters to be answered by dictaphone at night. His sweet and beautiful young wife is the most patient one we know. Once in a while the two of them join us in a dream about a flight to the South Seas; but instead Dick gets into his airplane and takes flight to some part of California where our clubs have got into a row, and have to be adjusted and pacified.

He has had the most thankless job in our movement. To him have come all the kickers and the cranks, the bores and the talkers, the self-seekers and job-hunters and chiselers—as well as the faithful hard workers whose opinions are not always in accord. All have to be patiently listened to; and those who don't get what they want, even some true and loyal ones, go off with the opinion that the campaign is being ruined because Dick Otto is incompetent or narrow-minded. For fifteen months it has been so: a string of people waiting outside his office—because each must see the "campaign manager," and nobody else will do; and if the wait is long, they say that he is dictatorial, "undemocratic," "high hat." Others complained that he would not delegate authority; they almost had me persuaded that this might be true; but after I had seen what some of the others did with the authority they got, I decided that there were reasons for the caution which the EPIC campaign manager had developed. His strictness in matters of finance arose out of one fact, which prevailed for many months: that if bills were contracted, either I had to pay them or he had to pay them—and we had both spent all our money!

After watching events for more than a year, and hearing all sides to many disagreements, I say that our people all over the State may trust Dick Otto: they must stick by him and cooperate with him. The movement we have built up is worth millions of dollars to the enemy—if they can capture it, or demoralize and disorganize it. They must not be allowed to get hold of it!

The board of directors of the End Poverty League consists of fifteen persons who may or may not be the most mature advisers, but they are experienced in the affairs of the EPIC movement and know every detail of it, and they are giving their time and labor for no other reward than the satisfaction of realizing their faith. They insisted upon placing their resignations into my hands and leaving them there. One or two changes will be made, but I don't ever expect to use the rest of them, because I have confidence in their sincerity of purpose and in their strength of character to safely guide the EPIC movement.

CHAPTER XLIII

The problems now confronting our EPIC movement arise out of that wedding which took place at Sacramento. Many insisted that it was a misalliance, and that two such incompatible parties could not continue in the bonds of political matrimony.

Our End Poverty League contained all the various kinds of social reformers to be found in California; and I assure you we have every kind there is. Speaking generally, the EPIC people were and are idealists, full of enthusiasm and willing to make sacrifices.

They married the Democratic party, a marriage by capture. The EPICS by that time had got a clear understanding of production for use and the theory of a planned economy; and they found that their new partners in marriage knew hardly anything about it. A good part of the Democrats were dominated by the psychology of the old parties in America, that the purpose of politics is to get you a job. Of course, the EPICS wanted jobs for everybody; but many of the Democrats wanted jobs for Democrats.

Now there are Democratic clubs, and there are EPIC clubs, and how are they going to get together, and who is going to run the political affairs of California? The Democrats maintain that the End Poverty League ought to limit itself to educational activities, but it so happens that our education is political education, and our purpose is to apply it here and now. The End Poverty League has elected many candidates to the assembly, and assuredly the members of the League expect to have some say as to how these legislators shall function. If they sell out to big business, as most California legislators have done hitherto, the End Poverty League is going in and recall them and put in others.

I stated in my speeches and editorials, again and again: "We are now the Democratic party, and we intend to remain the Democratic party." That was my challenge to those who deserted us for Merriam, and who now think that they can run the Democratic party. But I didn't mean by that, and I never thought of meaning, that the EPIC movement should sink its identity in the Democratic party. In the first place, there are many parts of the State where the reactionaries retained control, and the county central committees refused to endorse the State ticket, and in some cases repudiated it. In these places the EPIC clubs will continue the fight for our program, and will select their own candidates and endeavor to capture the Democratic party machinery at the next primary.

In places where we actually have control of the party machinery, we will use it. I don't see any reason why the same club can not be EPIC and Democratic at the same time. The two groups have to learn to cooperate, for certainly we are not going to turn the Democratic party back to the reactionaries, and we don't want to continue the factional strife which wrecked the party in the past.

Personally I believe that there should be a State EPIC convention within a reasonable time. Our EPIC clubs should send delegates to discuss our problems and perfect our program. We have work to do on the economic field, cooperatives to be started, with whatever funds we can get from any source. We have the problem of our attitude toward the new legislature, and with as little delay as possible we want to prepare our own initiative measures and put them before the electorate. Apparently the Federal Government is going in for individual subsistence homesteads, a reactionary program which I have summarized under the formula, "one acre, one mule, and one mortgage." If our unemployed are to have the benefit of modern machinery and large scale production, it can only be because we agitate for it, and get the people to vote for it.

Personally I should like to suggest some revisions in the EPIC Plan before it comes before the voters again. I think we made a mistake to call for income taxes as high as 30 per cent; not because such a tax is injust, but because one State cannot impose it without handicapping itself. The same thing applies to inheritance taxes if they are too high. We have to carry that agitation into the Federal field. I think also we should follow the Democratic platform, and limit our demand for exemption of homesteads from taxation to the first thousand dollars at the start, and raise it to three thousand later on. I think we should also follow the Democratic platform in calling for a repeal of the sales tax "on the necessities of life." We should call for a California Authority for Barter, instead of a California Authority for Money; because very certainly our enemies would tie us up in court proceedings if we tried to create anything along the line of "money" in our State.

Many times I wished that I might have gone over the "I, Governor" book, and changed a few phrases which furnished ammunition to our enemies. It wasn't up to me to tell how the profit system is going to crumble. It is crumbling every day before our eyes, but the people don't want to know it, and quarrel with anybody who points it out to them. It is the same impulse which in the old days caused the kings to cut off the head of the herald who brought bad tidings. Our EPIC Plan should confine itself to the measures we intend to enact during the period covered by the election.

We have got to win, because the crisis is coming on, faster and faster. The New Deal has been in operation for twenty-one months, and unemployment stands practically where it did, and real wages are a little lower. Any trace of improvement you can find is due to one cause, and one only: Government spending of borrowed money. The idea of borrowing one's self into prosperity seems childish, but it is a stage we have to go through. Our financial rulers insisted upon trying it over a period of years in connection with the German war debts—lending money to a bankrupt country so that it could pay that money back as interest. Now we are lending money to ourselves to pay our debts to ourselves.

Production for use must come, and it is only a question how much longer our people will suffer before they demand it; how much clamor it will take to overcome the greed and fear of business, and force real action to make the unemployed independent and self-sustaining.

Upon this question depends the future of American politics. If President Roosevelt keeps dickering with bankers and trust magnates, as he has been doing since he talked with me; if he lets them persuade him they can bring prosperity back and re-employ the idle—then there is going to build itself up through the coming winter such a mass of discontent that we shall see a third party movement all over the country. On the other hand, if the President acts quickly enough, he can make the Democratic party the instrument of the coming change.

Because I trusted him, and the young men whom I know in his Administration, I urged the people of California to join the Democratic party. I could see no reason for a new party, when it was so easy to take an old one, as we found it here. Of course, conditions vary in every State, and whether our program can be carried out in your State is something you have to judge. My general statement is that where the direct primary exists; where anyone can join the party of his choice and name its candidates, there is no sense in starting a third party. The same amount of effort will persuade the people to become Democrats, and the same number of votes that are needed to elect new party candidates will elect EPIC candidates on old party tickets.

What is needed is a program, and leadership which can be trusted. Old party politicians, with their crooked habits, need not trouble you too much; as soon as you have carried the election, they all move out. The advantage you gain is a certain large percentage of voters who automatically go with the old party; and vote the ticket regardless of who the nominees may be. When you capture the party you capture them, whereas, if you start a new party, you have them against you.

One thing, the all-important thing, our EPIC movement proved: the reserves of initiative and idealism which are in our people. I cannot speak for the East, with its crowded cities and beaten-down slum populations; but the West is all pretty much the same as California, and we have proved that the people can be taught and will act in their own behalf. I have seen them in action, and will carry the memory of it to my dying day. If I had suffered any weakening of faith, they would have restored it; if I had had any impulse towards cynicism, the "smart" tone of Broadway, these

California audiences would have brought me back to America and the faith of my youth.

I thank them for that: men and women whom I have met by the thousands, whose hands I have shaken, whose faces I have looked into. I say to them, this last word for the moment: Yes, my friends, we are going to bring back America. We are not going to sink, and make one more of the slave empires of history. We are going to revive Democracy, and make it work; we are going to apply it, not merely to politics, but to industry. We are not going to let ourselves be fooled by catchwords and buga-boos—regimentation, bureaucracy, loss of liberty, and the rest of the Hoover bunk. We are going to make our government work. We are not going to be afraid of it, because we know that it is ours, it is ourselves, acting in a collective capacity to carry out our collective will in our collective interest. Our only enemy is organized greed, which steals our government away from us; if we slay that monster, we have nothing to fear from government.

That is what we told the people of California, and they understood it—879,000 of them. It won't take them many months to convert a couple of hundred thousand more. Just a little more educational work— such as our people are doing right now. They tell me that our club meetings are twice as well attended as before the election; and our youth groups have added six new clubs in Los Angeles county in the past month. Keep your eyes on California, and follow along behind us.

Postscript. As this book is going to press, there is shown to me a letter from Robert A. Millikan, discussing my candidacy, and this reminds me that I have left the scientists out of this record.

At the height of the campaign, Prof. Millikan issued a blast against me, based upon the fact that once in my life I had invaded his field of physics, and had expressed an opinion about the ideas of Dr. Albert Abrams, which Millikan considers absurd. But how many scores of times has Millikan invaded *my* field of economics, expressing opinions which I consider unworthy of a child in high school!

Robert A. Millikan is a great scientist, and a Nobel prize winner. He runs the California Institute of Tech-

I, CANDIDATE FOR GOVERNOR

nology, where many scientists carry on research. What is the state of freedom of opinion at the institution? Dr. Millikan himself expresses his political, economic, and religious infantilities whenever he pleases; and his colleagues and subordinates keep silence at all times. A dozen of them are my friends; and I knew privately that most of them were for EPIC; but not one of them spoke one word. They did not even dare to be seen with old friends.

There is a greater scientist than Robert A. Millikan in America, and him no one has yet been able to silence. It will be pleasant to conclude this book with a little benediction from Albert Einstein.

Princeton, N.J.
November 23, 1934.

Dear Upton Sinclair:

My son, when he was about five years old, attempted to split wood with my razor. You can be sure that it was less bad for the wood than the razor.

I remembered that story when I heard from you that you had got yourself into this rude business. As I read that this cup had passed from you, I rejoiced even though it had not gone exactly according to your wish.

In economic affairs the logic of facts will work itself out somewhat slowly. You have contributed more than any other person. The direct action you can with good conscience turn over to men with tougher hands and nerves.

To you and your wife, the hearty greetings of your

A. EINSTEIN.

APPENDIX

A PROCLAMATION
To the People of California

My Fellow Citizens:

You have seen fit to elect me as your next Governor. Under the law approximately sixty days are to elapse before I can take office. In view of the crisis confronting us, it would be a blunder and failure of duty to delay for that long the setting in motion of our declared program.

We have in our State one and a quarter million persons dependent upon public charity. Assuming that each of these persons receives fifty cents per day to live on, our State stands to lose $37,500,000 by sixty days delay in starting the EPIC Plan. We have close to half a million able-bodied workers begging work and unable to find it. Assuming that each of these men by his labor creates four dollars worth of wealth per day, we will lose in that same period the sum of $120,000,000 which might have been created. It ought not to be necessary to present further argument in favor of prompt action.

For more than a year we have been building up our movement to End Poverty In California. We have nearly two thousand active clubs; we have district secretaries in each assembly district, and precinct captains in most of the ten thousand precincts of our State. A couple of months ago we combined our EPIC forces with those of the Democratic Party, and have built an organization which has proved its effectiveness in the recent balloting. This political machine has done its work, but must not be permitted to go to pieces for lack of use. The instrument of the people's political will must be converted into their instrument of industrial action.

I therefore call upon all EPIC committee members, secretaries, and other workers throughout the State, and likewise all Democrats who have pledged themselves to our program, to join immediately in the task of finding work for the unemployed.

Our opponents have accused us of a desire to "regiment" people and force them into paths along which they do not wish to travel. We shall answer these statements in action; demonstrating that our EPIC program can and will be carried out by the spontaneous action of the people, acting upon their own initiative in their own neighborhoods.

In the spring of 1917 the American people went to war. In liberty loan and other drives, they showed what are the capacities of the people for self-help, for immediate organization, for democratic action to meet an emergency. We confront today a need no less great, and the people of California will display the same capacities—but this time for the creation of wealth instead of its destruction, for brotherhood instead of for slaughter.

APPENDIX

I: Agriculture

Great quantities of fertile land are standing idle in our State, while at the same time great numbers of men and women and children are going hungry. We intend to start today to end that condition, and to put the idle people on the idle land to produce food for themselves.

Our EPIC movement has been made by the volunteer labor of devoted men and women. I have watched their work for a year and can name many who have proved their competence and loyalty. I have selected three of these to take charge of the task of food production for the use and benefit of the unemployed. I hereby establish the California Authority for Land, to be known for brevity as the CAL; and I name the following three persons as the Central Commission of this public body. I am today writing the Acting Governor of California, asking him to name these persons as an emergency commission in connection with the relief activities of the State.

In the event that the Acting Governor shall not see fit to grant this request, the three commissioners will function as volunteers until I become Governor. In any case they will receive the full and wholehearted cooperation of all EPIC and Democratic workers, and I hereby call upon these workers to place themselves under the orders of this Central Commission. All heads of EPIC clubs, all district secretaries and precinct captains, all officials of the Democratic Party, are invited to call together the EPIC workers in each of the ten thousand precincts of California and make immediate plans for getting facts and starting work.

How much acreage is there in your precinct which is capable of cultivation and which is not under adequate cultivation? A committee of persons experienced in the growing of crops must be appointed immediately to list such acreage and ascertain as follows: Who owns the land, and upon what terms will the owners consent for a crop to be grown upon it? What food or industrial crops can be grown advantageously? What is the proper time for planting, and who has had experience in the growing of such crops? Where can seed be obtained, and in what quantities, and upon what terms? Who has plows and other necessary tools? Who has horses and tractors, and how can the work be most economically done? What persons are desirous of labor on the land, and for what hours will they be willing to place themselves under the direction of qualified leaders?

A great deal of information has already been accumulated by our Research Associates. More is in the hands of groups at our State University. The Central Commission of the CAL will set to work to collect this material and make it available. It will prepare bulletins of information and advice, bearing on all aspects of the problem of growing food and industrial crops in various portions of California. It will accumulate a library of national and state bulletins, and digest these, and make the information available for the workers. It will assemble secretarial groups and establish a system of correspondence whereby questions may be answered and the needed authority given. It will arrange for experts to tour the State in demonstration cars under the authority of the CAL, and will send out organizers and supervisors to supply the necessary initiative and guidance wherever the people themselves may prove unequal to the emergency. But for immediate action the people must not wait for any orders. The various groups must seek and find qualified leaders from their midst. The task is a colossal one, and the Central Commission will be overwhelmed with the work of starting.

As guiding principles of action, I lay down the following:

1. Every effort should be made at the beginning to obtain the use of idle land for a purely nominal rental. As Governor-elect of California, I appeal to the patriotism and public spirit of landowners in our State. I point out to them that we are confronting the greatest crisis in our history. One and a quarter million people will not suffer want and humiliation indefinitely and we have no right to expect them to do so. It is contrary to public policy that needed land should be held out of use, and persons who hold it out of use are incurring a grave social risk. In making land temporarily available for the growing of crops, the owner will part with no permanent right, and in the present state of the real estate market landowners must realize that they are not apt to find a purchaser of their land before a crop can be grown upon it. In letting the people use the land in this emergency, the owners acquire a debt of gratitude which the people will not fail to pay. When the time comes to purchase land, preferential consideration will be given to land which has been proved.

I point out furthermore that the feeding of the unemployed by public charity comes back inevitably upon the taxpayers, because there is no one else to meet the cost; therefore, when the landowner permits the unemployed to grow food for themselves, he is saving himself future taxes on his land, and benefiting from the transaction as definitely as if he were paid in cash.

2. I believe that our movement can proceed by reliance upon the best impulses of our citizenry, and if there are landowners who do not freely cooperate, our workers should leave such persons alone, and let them learn from the wave of constructive activity which will soon be sweeping our State.

3. I make a tentative suggestion of the kind of contract which should be made with landowners by the local organization of the CAL. The land should be leased for a period of six months for the sum of one dollar, plus personal requirements of products, if desired.

4. If after due effort it should appear that sufficient land cannot be obtain on these terms, the Central Commission of the CAL will authorize the paying of larger shares of the expected crop, or for cash payments.

5. The compensation for seed, and for use of tools, machinery, horses, etc., will be fixed upon the basis of a share of the crops, and the current value of such services or rentals. In cases where the necessary materials or services cannot be obtained upon such basis, they will be obtained by cash payments from available means.

6. I point out that the fact that the land is located in cities is no barrier to its use for the growing of garden crops. All vacant land in and around the cities of Germany has been turned into flourishing gardens which the people of the neighborhood work in their off hours, producing food for themselves. The one question regarding an avail-

able tract of land is whether the food which can be grown on it will repay the labor called for.

7. The problem of water is of special urgency in California. Some crops can be grown without irrigation, and these are matters which call for local knowledge, which our local groups will obtain. In the case of garden plots in cities, I point out to the local authorities that it is far more economical to furnish the water free and let the people grow their own food than to furnish the food. I call upon all city and county authorities to do all things lawfully permitted in order to make possible the self-help activities of our needy people.

8. The working farmers of California have enormous stocks of food for which they can find no market. The present practice of relief authorities is to give to the unemployed money with which they buy food at four or five times what the farmers get for it. Very largely they buy in chain stores and the profit goes to Wall Street to wait until the Government borrows it again. We propose to eliminate this waste, and our workers are urged to find out what stocks the farmers have on hand, what prices they ask for them, and whether or not they will take the warehouse receipts of the CAL. It should be pointed out to the farmers and to all others interested that the paper of the CAL will speedily be exchangeable for a wide variety of products in the retail depots which will serve those in the system.

9. Compensation offered for services should be in general that to which people are accustomed, except that high salaries have no part in our system in the initial stages. It is our purpose to provide plenty for all, and with modern machinery this can be done with the greatest ease. But naturally that cannot be done in the first few months.

10. The local committees of the CAL are authorized to make contracts which involve a share of the proceeds of their labor, and for the expenditures of any cash which they themselves raise. But no one is authorized to pledge any expenditures in behalf of the Central Commission of the CAL, or to assume any responsibility in the name of the State of California. The Central Commission will make no expenditures until it has the funds in hand, and no responsibility may be incurred in the name of the State of California until I have been inaugurated as Governor and have given the necessary authority under the law.

II: Industry

For the purpose of bringing idle factory workers into the factories and starting the machines, I hereby establish a commission entitled the California Authority for Production, hereinafter called the CAP. As members of the Central Commission of this organization, I appoint: I name this commission to serve in the manner and upon the same terms as in the case of the CAL.

The local committees are charged to find persons familiar with industrial production in each assembly district. They will list the factories in the neighborhood, those which are entirely idle and those which are operating on part time. Contact will be made with executives and owners of these factories, and efforts will be made to obtain exact and careful information as to what products the factories are turning out, which are idle or part idle, and what is their present financial condition. In the case of idle factories and processing plants, have they been dismantled, and if so, what is the estimated cost of putting them in repair, and where can machinery be found to be installed? What is the condition of the machinery and its potential capacity? What raw materials are needed, and from what sources can these materials be most economically obtained?

Such questions are apt to be more technical in the case of factory production than of agriculture. The knowledge is more specialized and the persons who possess such accurate knowledge are less easily found. The Central Commission of the CAP will start a file of all persons who possess such knowledge. Such persons are urged to send their names to the CAP, and local organizations must collect lists of names with all necessary data, and forward them to the central office. The EPIC movement has had an organization known as the Research Associates, consisting of engineers, statisticians, accountants, etc., and similar local groups will be formed to conduct the necessary work in each and every neighborhood where industrial operations are possible, or where the raw materials of industry can be obtained or produced.

A joint committee of CAL and CAP must be set up to arrange for the producing of industrial crops needed for factories, and for tools and other CAP products required for the operations of CAL.

The problem of renting factories will be found more complicated than that of renting land for the growing of crops. The owners of factories will have to be compensated to the extent of their taxes, overhead charges and depreciation, plus a small profit when earned. It is my hope that State authorities will accept the verdict of the people of California that the unemployed are to be made self-sustaining and be permitted to produce what they consume. I am making immediate application to relief authorities so that as large a share of funds as possible may be used for the renting of factories and the purchase of raw materials. I am furthermore making application to all Federal authorities who are interested in remedying the depression, asking their help in the form of credits which may be applied to the starting of industry for use.

For the local committees of the CAP I set forth the following general principles:

1. The first problem is to get full information as to the possible cooperation of factory owners and executives. Our people must appeal to the public spirit and patriotism of the owners of idle and semi-idle plants. Each owner shall be asked to make as liberal a proposition as he can afford.

2. Local committees are authorized to conclude contracts wherever they and the owners are willing and able to become responsible for carrying out the terms.

3. The terms should indicate wherever possible a share in the product as the price of the lease. Stocks of raw material in hand should be taken over at their actual purchase price.

4. In the case of factories which have to be reconditioned, the local committee reporting the matter to the CAP may arrange for the

cost of the repairs, to be charged against the factory either on the basis of day labor at current wages or for a fixed contract price. Periods of lease should be not less than one year nor more than three years.

5. No contracts shall be made involving expenditures on the part of the Central Commission of the CAP without authority from the Central Commission. No contract shall be made upon the authority of the State of California until after I have become Governor and shall have delegated the necessary authority.

Local committees are authorized to make any arrangements with local relief authorities for such contributions as these authorities may be willing to give. It is earnestly hoped that relief authorities will adjust their proceedings to the new plan.

7. In the case of factories which are running on part time, and whose owners care to lease to the CAP, it is recommended that executive staffs shall be retained. Administrators of the CAP should endeavor to cooperate with present managers, and remove them only in the event that they prove themselves in action to be incompetent or disloyal.

8. It should be borne in mind that the purpose in taking over plants is to increase production. The sole reason for leasing any going concern is that more workers may be put to work and more products turned out. All plants leased by the CAP must immediately be started at their utmost possible capacity, and worked the maximum number of shifts consistent with the welfare of the workers and economy of production. Only experienced persons must ever be placed in charge, and favoritism and political influence of all kinds are to be rigidly excluded.

9. Great numbers of self-help groups have sprung up all over our State. These groups should now serve as the centers of the new production system. Our workers should get in touch with the cooperatives and learn from them how to function. They should find out what the cooperatives need in order to increase production, and should help in every way to get the necessary materials and arrange for their transportation and exchange.

10. To all persons interested in the work of CAP it should be made plain that its paper will speedily be exchangeable for a wide variety of products to be made available at retail depots.

III: EXCHANGE

For the purpose of arranging for the exchange of goods produced by CAL and CAP, I hereby establish the California Authority for Barter, hereinafter called the CAB. The purpose of this organization is to arrange for the warehousing, distribution, and exchange of the products of CAL and CAP, and to devise one or more mediums of exchange for the goods produced. As a Central Commission, I appoint the following three persons:

We desire to use United States money in so far as we can get it. We shall ask it of relief authorities, and urge the Federal administration to back our Plan to the limit. But it takes time for their machinery to move, and meantime our people are hungry, our taxpayers are losing their homes, and our State is close to bankruptcy. Therefore the CAB will study the problems of other means of exchange: warehouse receipts, credit accounts, certificates of service, and other lawful devices which may serve in making the products of CAL and CAP available to those who work within the system.

They shall arrange for a credit institution which will see to the issuing of the necessary certificates, warehouse receipts, etc., and balance the accounts of the various groups occupied in producing, transporting, and exchanging goods. They shall make any immediate emergency arrangements which may be lawful and practicable, and they will carry on a research to determine the permanent forms under which credits may be issued and debts be paid within our system of production for use.

As to the immediate financing of the three Commissions: I am requesting the Acting Governor to make an appropriation of fifty thousand dollars out of the relief funds of the State over which he has control. I am informed that he has the legal power to do this; for the starting of the unemployed at productive labor is a form of relief activity and the most productive use to which relief funds can possibly be put. In the event that the Acting Governor grants my request, this money will serve to cover the necessary expenses for the next two months—clerical hire, postage, telephones, telegrams, etc. The nine commissioners will receive three hundred dollars per month each. No higher compensation than this will be paid to anyone in the system until after this emergency stage has been passed and production is fully under way.

In the event that the Acting Governor should not see fit to grant my request, the Commissioners will have to wait for their salaries. All EPIC and Democratic workers and organizations are asked to continue their voluntary services. The EPIC headquarters must be continued as headquarters for this work, and it will be necessary to raise funds by private subscription, so that all who have helped the EPIC movement or the Democratic party during the campaign, will be asked for contributions to continue the work in the next stage.

I have every reason to expect that generous allotments of Federal funds will be made to assist this work. I am making immediate application for such funds, but I do not know whether they can be paid until after I have actually become Governor. Manifestly we are more apt to get funds if we are a going concern and are able to point to actual achievements. I am, of course, acquainting the Federal authorities with our actions and plans, and hope for prompt decisions from them. If we get a generous allotment of Federal funds our task will be made easier, but it is the part of wisdom to make these preliminary plans upon the basis of what we ourselves can do by our own efforts.

The tasks which are here outlined have been ordered by the collective wisdom of the people of California, expressing themselves through the medium of the ballot box. In issuing this call for action I am merely summoning the people to the carrying out of their own recorded purposes, and counting with full confidence upon their determination, intelligence and loyalty, in the process of ending poverty in California, and obtaining for all men and women in our State the right to labor and to enjoy the products of their labor. We of the EPIC movement have staked our existence upon faith in cooperative production and its ability to produce more wealth and security and happiness for the masses of the people than the system of competitive commercialism. It is up to us now to prove our faith in action; to do it individually by unselfish labor and collectively by sound judgment and Democratic solidarity.

In this spirit and with these hopes I commend the CAL, the CAP, and the CAB to the people of California. You are to create them, you are to manage them, and you are to reap the benefits of them. Every man and woman in the State who has an interest in the common welfare and who has any talent or skill to contribute, is urged to come forward and help. There is nothing political or partisan about this invitation. Our former opponents will be welcomed just as cordially as our old-time friends. No one will be asked anything except: "Do you really want to help, and if so, what are you qualified to do?" The rest will prove itself in action. We have all the necessary means of making comfort and security for ourselves, and with God's help we shall go forward to do it.

THE EPIC PLAN
(Revised 1935)

1. A legislative enactment for the establishment of State land colonies, whereby the unemployed may become self-sustaining and cease to be a burden upon the taxpayers. A public body, the California Authority for Land (the CAL) will rent or purchase idle land, and land sold for taxes and at foreclosure sales, and erect dormitories, kitchens, cafeterias, and social rooms, and cultivate the land, using modern machinery under the guidance of experts.

2. A public body entitled the California Authority for Production (the CAP), will be authorized to rent or purchase production plants whereby the unemployed may produce the basic necessities required for themselves and for the land colonies, and to operate these factories and house and feed and care for the workers. CAL and CAP will maintain a distribution system for the exchange of each other's products. The industries will include laundries, bakeries, canneries, clothing and shoe factories, cement-plants, brick-yards, lumber yards, thus constituting a complete industrial system, a new and self-sustaining world for those our present system cannot employ.

3. A public body entitled the California Authority for Barter (the CAB) will devise and issue warehouse receipts, certificates of service, credit accounts, and other means of exchanging the products within the system. It will also issue bonds to cover the purchase of land and factories, the erection of buildings and the purchase of machinery.

4. An act of the legislature repealing the present sales tax on the necessities of life.

5. An act of the legislature providing for a State income tax graduated after the fashion of the Federal tax, but preceding that tax.

6. An increase in the State inheritance tax, steeply graduated and applying to all property in the State regardless of where the owner may reside.

7. A law increasing the taxes on privately owned public utility corporations and banks.

8. A constitutional amendment revising the tax code of the State, providing that cities and counties shall exempt from taxation the first $1000 of asessment on homes occupied by the owners and ranches cultivated by the owners. This exemption later to be increased to $3000.

9. A constitutional amendment providing for a State land tax upon unimproved building land and agricultural land which is not under cultivation. The first $1000 of assessed valuation to be exempt, and the tax to be graduated according to the value of land held by the individual. Provision to be made for a state building loan fund for those who wish to erect homes.

10. A law providing for the payment of a pension of $50 per month to every needy person over sixty years of age who has lived in the State of California three years prior to the date of the coming into effect of the law.

11. A law providing for the payment of $50 per month to all persons who are blind, or who by medical examination are proved to be physically unable to earn a living; these persons also having been residents of the State for three years.

12. A pension of $50 per month to all widowed women who have dependent children; if the children are more than two in number, the pension to be increased by $25 per month for each additional child. These also to have been residents three years in the State.

DATE DUE

GAYLORD

PRINTED IN U.S.A.